The Future of Modular Architecture

The Future of Modular Architecture presents an unprecedented proposal for mass-customized mid- and high-rise modular housing that can be manufactured and distributed on a global scale. Advocating for the adoption of open-source design based on a new modular standard, the book shows how the construction industry and architectural practice may soon be radically reshaped. By leveraging the existing intermodal freight transport system, global supply chains can be harnessed to realize the long-held promise that housing will be a well-designed and affordable industrial product. We are on the cusp of a transformative change in the way we design and build our cities.

Author David Wallance argues that modular architecture is profoundly intertwined with globalization, equitable urbanism, and sustainable development. His book addresses these timely issues through a specific approach grounded in fundamental concepts. Going beyond the individual modular building, Wallance forecasts the emergence of a new type of design, manufacturing, and construction enterprise.

Written in an approachable style with illustrated examples, the book is a must read for professionals in architecture and design, city planning, construction, real estate, as well as the general reader with an interest in these topics.

David Wallance, FAIA is an architect, educator, and author. He is the founder of DRA/W, an architectural practice based in Brooklyn, NY.

"David Wallance's work in intermodal modular architecture opens a future for sustainable, less expensive and factory-perfect buildings going well beyond the building typologies typically associated with pre-built structures. Since the introduction of curtain wall design nearly 70 years ago, building construction methods have changed little and remain profoundly inefficient in comparison with the enormous technical progress made in other areas of goods production. David's comprehensive exploration of modular design confronts systemic anachronisms that are deeply intrenched in the construction industry and forces consideration of why it is that we continue to tolerate them."

Daniel Alpert, Founding Managing Partner and Chief Economist, Westwood Capital, LLC, Author of *The Age of Oversupply: Overcoming the Greatest Challenge to the Global Economy*

The Future of Modular Architecture

David Wallance

Foreword by Susan Szenasy

Routledge
Taylor & Francis Group

NEW YORK AND LONDON

First published 2021
by Routledge
605 Third Avenue, New York, NY 10158

and by Routledge
2 Park Square, Milton Park, Abingdon, Oxon, OX14 4RN

Routledge is an imprint of the Taylor & Francis Group, an informa business

© 2021 Taylor & Francis

The right of David Wallance to be identified as author of this work has been asserted by him in accordance with sections 77 and 78 of the Copyright, Designs and Patents Act 1988.

Trademark notice: Product or corporate names may be trademarks or registered trademarks, and are used only for identification and explanation without intent to infringe.

Library of Congress Cataloging-in-Publication Data
A catalog record for this title has been requested

ISBN: 9780367469146 (hbk)
ISBN: 9780367467227 (pbk)
ISBN: 9781003031932 (ebk)

Typeset in Univers
by codeMantra

In memory of my parents, Don and Shula Wallance, from whom
I absorbed a design education and a design ethos long
before I became an architect.

Contents

About the Author

David Wallance, FAIA has worked on numerous award-winning buildings over the course of his 40-year career as an architect. For 20 years he taught advanced building technology at the Columbia University Graduate School of Architecture, Planning and Preservation. Highly regarded as a technically innovative designer, Wallance spearheaded the ultra-transparent glass façade at the Rose Center for Earth and Space in New York, hailed by the *New York Times* as "what may well be the finest example of glass curtain wall construction ever realized in the United States". Turning his attention to the problem of urban housing affordability, in 2005 he began developing a next-generation system of mid- and high-rise modular architecture.

Wallance has been an invited speaker at international conferences, including Greenbuild and Council on Tall Buildings and Urban Habitat, where he has presented and published his work. This book is the result of 15 years of research, design, and thinking about a scalable approach to modular housing, and how that approach is situated in the broadest possible context.

Wallance studied architecture at The Cooper Union in New York City.

Acknowledgments

Much of the material included in this book originated during an intense and exciting two-year collaboration, from 2005 to 2007, at Global Building Modules (GBM). I want to thank Alex Abrams, GBM's former co-founder, for his continued friendship and enthusiasm. Thanks as well to former co-founder Eldon Scott, and to Jason Buchheit, Karl Hirschmann, and the rest of the GBM team (see project credits) for their invaluable contributions.

Among various consultants who have been involved with the GBM system over the years, I want to first thank Dan Sesil and his team at LERA Consulting Structural Engineers for their innovative contributions and sustained interest. Thanks also to Greg Romine, the founder of Axis Materials USA, for opening my eyes to global construction product supply chains; to Elias Dagher and Dagher Engineering; and especially to Jamy Bacchus, an engineer and energy expert, on whose knowledge and advice I drew for Chapter 7.

One pivotal morning in 2008, I met Mark Strauss for breakfast to show him the work I had done with GBM, which led to a ten-year affiliation with his firm, FXCollaborative. In addition to thanking Mark for opening that door, I want to express my gratitude to senior partner Dan Kaplan for so generously sharing his time over the years. Thanks as well to partner Jack Robbins for championing the London innovative housing competition submission illustrated in the book. I am grateful to the firm for facilitating opportunities to continue the modular research through feasibility studies, competitions, publication, and speaking engagements.

I want to express my appreciation to Ilana Judah, Carl Stein, Dan Hoffman, Jeffrey Raven, Gabriella Mirabelli, and Allie Tepper for taking time from their busy schedules to read selected chapters and for providing insightful comments. It's also time to thank Nancy Kleppel, who read the first draft from start to finish in 2012 and offered invaluable suggestions for improving the manuscript. My special thanks go to Stephen Kieran for his support for the book during the proposal stage.

I'm grateful to Professors James Garrison and Deborah Gans for inviting me in 2019 to join them to teach "The Prefabricators Workshop" at Pratt Institute, where I was able to advance the modular façade concepts discussed in the book. I want to highlight the contribution of Sidhant Seth, a former Pratt student, who worked with me to create a beautiful series of modular apartment illustrations shown in Chapter 6.

My thanks as well to Erica Stoller, Cynthia Ehrenkrantz, Joshua Lee, and David Meerman Scott for going out of their way to help with image sourcing, and to Kate Wittels and Ariel Benjamin of HR&A Advisors for sharing cost data on the Sunnyside Yards feasibility study discussed in Chapter 7.

The cost of writing a book is the time one spends alone rather than with family and friends. While inadequate as a gesture of appreciation, this is at least a place to start. To Beth Wallance, a long overdue thank you for your encouragement and support when I wrote the first draft ten years ago. To my capable research assistant (and daughter) Rebecca Wallance: I could not have completed this project without your help sourcing images, tracking down copyrights, fixing my citations, and preparing the index. Your knowledge and professionalism make me proud.

The killing of darlings is unpleasant. To the extent that this book has been purged of them is due to Deborah Posner, who had the patience and fortitude to read every word and unerringly target darlings, digressions, and mangled sentences. Thank you, Deborah, for saving me from myself.

It was an unexpected honor when Susan Szenasy offered to write the Foreword, and I could not have asked for a more eloquent statement. She has situated the book in the broadest possible context, endowing it with a sense of urgency. Thank you, Susan.

Finally, my sincere appreciation to my publisher, Routledge, for their willingness to take on this project. I understand that there was a "lively discussion" among the publishing committee about whether to give my proposal the green light. I hope the book sparks an equally lively discussion among its readers.

Foreword

When architect Walter Gropius moved his newly founded, progressive design school from Weimar, the politically innovative but physically sleepy German town, he set in motion the massive change that was about to shape the 20th century, worldwide. His newly designed and built school rose in Dessau, a city known for its industrial innovations, like Junkers aircraft, known to progressives far beyond Germany. This technology foreshadowed more than a new era of long-distance transportation. Like many informed Europeans of his time, Gropius admired the mass production in his new town as well as its high-volume counterpart in the American Midwest where Ford's assembly lines turned out affordable cars for growing markets.

This new world order promised entirely new opportunities for Gropius's design students trained to create prototypes for industry. Architecture, itself, as the Bauhaus campus made it palpable, as well as visible, needed a massive overhaul. As one early modernist practitioner remembered, "We had to design everything!" He talked about working with manufacturers on wall systems, building parts and joinery details, lighting, and heating systems—literally EVERYTHING! The beneficiaries of these new buildings were the workers, as much as their employers. Gropius, though a creature of his male dominated culture, nevertheless imparted his ethic of social equity to his staff and students. He saw the redeeming qualities sensitively designed environments could offer to ease the physical and emotional damages wreaked by World War I, in which he served.

Somehow the early modernists' enthusiasm for overhauling familiar systems has bypassed subsequent practitioners. Yet now, once again, we too are face to face with the challenges of our own century: catastrophic climate change is about to set in motion massive migrations of hungry humans roaming the polluted planet; the air we breathe is poisoned, our waters polluted; outdated, racially biased planning policies enforce racial segregation in our cities; the relentless pandemic has revealed that racial segregation can wreak havoc on black and brown populations while calling attention to our outdated public health system. Each of these challenges is connected to how the built environment is planned, designed, and built.

We hear about the plight of the poor and unemployed, their numbers growing exponentially. The desperate need for affordable housing and other essentials harken back to the societal issues that Gropius's design school put in the service of mass production and expanding markets. Rising to the new and growing challenge is architect David Wallance and his brilliant multi-disciplinary team. What follows is the inspiring story of creating a new approach to affordable urban housing from a product of worldwide commerce; and a deep understanding of global connections between the peoples of the Earth, in the 21st century.

Susan S. Szenasy

Historian, Educator, former Editor in Chief, *Metropolis*

Preface

In 2015, I organized a panel discussion advertised as "The Future of Modular" at the Center for Architecture in New York. The event was well attended by an engaged audience, and it generated some buzz in the local real estate and design press. An article appeared in Crain's New York the next day that was headlined: "Modular Housing Stuck in Never Ever Land".

Ouch.

I was initially indignant, but I had to admit that the writer hit a nerve because, well, he had a point. Every now and then, a modular project gets built, attracts attention, and... the future is on its way! But the reality is that multi-story modular construction remains a marginal segment of the urban housing industry even if there is an occasional newsworthy project.

Here is the book's background: from 2005 to 2007, after 25 years in architectural practice, I went to work with a well-funded start-up to spearhead design and R&D of a next-generation system of modular construction. That enterprise ended abruptly with the onset of the 2008 global financial crisis. The work we did during those two years was foundational but remained theoretical—the crisis stopped our progress before we could put up our first building. However, I could not let the idea go and wrote the first version of this book. It has been a work in progress for a decade. If anything, the ideas embodied in the current version have matured and are as relevant, if not more so, than when I began.

Why is there a need for modular housing, and why is it stuck in never ever land? To the first part of that question, there is a housing crisis in every major American city, a crisis not just of homelessness, but also of affordability at all income levels, from the urban workforce to middle-class professionals. Cites around the world are experiencing rapid population growth and at the same time spreading out, American style. Our anachronistic, labor-intensive methods of construction are too costly.

The long-held dream of housing made in factories remains unrealized, which brings us to the second part of the question. If the future of modular architecture were simply a matter of technology, the future would have arrived by now. But the future has not arrived because technical solutions, while necessary, are insufficient. Technical problems are linear and solvable. Cultural problems, however, are not solvable in any linear sense. If we want the world to accept—no, to desire—housing that is designed and manufactured as an industrial product, we must change millennia of customs and habits in the way we think about our built environment. The concerns of all stakeholders—architects, manufacturers, builders, trade unions, public officials, and, not least, the consumers of housing—must be addressed.

Accordingly, this book offers a theory of modular architecture grounded in first principles, and frames its technical subject matter within a social, cultural, and historical context. Without theory, we are navigating without a map, without a way out of never land. I do not wish to claim that the theory put forward in this book is the only possible theory. I expect others to challenge it and offer alternatives. I also expect that the best alternatives will reach for the same scope and will reasonably refute, improve, or elaborate on the logic of the book's argument.

One element of the argument is that modular architecture is a distinct discipline that cannot be separated from business enterprise. This suggests that certain entrenched professional structures must be rearranged. I believe that architects must lead modular business enterprises, not merely furnish design services to them. Architectural training and our method of design thinking provide the tools needed for dealing with the kind of complex non-linear problems that must be solved for modular architecture to succeed. This cannot be accomplished from the arm's length distance of the design studio, and it means blurring the bright line that separates the commercial and professional realms. Design brilliance in commercial enterprise as exemplified by Apple under Steve Jobs and Jony Ive is the model.

The book's argument is situated within the changing context of globalization. I am unpersuaded that globalization is on the way out, but it is clearly evolving. During my publisher's peer review process, I received a comment that the book was uncritical in its acceptance of certain outmoded neo-liberal ideas pertaining to globalization. The discomfort I felt caused me to reflect. I don't subscribe to neo-liberalism, understood as the belief in an unregulated free market. I agree with those who believe that neo-liberal ideology has contributed to the inequities of globalism. I do argue for global markets for modular housing because I believe that is the only way to achieve truly significant economies of both scale and scope. However, while private enterprise is best equipped to implement an industrialized housing solution, public policy makers must step in to ensure that the economic benefits of that solution are equitably distributed. Good-quality affordable housing is a right, not a privilege.

Cities are central to the book's argument. Efficient land use, walkability, sustainability, innovation, culture, diversity, and tolerance are all connected to density. The high cost of urban mid- and high-rise housing, however, is a major barrier to an economically diverse urbanism. As I was nearing completion of the manuscript, two events occurred that suddenly changed our understanding of the urban context. These are, of course, the global pandemic, followed by the killing of George Floyd and the ensuing Black Lives Matter protests. The idea has taken hold that cities are centers of disease spread, and many who can afford to are moving away from cities or are talking about it. The echoes of white flight during the 1960s are unmistakable, although the impetus this time is not explicitly related to racial prejudice. Still, it is clearly related to racial disparities in income and housing. Decades of redlining, economic injustice, and overcrowded housing have been a significant contributor to the disproportionate impact of the pandemic on Black people and people of color. The Black Lives Matter protests have focused our attention on centuries of structural racism. While it is beyond the scope of this book to discuss these issues in depth, they cannot go unmentioned. I hope that readers will bear this changed context in mind while reading the book.

Part 1

1 Introduction

Housing construction and city-building are now targeted for disruptive innovation. Initiatives by tech firms, including Google, Amazon, and others, indicate that 21st-century advances in information technology and artificial intelligence will soon intersect with 20th-century industry to move construction off the jobsite and into the factory. Venture capital is starting to flow into modular technology start-ups.[1] These trends suggest the possibility, if not the likelihood, that the construction industry and architectural practice will soon be radically reshaped.

This book is as much about globalization as it is about the future of modular architecture.[2] It's also a book about cities for the growing global middle class, about sustainable development, and about the way housing will be designed and by whom. The book's argument is that these five topics are profoundly intertwined, and that this moment is indeed ripe for transformation.

It is not my intention to make a case for globalization; it is, rather, to start from the recognition that, as problematic as it may be, globalization is simply the contemporary condition. Ninety percent of the world's goods are transported overseas, with 70 percent in shipping containers.[3] It is hard to imagine that transnational corporations, the borderless flow of capital, global supply chains, and social media can somehow be constrained within national boundaries, despite current political winds.[4] To be clear: while globalization is the contemporary condition, how we respond to it can either exacerbate or rectify its inequities. One of my underlying aims in writing this book is to show how global forces can be harnessed to build equitable housing and cities, and to realize the long-held promise of modern architecture that housing will one day be a well-designed and affordable industrial product.

How the Seed Was Planted

I never expected that I would find myself deeply involved with an idea that might change the world. There are no new ideas under the sun, as the saying goes, and that may or may not be true. But there are, without a doubt, new combinations of old ideas. Fifteen years ago, as of this writing, I happened upon a new combination of ideas that in retrospect seems even more compelling than when I first encountered it.

In the spring of 2005, I was approached by a friend, a restaurateur and aspiring hotel developer who wanted to build an affordable urban student hostel. He had just been to a photography exhibition on Manhattan's West Side piers, held in a temporary pavilion designed by Shiguru Ban, the Japanese architect who made his reputation building with cardboard tubing as a structural material. The Nomadic Museum, as the pavilion was called, was designed to be disassembled and moved to other locations. To accomplish that, Ban had used shipping containers stacked four high to form the walls.[5]

My developer friend asked me: "why not order shipping containers from China already fitted out as rooms for a low-cost student hostel, and stack them into a building in New York?"

I thought of a few reasons why not.

How would you get those shipping container modules to meet building codes? How would the interiors hold up during a sea voyage, with all the pitching and rolling of a ship? Would windows survive sea transport? What about fireproof construction? How would you connect them together? What about unions? But even as I was raising these questions, I was thinking that maybe they were mostly technical problems, really not all that difficult, if you had some money and time to think through solutions and test them out.

I'd already been aware for a few years that prefabricated building components were being sourced from China at an unheard-of low cost. Contractors were having architectural metalwork, for example, fabricated overseas to a surprisingly high standard of quality. New design possibilities that previously could not have been contemplated for being too expensive were suddenly attainable within tight budget constraints. In 2005, the idea of attempting overseas fabrication of elements for building construction may have been somewhat cutting edge, but it didn't require a big imaginative leap to think that in a few years, we would be seeing much of the building construction supply chain coming over in shipping containers. So *why not* just make buildings in China from shipping containers, fit them out over there, and ship them to the U.S. ready to stack into a building?

Shipping container architecture was not new. Architects around the world were experimenting with habitable shipping container designs. On the banks of the Thames River in London, an enclave of five-story shipping container live-work spaces had recently been constructed. Most of these projects celebrated the notion of shipping container reuse. A few were done with new shipping containers procured from China for local fit and finish into a building. But no one had yet attempted to manufacture modules with wiring, plumbing, and finished interiors, meant for overseas shipping and ready like plug-and-play components to stack into a building.

• • •

The shipping container student hostel didn't go anywhere, and I continued in my career with the well-known architectural firm, the Polshek Partnership,[6] where I had been working on high-profile projects, like the Rose Center for Earth and Space at the American Museum of Natural History. One of my contributions on the Rose Center was the design of its ultra-transparent glass facade,[7] which entailed technical innovation and close collaboration with engineers and manufacturers. That kind of integration of design, engineering, and fabrication has always been my passion as an architect.

Despite successes like the Rose Center, it had become increasingly clear to me that much of conventional practice was an anachronism. The design of exceptional one-off projects built using techniques rooted in craft[8] is workable only with exceptional budgets. What about the rest of the urban built environment, the vast majority of which is comprised of "everyday" buildings? Our everyday architecture too often fails to satisfy our human need for well-designed and crafted environments. As a natural extension of my inclinations as an architect, I had been thinking for some time about the potential for modular architecture to take "everyday architecture" to a new level.

A Modular Start-Up

A few months after my conversation about a student hostel made of shipping containers, a colleague at the Polshek office came to me with another shipping container proposition. Two Manhattan real estate developers had approached him to head up the design and technical side of a start-up enterprise that would manufacture modular apartment buildings out of recycled shipping containers. My colleague had decided it wasn't right for him, but he thought it might be a good fit for me. I was simultaneously intrigued as well as concerned about the risks.

The prospect of joining the start-up resonated with my interest as a designer in modularity, rigor, and execution of details. During the previous ten years, while working at Polshek, I had designed and built two houses in the Hudson Valley that were based on a modular grid. I drew every stud, positioned on 16-inch centers, spaced evenly within the grid. I detailed ship-lap siding on the elevations to express the module with a vertical shadow joint on the grid centerline. Every exposed stainless-steel nail head in the ship-lap siding was located on my drawings, positioned to land on a stud so that the nail would hold fast. Windows, partitions, cabinetry—it all related back to that module.

The start-up enterprise was an opportunity to pursue my interest in modularity on a larger canvas, and I began discussions with the two developers. Toward the end of 2005, I signed a two-year contract as the Senior Vice President of Design and Development of Global Building Modules, Inc., or GBM. As an active enterprise, with an office and staff, GBM lasted a brief two years. With the first rumblings of the sub-prime real estate debacle during the summer of 2007, funding for the company came to a halt as our main investor ran for cover. One by one, our staff departed. By Christmas that year, the office had closed its doors. I went on to set up a small architectural firm, and the co-founders moved on to other businesses.

• • •

We did fundamental work during the two years that GBM was an active enterprise—fundamental in that we re-thought the entire process of design and construction from the standpoint of what I'll be referring to throughout the book as "intermodal modular architecture".

Our most important breakthrough came when we recognized the deficiencies of shipping containers as modules for mid- and high-rise building construction. This led to our realization that the key virtues of the intermodal shipping system were its standard dimensions and fittings for economical transport and automated handling. That prompted our seminal decision to move away from containers and to redesign our building module from scratch. Our redesigned module retains the essential property of intermodal transport while being engineered expressly as an open frame for mid- and high-rise building construction. We named it the "Volumetric Unit of Construction", or VUC, to clearly distinguish it from a shipping container. Stemming from that breakthrough, we introduced numerous technical innovations geared to a systematic approach that integrates structure, facades, interior components, environmental systems, and cores. While GBM's progress ended prematurely, we had enough time and resources during those two years to establish the basis for a comprehensive "plug-and-play" system for manufacturing modular multi-story housing.

What the Book Is About

The interwoven strands of modular architecture, globalization, urbanism, sustainability, and architectural practice call for an extended, book-length treatment. The book's argument is built on a theory of modular architecture grounded in 12 interrelated principles, which will be explained further as the book unfolds.

Principle #1: Economies of Scale
Principle #2: Economical Long-Distance Transportation
Principle #3: Intermodal Standards
Principle #4: Global Supply Chains
Principle #5: Leverage Existing Infrastructures
Principle #6: Use Intermodal Standards, but Don't Use Shipping Containers.
Principle #7: Spatially Indeterminate Modular Planning
Principle #8: Component Assembly
Principle #9: Location Efficiency Matters. Local Sourcing Does Not.
Principle #10: Design Thinking
Principle #11: Open Source
Principle #12: Differentiation within Standards

• • •

The book is broadly organized in a three-part structure. The first part provides the urban, technical, and historical contexts within which intermodal modular architecture is situated. In the middle is an illustrated design and technical discussion of the intermodal modular system itself. In the third part, we explore the broader ramifications of intermodal modular architecture, including questions of sustainability, disruptive innovation, and cultural acceptance. We will speculate on changes that will be experienced by all of the participants in the housing process: architects, developers, builders and the building trades, manufacturers, policy makers, and not least, consumers of housing.

Here is a brief outline of the book's argument, by chapter.

Chapter 1—Introduction

The design and construction professions, despite enormous advances in digital technology, are mired in outmoded practices. Architects design exceptional one-off projects, but the vast majority of our everyday buildings fail to satisfy our need for well-designed and crafted environments. Modular construction has the potential to take everyday architecture to a new level of quality.

The prevalence at American construction sites of building components manufactured overseas points to the reality of a global construction supply chain, which leads us to the concept of intermodal modular architecture: instead of delivering those components packed inside a shipping container, we can deliver them as an integrated "plug-and-play" system, with the shipping container itself re-purposed as a standardized building module. The VUC retains the essential properties of shipping containers for intermodal transport while being engineered expressly as an open frame for mid- and high-rise building construction.

Chapter 2—The Global Housing Crisis

A scalable solution to mid- and high-rise housing suitable for dense urban development is urgently needed to cope with projected global urban population growth. At the same time, the global middle class is growing rapidly, and land use patterns associated with housing for the middle class—automobile dependence and its concomitant urban sprawl—are unsustainable. A transformation in construction technology that brings down the cost of multi-story housing will encourage a shift in settlement patterns, re-populating cities not just with young creatives but also with families and retirees, changing the way land has been developed in the U.S. since the end of World War II.

While much of the book's focus is on urban housing for the global middle class, it also addresses the pressing needs of the homeless, the poor, and the working poor. Much as an automobile chassis can support a range of models from economy to luxury, intermodal modular architecture supports inclusionary housing at all income levels.

Chapter 3—The Argument for Economical Transportation

The essential nature of the construction process has not changed for thousands of years. Buildings have always been and still are put together from small parts and pieces brought to the building site and assembled in place. Modular solutions have been proposed for decades but have not been widely adopted. Why not?

The existing legacy modular industry is constrained by regional markets out of a widely held but erroneous conviction that maximum-size modules minimize cost. Trapped in conventional thinking, modular manufacturers cannot effectively market beyond a distribution range of about 125 miles. A true industrial solution requires global distribution to attain meaningful economies of scale. Here is our fundamental insight: low-cost transportation is the key to a robust modular building industry. Low-cost transportation using the existing intermodal shipping system opens global markets and global supply chains. The right size for a building module is the size of the shipping container.

Chapter 4—The Disruptive Advent of Intermodal Shipping

A book that proposes a system of construction based on intermodal transportation would be remiss if it overlooked the origin of the shipping container, conceived in 1954 by an American trucking tycoon named Malcom McLean. We'll take stock of the revolution in global transport and trade as well as in labor relations brought about by those ubiquitous corrugated steel boxes. Modern intermodal shipping finally arrived when uniform dimensional standards for shipping containers were adopted internationally in the 1970s.

A half-century ago, longshoremen were on the front lines of globalization. The struggle of the longshoremen's unions to maintain a foothold during a period of disruptive change in the shipping industry foreshadows what is likely to be resistance by trade unions to the widespread adoption of intermodal modular architecture. The conflict on the waterfront was resolved equitably for the longshoremen's unions, and suggests a model for resolving similar conflicts in construction.

Chapter 5—Promises of Progress: Four Case Histories

Turning to the history of modular architecture and pre-fabrication in construction, we discover a paradox: modern architects have been advocating the use of industrial techniques for almost a century, and yet with few exceptions, architects have been averse to associating with commercial ventures. Four case histories of modular and prefab commercial enterprises—the Sears Modern Homes program, the Lustron Corporation, the Techbuilt House, and the School Construction Systems Development Project (SCSD)—have lessons to offer. Each leveraged one or more existing infrastructures for marketing, transportation, manufacturing, distribution, and procurement. We'll see how technical ingenuity and resourceful problem-solving, as well as effective branding and marketing, were the ingredients of success, and how external factors, including economic cycles, cultural shifts, and even politics, played a role in failure. If modular architecture is going to succeed, it must be an integrated architectural and commercial enterprise in which logistics, marketing, finance, economics, and politics are considered together with design.

Chapter 6—The Intermodal Modular System

This chapter, at the heart of the book, is an illustrated and detailed explanation of how intermodal modular architecture works. At GBM, we created an integrated system around the Volumetric Unit of Construction, or VUC. The VUC transcends numerous limitations of re-purposed shipping containers, having been engineered for optimal performance as a stackable high-rise module with extensive design flexibility. With stackable cores, including elevators and fires stairs, VUCs can be arranged in four fundamental housing typologies—row housing, perimeter block, slab, and tower, with the potential for hybrid solutions.

The VUC is geared for component-based supply chain manufacturing and is internally standardized on a four-inch grid for plug-and-play integration of prefabricated facades, environmental systems, interior partitions and doors, bathrooms, kitchens and storage units. Comprehensive dimensional standardization enables the VUC to be the physical counterpart to object-based design software that will link directly to a digitally driven manufacturing process.

The technical aspects of the VUC are presented along with projects that demonstrate its application to mid- and high-rise housing design.

Chapter 7—Is Intermodal Modular Architecture Sustainable?

Globalization of the building process, as this book proposes, appears at first glance to be at cross purposes with sustainability. Aspects of sustainability that are addressed in this chapter include GHG emissions, embodied energy, transportation energy, and operating energy; the cradle-to-grave and cradle-to-cradle life cycles; and neighborhood disruption during construction. Using Life Cycle Assessment to establish objective and verifiable green metrics, we'll look at the impacts of long-distance transportation of VUCs. We'll find that in the broader context, long-distance transportation is not a significant contributor to an intermodal modular building's GHG footprint. More important, the standardized all-steel VUC is inherently demountable and reusable, which means that it need never enter the waste stream. Of the greatest importance, however, is the need for sensible land use policies that encourage dense urban development and that discourage sprawl, policies for which intermodal modular architecture can be an effective tool.

Chapter 8—Innovators, Entrenched Interests, and Early Adopters

Disruptive technology forces change upon us, often faster than our social, economic, and cultural institutions can absorb and adjust to it. To take an early example, the invention of interchangeable parts at the beginning of the industrial revolution pitted artisans against industrialists in a struggle that the artisans were foreordained to lose. "Made-to-measure" craftsmanship gave way to new concepts of "tolerance", or standardized error.

Innovation in the tradition-bound construction industry is notoriously difficult to accomplish amidst resistance mounted by entrenched interests. Labor practices are slow to change, and productivity is stagnant. Pressures on construction firms to earn a profit in the face of stagnant productivity mean that resources for research and development are scarce. By contrast, R&D funding in the industrial sector is ample, and central to the product development process.

The complex array of forces that have made innovation in design and construction so difficult to accomplish are stubbornly resistant. By adopting design thinking, a methodology for dealing with "wicked problems", the intermodal modular enterprise can resolve the conflicting and competing interests in the construction sector by engaging all stakeholders in an ongoing, collaborative, and iterative process.

Chapter 9—Toward a Global Vernacular

The history of architecture is mainly the history of monuments, public buildings, palaces, and religious edifices. The everyday architecture of indigenous dwellings went mostly unnoticed until the industrial revolution triggered mass migrations from the countryside to cities, and as a living vernacular building culture vanished, a heightened awareness emerged among architects and historians of its importance.

We'll explore how this loss of "architecture without architects"[9] has upset the balance in quality between our background urban fabric of everyday buildings and the architecture of our signature public, cultural, and institutional buildings. Can that balance be restored by the widespread adoption of intermodal modular architecture?

A 21st-century vernacular, based on the VUC with its standardized dimensions and connections, will be an open-source language shared among architects, designers, and product manufacturers worldwide that will lead to virtually limitless variety in design expression. By leveraging the power of distributed intelligence, the new global vernacular will raise everyday architecture to a previously unattainable level of excellence in design and quality.

Chapter 10—The Collaborative Open-Source Project

We'll speculate further on the idea of a new global vernacular, and how the traditional role of the architect can be expected to change. The design and technical development of housing based on the VUC and its myriad components will shift to the manufacturing enterprise, while the site-specific and local aspects of intermodal modular architecture will remain situated within the traditional firm.

The apartment buyer of modest means will be presented with new choices—finding it possible to be involved, say, in the customizing of a yet-to-be-built urban apartment, along the lines in which suburban builders offer homebuyers selections in layout, finishes, and appointments. Influencers on social media platforms will reshape the relationships among architects, developers, clients, and the intermodal modular enterprise. The open-source approach and access to global markets will offer new economic opportunities for architects, especially for those in small practices.

At the same time, the creative interplay between the new global vernacular and the signature architecture of public, cultural, and institutional buildings will invigorate both.

Chapter 11—The Place of Intermodal Modular Architecture

The final chapter situates intermodal modular architecture within the larger built environment, by considering what intermodal modular architecture is not: namely, the urban landscape—the space between and around our buildings—that is our shared public realm, and the furnishings, textiles, and other objects with which we create personal interior spaces in which to live comfortably and pleasurably. We'll draw a sharp distinction between urban multi-story housing, which is well-suited to industrial production, and those aspects of our built environment that can and should remain in large degree local, idiosyncratic, and contingent on made-to-measure craftsmanship. An excellent localism can be in dialogue with industrialized housing, to harness the economic, social, and cultural forces at work in the hyper-connected modern world to human ends.

Reintegrating Architecture

VUCs can be manufactured wherever there is a suitable industrial infrastructure, and because VUCs are designed for intermodal transport, they can be inexpensively shipped from the factory to a building site that might be thousands of miles away. The VUC opens the door for a new industry operating on a global scale. It seems counter-intuitive: how can a modular system based on intermodal transportation contribute to solving our pressing economic, social, and environmental problems? More manufacturing jobs overseas or replaced by automation? Shipping thousands of miles? The argument presented in the following chapters will show how a method of construction based on intermodal transportation can be a tool for solving these problems, to demonstrate that it is feasible, and to convince skeptics why this approach should be widely adopted. With advanced manufacturing techniques, including robotics, it could even become the basis for a new American export industry.

Received notions about how we build and house ourselves are deeply rooted, and the future of modular architecture will entail a break with traditional ways. I want to frame that break and its implications in as broad a context as possible, including the quality of urban life, housing equity, the allocation of economic resources, and environmental impact. Globalization, the leveling of economies, nations, and cultures brought on by technology in general and the information revolution in particular, is a blessing with a mix of curses. The solution put forward in this book aims to reconcile some of the impersonal forces at work in the modern world with the individual agency made possible by digital tools. A global platform for open-source design can be a path toward local expression in urban housing.

In our flat, networked, and lightning fast world, the lack of a systematic approach to the dimensions and interconnections of building components confounds our aspirations as architects and builders. By thinking through a common language of construction, we can restore for ourselves a healthy relationship to our built environment and reintegrate architecture—that ennobling art and science that transcends mere building—into our everyday lives.

Notes

1 Konrad Putzier, "Momentum Builds for Automation in Construction," *Wall Street Journal*, July 2, 2019, https://www.wsj.com/articles/momentum-builds-for-automation-in-construction-11562073426.
2 *Merriam-Webster.com Dictionary*, s.v. "modular," accessed July 20, 2020, https://www.merriam-webster.com/dictionary/modular.
  Definition of modular:

  1: of, relating to, or based on a module or a modulus
  2: constructed with standardized units or dimensions for flexibility and variety in use

3 James Castonguay, "International Shipping: Globalization in Crisis," *Witness*, accessed July 20, 2020, https://www.visionproject.org/images/img_magazine/pdfs/international_shipping.pdf.
4 Douglas A. Irwin, "The False Promise of Protectionism," *Foreign Affairs*, May/June 2017, https://www.foreignaffairs.com/articles/united-states/2017-04-17/false-promise-protectionism.
5 "Nomadic Museum," World-Architects.com, accessed July 20, 2020, https://www.world-architects.com/en/shigeru-ban-architects-tokyo/project/nomadic-museum.
6 Now Ennead Architects.
7 Herbert Muschamp, "It's Something New Under the Stars (And Looking Up)," *New York Times*, February 13, 2000.
8 I use the term craft here broadly, to encompass materials and components that may be pre-fabricated using industrial methods but which are still customized and dependent on the traditional sequences and procedures of on-site construction.
9 Bernard Rudofsky, *Architecture Without Architects* (Garden City, NJ: Doubleday, 1964).

2 The Global Housing Crisis

By the time you finish reading this sentence, the world's urban population will have grown by one new household. And as you pause for a moment to consider that, another household will have been added... pause... and another. Cities are growing at a rate of 1.5 million people per week.[1] At roughly five persons per household,[2] that's 300,000 households every week, which of course also means that the same number of dwelling units need to be constructed to keep up with household formation. Virtually, every breath you take marks the need to add one urban dwelling unit somewhere on the face of the globe, most likely in a developing country. The world's population is not only growing, it is urbanizing... rapidly. In 2008, for the first time in human history, the proportion of people living in a city exceeded 50 percent,[3] and urban population will continue to grow into the foreseeable future, with the figure rising to 68 percent by 2050.[4] During the period between 2018 and 2050, urban populations have been projected to increase by 2.5 billion.[5] Ninety percent of this growth will be in Asia and Africa.[6]

It's estimated that by 2025, there will be 440 million existing urban dwellings that are substandard, not fit for a healthy, dignified existence.[7] The need for replacement dwellings in fact overshadows the need for new dwellings. If replacement dwellings were to be built at the same pace that new urban households are formed, or 300,000 per week, it would take 28 years just to replace the existing substandard stock—assuming that the number of substandard units simply remains static. The arithmetic is simple, but staggering.

• • •

The argument presented in this chapter is that a global-scale solution to mid- and high-rise housing for dense urban development is urgently needed to cope with projected global urban population growth. The global middle class is growing rapidly, and land use patterns associated with housing for the middle class—automobile dependence and its concomitant development sprawl—are unsustainable. The American post-World War II suburban model has outlived its usefulness. The revitalization of cities has been underway for several decades largely due to the influx of young creatives, but those creatives revert to suburban living to raise families. A transformation in construction technology that brings down the cost of multi-story housing can encourage a shift in settlement patterns, re-populating cities not just with young singles but also with families and retirees. An equitable urbanism will require a cost-effective solution to housing construction at all price levels. Cities must attract the middle class and be affordable for the poor and working poor at the same time.

The Global Middle Class and Sprawl

The emergent economies in the developing world are, in fact, rapidly modernizing as well as urbanizing, with an expanding middle class. According to Kishore Mahbubani, author of *Convergence: Asia, the West, and the Logic of One World*, the global middle class will reach 4.9 billion by 2030,[8] an order-of-magnitude larger than the middle class of the U.S. and Europe combined. To discuss global housing needs is no longer to talk solely about meeting the minimum requirements of shelter. Adequate living space, with finishes, fixtures, and furnishings that reflect the aspirations of upwardly mobile societies are needed.

The growth of the middle class in emergent economies is accompanied by a demographic "youth bulge". In India, there are 560 million people under the age of 25, of whom 40 percent are between 10 and 19.[9] Cities are where young people come for education and jobs and are where young singles find mates and start families. The youth bulge and the urbanization bulge are related trends.

Uri Dadush, co-author of *The Global Middle Class Is Bigger Than We Thought*, has found that "the number of passenger cars in circulation can act as a direct measure of the middle class in developing countries".[10] Roughly seventy developing countries, altogether containing about four billion people, are poised to see rapid increases in car ownership in the years ahead.[11] The global rise in car ownership, while marking economic improvement for tens of millions of people a year, is at the same time an ominous trend, because with widespread automobile ownership comes the tendency toward American-style sprawl. Land use patterns in the developing world increasingly resemble our own, with urban surface area worldwide increasing, on average, at twice the rate of urban population growth.[12] On a global scale, a growing and urbanizing middle class is buying cars and using them to live on the outskirts, away from dense city cores.

2.1
Automobile dependence is facilitated by investment in limited-access highways instead of mass transit.

In the U.S., access to transit systems is inadequate. A report by the Brookings Institute states that "the typical metropolitan resident can reach about 30 percent of jobs in their metropolitan area via transit in 90 minutes".[13] The report points out that "while owning a car improves chances of employment, a growing body of work quantifies the crushing impact of housing and transportation costs on households' economic bottom lines".[14] For most people, there is no choice but to drive. For the poorest, the cost of owning and operating a car is too great, a factor contributing to recent trends in the American suburbanization of poverty.[15] A study by the Center for Neighborhood Technology showed that between 2000 and 2010, the combined cost of housing and transportation rose faster than incomes for median-income families.[16]

2.2
Typical pattern of automobile-dependent housing sprawl fostered by limited-access highways that encourage development on cheap land distant from city cores.

The trend toward automobile-dependent sprawl can only be reversed with planning policies that encourage density. Such policies include investment in mass transit; schools; public safety; and sanitation, electrification, and other infrastructure. We need zoning regulations that encourage multi-story housing, and we need safe, economical, high-quality multi-story dwellings that can be built at a rate that keeps pace with urban population growth.

• • •

As this is written, the coronavirus pandemic has created uncertainty about the future of city living. Still, there is a strong argument being made that cities will remain essential centers of economic life, education, innovation, and culture.[17] According to Dr. Mary T. Bassett, director of the FSB Center for Health and Human Rights at Harvard University, urban density is not the cause of viral transmission. "Factors that do seem to explain clusters of Covid-19 deaths in the United States are household crowding, poverty, racialized economic segregation and participation in the work force".[18] The disproportionate impact of the pandemic on lower-income communities is partly due to inequitable and crowded housing.[19] Crowding, a direct result of the high cost of housing, is not the same as density.

Equitable housing must be affordable and inclusionary.[20] We need a solution for multi-story urban housing that works for people at all income levels. Decades of segregated housing patterns created by redlining[21] will have to be reversed. In one installment of *The America We Need*, a recent editorial series responding to the pandemic with proposals for a "fair, resilient society", *The New York Times* writes: "Our cities are broken because affluent Americans have been segregating themselves from the poor, and our best hope for building a fairer, stronger nation is to break down those barriers".[22] To use a phrase that takes on new meaning in the context of Black Lives Matter, the middle class must have skin in the game.

Housing: In Transition?

The home-building industry in the U.S. is geared to the single-family house, laid out on small lots in planned suburban communities built on subdivided open space. Production builders like Clayton Homes, Howard Hughes Corporation, and Toll Brothers, among others, dominate this sector and have evolved to incorporate integrated planning, design, marketing, sales, and financing under one roof. These sophisticated companies deliver a reliable product at good value, geared to a market that wants large houses with status kitchens, walk-in closets, covered patios, and a nearby golf course.[23]

But suburban sprawl with its social and environmental costs is unsustainable. Within the suburbs, architects and planners are challenging the notion of the single-family home on a quarter- or half-acre lot. Transit Oriented Development (TOD) is based on principles of densely planned neighborhoods within walking distance of mass transit. TODs are today being planned and built around existing commuter rail hubs in small towns throughout the U.S. High-speed rail projects will, if implemented, spur further TOD in the decades ahead.

The seemingly intractable post-World War II housing crisis precipitated by the return of American soldiers from Europe and the Pacific was solved through a great suburban expansion, fueled by a variety of influences, ranging from enlightened social policy to national security strategy. Cold-war-era planners, fearing nuclear attack, successfully encouraged the "defensive dispersal" of population away from vulnerable cities.[24] This dispersal could not have been achieved without the interstate highway system, which, in turn, depended on the availability of cheap and abundant gasoline. At the same time, electric-traction streetcars, which once comprised 17,000 miles of track, were going into bankruptcy.[25] Builders such as William Levitt achieved unprecedented economies in "mass-constructing" the single-family house by the thousands on cheap, easy-to-build subdivided farm tracts. Thus, the American Dream: a house, a yard, a picket fence, symbolizing upward mobility and the attainment of a middle-class standard of living.

It is a familiar litany. Upon examining those received ideas in a contemporary context, the arguments for suburban development are not so compelling as they once might have seemed, and the arguments for a return to densely settled urban neighborhoods become persuasive.

The pandemic has exposed the fact that infectious disease spread is a function of crowding, but we must not repeat the mistake of post-war planners who advocated for defensive dispersal as a remedy. The suburban expansion left poor people behind, while affluent whites fled urban cores, leading to a spiral of economic decline in the nation's cities. The answer is not to abandon cities once again, but to make them more livable at all economic levels.

On the other hand, there is an epidemic of suburban disease associated with sedentary, automobile-dependent culture—obesity, childhood diabetes, and cardiovascular disease, among other afflictions.[26] Urban environments encourage walking as well as bicycle use, and discourage driving, increasing physical activity, and promoting better health among people of all ages. Local food opportunities in suburbs are frequently limited to fast foods, or convenience stores that stock processed snacks lacking nutritional value. Supermarkets are too often located in malls accessible only by car. Walkable urban neighborhoods, owing to density, support small-scale produce markets, delicatessens, and bodegas that offer affordable unprocessed foods.

How much time, money, and anxiety go into the maintenance of a quarter-acre patch of lawn? And what is the purpose of that lawn other than to be compared invidiously in terms of color, texture, cut, and consistency to the neighbor's lawn? The financial resources, not to mention the vast quantities of water, chemical nutrients, and weed killers that are poured into the suburban lawn, are hardly the ingredients of well-being or a sustainable water supply.

The suburban tract house may have been a valid aspiration for World War II veterans returning home by the hundreds of thousands. There was a housing crisis, with families doubled up in cramped city apartments. Levittowns across the nation—affordable dwellings for the middle class—were the answer to that generation's urgent needs. Today's needs are different, and a different American dream is called for.

Upward mobility in the U.S. lags other developed nations,[27] including formerly class-stratified European countries. Could our land use patterns and development models have something to do with it? Density, or lack thereof, is a significant factor that affects the ability of families to rise out of poverty and enter the middle class.[28] Sprawling metropolitan regions unable to support rapid transit leave poorer families stranded far from jobs. Commuters are saddled with three or four hours of commuting that can involve traffic jams and/or multiple bus connections. Combine that with the challenging logistics of childcare, and the obstacles to economic improvement are difficult at best to surmount. Housing closer to the central business core is too expensive. Physical immobility leads to economic immobility.

Pedestrian and stroller-friendly urban environments encourage spontaneous social interactions that alleviate the isolation of caring for small children. Nearby playgrounds ease the burden of child supervision by sharing it with other parents. Perhaps the suburbs offer easier access for children to take part in weekend soccer, although this can certainly be found in cities. When they reach adolescence, car (meaning parental) dependence is an anchor that stunts self-reliance and limits access to cultural opportunities that urban public transportation can provide. Alarms are often raised about the kind of harm that can come to a teenager getting about alone in the city. In the suburbs, teenagers and cars can be a lethal combination, worsened by the easy availability of drugs and alcohol behind the suburban school gym. To create a bucolic world for children, we have allowed—encouraged—not just suburban settlement patterns but also their attendant dysfunctions to spread and sprawl.

Then, what happens when the children are gone? The entire raison d'être of suburban living disappears. Why exactly did we move here? I can't remember. Cities, on the other hand, make sense for all generations. Children can grow up, move out, and still be a subway ride away. Grandparents can babysit downstairs. If family values are what you are looking for, move to a city.

The Creative City

The scholar and cultural critic Richard Florida has studied the successes and failures of economic development and related social phenomena in cities across the U.S. His analysis of patterns in education, employment, cultural, sexual and ethnic tolerance, and technology led to his concept of the *creative class*—a group whose occupations involve creative work broadly defined, from industrial design to advertising to high-tech engineering. Florida cites data showing that "creatives" comprise nearly a third of the American workforce. He talks about nurturing "creative ecosystems" by attracting young talented creatives to cities to promote urban economic development.

Writing in 2002, Florida posited that careers of this new generation are "horizontal" instead of "vertical" as they had been for previous generations. A young professional might expect to work for many companies during a career, rather than rise through the ranks and ultimately retire from one firm the way her parents might have done. A re-ordering of priorities follows from this shift to the horizontal career, in which a geographic location is chosen first, and then job opportunities are pursued based on that choice. In past years, the young upwardly mobile college graduate would be more likely to take a career-long job with an established company and then re-locate accordingly. Today's young professional seeks a place to live that offers attractive lifestyle opportunities that might include culture, night life, urbanity, access to outdoor recreation, a lively music scene, and so on.

Florida identifies three essential components of a successful contemporary urban economy—the "three T's"—talent, technology, and tolerance. The importance to an urban economy of talent and technology seems self-evident. Interestingly, he finds a correlation between cities that have thriving gay communities and cities that are economically successful, which he views as being due to general attitudes that value openness to diverse and divergent ideas and lifestyles, attitudes that nourish creative thinking.

Viewed 18 years after the publication of Florida's influential book, *The Rise of the Creative Class*, we see that the economic benefits of the creative urban economy have been unequally distributed. In 2017, Florida published *The New Urban Crisis: How Our Cities Are Increasing Inequality, Deepening Segregation, and Failing the Middle Class – and What We Can Do about It*. Among the policy strategies that he advocates are land use policies that encourage growth without creating pockets of creative class affluence[29] and the construction of more affordable rental housing.[30] Florida acknowledges that simply deregulating land use to encourage greater density and verticality is insufficient. He writes:

> the high cost of urban land combined with *the high cost of high-rise construction* (emphasis added) mean it is likely to mainly add more luxury towers and that it will do little to provide the kinds of affordable housing that our cities really need.[31]

The notion of a creative urban ecosystem resonates with the ideas of Jane Jacobs, the pioneering urbanist who changed the way we think about cities. Jacobs' writings and her epic battles with Robert Moses turned the tide against large-scale urban renewal. Jacobs believed that neighborhoods are complex webs of relationships, based as much on diverse social structures as physical structures, accreted over time. Wholesale bulldozing to construct high-rise housing in isolated superblocks destroyed diverse urban ecologies and replaced them with residential mono-cultures, draining character and life from city streets, and fomenting social ills and crime.

We are only just now coming to a more nuanced understanding that recognizes some virtues of Moses' urbanism and some limitations of Jacobs. For decades, the idea of large-scale public housing was anathema. The favorite dead horse to flog was Pruitt-Igoe, a project in St. Louis that was dynamited in 1972 as being crime-riddled and too decrepit to be worth saving. In books, essays, and lectures widely disseminated 40 years ago, post-modern critics like the late Charles Jencks used the image of Pruitt-Igoe imploding into dust as a metaphor to proclaim the "death" of modern architecture. A recent documentary by filmmaker Chad Freidrichs called "The Pruitt-Igoe Myth"[32] demolishes Jencks' and others selectively argued interpretation of the facts.

Writing about the film in *The New York Times*,[33] architecture critic Michael Kimmelman tells the story of two housing projects of very similar design with very different fates. Both were high-rise slabs set in a park-like site spreading over several city blocks. One is Pruitt-Igoe, and the other is Penn South in Manhattan's Chelsea neighborhood. Penn South, it turns out, is a successful, affordable, and sought-after place to live. The interior park spaces at Penn South, so reviled by Jacobs, are well-used by elderly people who want to sit outdoors near their homes within a garden-like setting. Pruit-Igoe, finally given a fair hearing, is revealed to have been successful at first, but was ruined long before demolition by a combination of inadequate maintenance, benighted welfare policies, and white flight to the suburbs.

Kimmelman's larger point is that the high-rise model of urban housing is not inherently bad or good. Rather, it is the context into which that model is placed, and the policies that are administered after it is built that determine success or failure.

The principles and concepts of modular architecture discussed in this book do not have a direct bearing on theories of city planning per se, or whether planning should aim toward the large-scale approach of Robert Moses or the incremental approach favored by adherents of Jane Jacobs' ideas. On city planning principles, this book is agnostic. But what any approach to a sustainable city must have is a way of building mid- and high-rise, high-quality housing that is within the financial means of the aspiring, the emergent, and the established middle class. Too many professionals and creatives flock to urban centers as young people stay long enough to mate, but then find that the costs of housing in the heart of desirable cities are too high to remain and raise a family. The approach to intermodal modular architecture that will unfold in later chapters is equally suited to towers in the park, to urban infill housing of four to six stories, as well as to hybrid typologies that might not fit so neatly into either category.[34]

City Living within Reach

Our growing awareness of the scale of global urban growth makes us wonder: how will we achieve the scale that demographic trends are thrusting upon us, and avoid the ills of unsustainable sprawl? How can we encourage the growth of diverse urban neighborhoods that will attract a stable middle class while also meeting the housing needs of those less affluent?

If one were to only know the recently built environment through the pages of the architectural trade glossies, monographs, and real estate advertising, one would think that a glittering world of fluid forms and luminous spaces set off against a twilit sky is the world we actually inhabit. But we do not *dwell* in that photogenic world. Allowing for exceptions, our everyday urban world of domestic architecture ranges between two very different kinds of experiences: that of the old (mainly pre-20th century) mixed-use urban districts that give us a sense of well-being and charm; and the experience of modern "condo canyons" with automobile-scaled streets and the bulked up and slick buildings that increasingly define the modern city. When we imagine a home in the metropolis, we often find ourselves thinking of urbanity from an earlier era—perhaps brownstone Brooklyn or the converted 19th-century industrial neighborhoods of downtown Manhattan. There is an exhilarating modern alternative available to the wealthy, that of living in an architect-designed luxury-appointed glass tower. This has its undeniable appeal, but if it were to be replicated in a down-market version on a vast scale, it would almost certainly lose that appeal. Much the way the Seagram Building was once a startling counterpoint to the traditional masonry street wall of Park Avenue, as one glass tower after another eventually lined the entire avenue, Mies van der Rohe's exceptional work of architecture was recontextualized alongside commercial steel-and-glass simulacra. The exceptional building requires a fabric of ordinary buildings to provide a setting within which to stand out. Equally important, ordinary buildings can be honorable as architecture even if they are not signature statements.

We've defined our expectations downward and have come to accept a diminished tactile experience of everyday architecture, especially at the scale of the detail. Yet, it is in our living spaces where we are most sensitized to details, given that we experience every surface, joint, and corner at close hand, day in and day out. At the same time, we take joy in objects that embody sophisticated industrial design and with which we interact intimately—our cars, our hand-held gadgets, our kitchen appliances. The contrast between our merely tolerable yet costly contemporary urban living environments and our extraordinary consumer products is striking. Is it not possible to apply the same combination of innovation and design rigor that companies like Apple have forged, to build a new kind of urban habitat?

The quality of consumer products is made possible by economies of scale. The resources needed for R&D, design, prototyping, production engineering, and tooling are only available to enterprises that manufacture efficiently and sell to the largest possible markets. It is simply too expensive and wasteful to build affordable and at the same time desirable multi-story urban housing using our current archaic methods. Housing made in factories, the cherished dream of modernism, remains unrealized. This book's thesis is that it is indeed possible to transfer industrial methods to housing, but it will require a transformation in every aspect of the way we design and build. First and foremost, it will require scale.

PRINCIPLE #1   ECONOMIES OF SCALE

The challenge, then, is how to achieve scale with diversity, differentiation, and local adaptation, and to encourage density and discourage sprawl. A shift in patterns of land use requires a concerted effort on multiple fronts, including land use policy, investment in transit, tax incentives, and not least, the cost of construction. If we are to reverse the unsustainable and inequitable growth of suburbs, we will have to bring down the cost of multi-story urban housing. The land use problem is inextricable from the problem of construction economics.

In order to attract the global middle class across generations to live in cities and at the same time provide affordable housing for the less affluent, we need a scalable solution that, like the automotive industry, can offer a range of models from economy to luxury built on the same basic chassis.

As we consider our approach to urban housing, we are obliged to do more than simply meet a minimal standard of health, safety, and welfare. We are also obliged to resolve the tension between our enormous productive/technological capability on the one hand, and our unfulfilled aspiration to shape the built environment to meet our psychological, cultural, and social needs on the other. Meanwhile, the construction of the world's cities proceeds at an unprecedented scale and speed.

Notes

1 "68% of the World Population Projected to Live in Urban Areas by 2050, Says UN," United Nations Department of Economic and Social Affairs, May 16, 2018, https://www.un.org/development/desa/en/news/population/2018-revision-of-world-urbanization-prospects.html. Based on projections of 2.5 billion new urban inhabitants between 2018 and 2030.
2 John Bongaarts, "Household Size and Composition in the Developing World in the 1990s," *Population Studies* 55, no. 3 (2001): 8.
3 Alidad Vassigh and Tann vom Hove, "Urban Population Growth between 1950 and 2030," last modified August 7, 2012, http://www.citymayors.com/statistics/urban-population-intro.html.
4 United Nations Department of Economic and Social Affairs, 2018.
5 United Nations Department of Economic and Social Affairs, 2018.
6 United Nations Department of Economic and Social Affairs, 2018.
7 Jonathan Woetzel, Jan Mischke and Sangeeth Ram, "The World's Housing Crisis Doesn't Need a Revolutionary Solution," Policy, *Harvard Business Review*,

December 25, 2014, https://hbr.org/2014/12/the-worlds-housing-crisis-doesnt-need-a-revolutionary-solution.

8   Jimmy Yapp, "Singaporean Former Diplomat Kishore Mahbubani on Why He Is Optimistic about the Future," ACCA, published October 1, 2016, https://www.accaglobal.com/in/en/member/member/accounting-business/2016/10/interviews/kishore-mahbubani.html.

9   Thomas Friedman, "India vs. China vs. Egypt," Opinion, *New York Times*, February 6, 2013, https://www.nytimes.com/2013/02/06/opinion/friedman-india-vs-china-vs-egypt.html.

10 Uri Dash and Shimelse Ali, "In Search of the Global Middle Class: A New Index," published July 23, 2012, https://carnegieendowment.org/2012/07/23/in-search-of-global-middle-class-new-index-pub-48908.

11 Shimelse Ali and Uri Dadush, "The Global Middle Class is Bigger than We Thought," Argument, *Foreign Policy*, May 16, 2012, https://foreignpolicy.com/2012/05/16/the-global-middle-class-is-bigger-than-we-thought/.

12 Karen C. Seto, Burak Güneralp and Lucy R. Hutyra, "Global Forcasts of Urban Expansion to 2030 and Direct Impacts on Biodiversity and Carbon Pools," *Proceedings of the National Academy of Sciences of the United States of America* 109, no. 40 (2012): 16083

13 Adie Tomer, Elizabeth Kneebone, Robert Puentes and Alan Berube, "Metropolitan Opportunity: Transit and Jobs in Metropolitan America," *Metropolitan Infrastructure Initiative Series and Metropolitan Opportunity Series* (2011): 1. https://www.brookings.edu/wp-content/uploads/2016/06/0512_jobs_transit.pdf.

14 Tomer, Kneebone, Puentes and Berube, 4.

15 Tomer, Kneebone, Puentes and Berube, 3.

16 Robert Hickey, Jeffrey Lubell, Peter Haas and Stephanie Morse, "Losing Ground: The Struggle of Moderate-Income Households to Afford the Rising Costs of Housing and Transportation," *Center for Housing Policy* and *Center for Neighborhood Technology* (2012): 6, https://www.novoco.com/sites/default/files/atoms/files/nhc_losing_ground_101812.pdf.

17 Editorial Board, "The Cities We Need," Opinion, *New York Times*, May 11, 2020, https://www.nytimes.com/2020/05/11/opinion/sunday/coronavirus-us-cities-inequality.html.

18 Mary T. Bassett, "Just Because You Can Afford to Leave the City Doesn't Mean You Should," Opinion, *New York Times*, May 15, 2020, https://www.nytimes.com/2020/05/15/opinion/sunday/coronavirus-cities-density.html.

19 Bassett, 2020.

20 "What Is Inclusionary Housing?" Inclusionary Housing, accessed July 4, 2020, https://inclusionaryhousing.org/inclusionary-housing-explained/what-is-inclusionary-housing/#:~:text=Inclusionary%20housing%20programs%20are%20local,units%20to%20lower%2Dincome%20residents.

21 Tyler Cukar, "Orchestrated Urbanism: The Race Built City," *FXCollaborative Podium*, 2020, accessed July 4, 2020, http://www.fxcollaborative.com/activity/publications/13/orchestrated-urbanism/.

22 Editorial Board, 2020.

23 Alana Semuels, "Why Are Developers Still Building Sprawl?" Business, *Atlantic*, February 24, 2015, https://www.theatlantic.com/business/archive/2015/02/why-are-people-still-building-sprawl/385741/.

24 Michael Quinn Dudley, "Sprawl As Strategy: City Planners Face the Bomb," *Journal of Planning Education and Research* 21, no. 1 (2001): 52–63.

25 Joseph Stromberg, "The Real Story behind the Demise of America's Once-mighty Streetcars" *Vox*, May 7, 2015 https://www.vox.com/2015/5/7/8562007/streetcar-history-demise.

26 Howard Frumkin, "Urban Sprawl and Public Health," *Public Health Reports* 117, no. 3 (2002): 201–217, https://doi.org/10.1093/phr/117.3.201.

27 Julia B. Isaacs, "International Comparisons of Economic Mobility," *The Brookings Institution* (2016): 6, https://www.brookings.edu/wp-content/uploads/2016/07/02_economic_mobility_sawhill_ch3.pdf.

28 Raj Chetty, Nathaniel Hendren, Patrick Kline and Emmanuel Saez, "The Equality of Opportunity Project," Harvard University, University of California Berkeley, 2013. Paul Krugman, "Stranded by Sprawl," Opinion, *New York Times*, July 28, 2013, https://www.nytimes.com/2013/07/29/opinion/krugman-stranded-by-sprawl.html. Dave Leonhardt, "In Climbing Income Ladder, Location Matters," *New York Times*, July 22, 2013, https://www.nytimes.com/2013/07/22/business/in-climbing-income-ladder-location-matters.html.

29 Richard Florida, *The New Urban Crisis: How Our Cities Are Increasing Inequality, Deepening Segregation, And Failing The Middle Class – And What We Can Do About It* (New York: Basic Books, 2017): 191–195.

30 Florida, 199–202.

31 Florida, 192.

32 *The Pruitt-Igoe Myth*, directed by Chad Freidrichs (St. Louis, MO: Unicorn Stencil, 2011), DVD.

33 Michael Kimmelman, "Towers of Dreams: One Ended in Nightmare," Critic's Notebook, *New York Times*, January 25, 2012, https://www.nytimes.com/2012/01/26/arts/design/penn-south-and-pruitt-igoe-starkly-different-housing-plans.html.

34 David Wallance and Austin Sakong, "Boundary Issues: Building Form, Site Form, Urban Form," *FXCollaborative Podium*, 2020, accessed July 4, 2020, https://issuu.com/fxfowle/docs/190220_boundaryissues.

3 The Argument for Economical Transportation

When we think of building (the noun), we think of building (the verb). We peer through the eyehole in our mental sidewalk fence and see truckloads of steel, bricks, and mortar unloaded at the building site and laboriously joined piece by piece, as a structure slowly rises out of the excavation. Lots of noise, dust, and a small army of construction workers shouting and waving instructions to one another above the din. This is the nature of the construction process as it has been since the mythical Tower of Babel.

We'll begin this chapter with an overview of construction the way it has been for millennia, which will set the stage for a review of what we'll call the "legacy" modular industry as it currently exists in the U.S. Within the legacy industry, we'll classify several categories of modular construction. Among these categories, one is scalable, some have design flexibility, and some are economical, but none are all three. In looking at scalability, we'll analyze the mismatch between the legacy industry's production capacity in the factory and crane capacity at the jobsite. We'll also note the mismatch between architects' design expectations and the legacy industry's ability to meet those expectations. With that background in mind, we'll question received ideas about module size and transportation to arrive at critical insights about scalability, transportation, standards, economy, and design flexibility. Our thesis is that limited transportation distance prevents the modular industry from achieving economies of scale, and that intermodal standards are necessary for economical long-distance transportation and

3.1
The Construction of
the Tower of Babel,
Hendrick van Cleve III, c.
1525–1589, via Snark / Art
Resources, NY.

thereby to achieve scale. Design flexibility is also central to the argument for intermodal modular architecture, but we'll save that topic for an in-depth discussion in Chapter 6.

• • •

From the earliest history of construction, building techniques have been constrained by the strength and durability of available materials, the technology for shaping, finishing, and joining materials together, and the means at hand for transporting, lifting, and assembling those materials into a building. For thousands of years, the essential technical and physical characteristics of buildings (formal, cultural, and stylistic differences aside) remained unchanged.

Until the 19th century, building materials were mainly limited to harvested (wood), quarried (stone), and earthen (brick) materials, with very limited use of metal and glass. Then, in the last great transformative phase in

3.2
"The future is already here—it's just not very evenly distributed"—William Gibson.

building technology, along came some radically new materials. Hand-craft began its slow decline. Steam, and later, electric and internal combustion engines multiplied our ability to transport and lift heavy objects, which up to that point was limited by the energy that could be extracted from human and animal muscle. New processes were invented to manufacture steel and glass in large quantities.

Buildings are massive structures weighing hundreds if not hundreds of thousands of tons. You can't build a large building in one place and move it to another place. Buildings, being uniquely large objects, must be put together at the building site by carpenters, masons, welders, electricians, plumbers... the list goes on to include dozens of trades on a typical high-rise residential project. The three-dimensional geography of the job site discourages coordination, quality control, and labor efficiency. The workforce is spread out on multiple floors, and simply moving workers and materials up and down the building eats away at the efficient use of time. At the morning and afternoon "rush hours", there can be a 45-minute commute just to get up or down the construction elevator on a high-rise building. Contractors in New York City assume that they will net about four to five hours of productive work from a seven-hour day.[1] On unionized projects, archaic work rules and self-interested labor agreements further erode productivity.[2]

Construction is a conservative industry, slow to innovate, slow to adapt and adopt. Innovations accrue as new products are introduced that work with old products and methods. The order in which the pieces are joined has the logic of a time-tested recipe handed down through generations. You don't add the sheet rock before the plumbing. You don't add the wiring before the framing. In building construction, a "disruptive" technology, one that writes not just a new recipe but an entirely new way of cooking, rarely comes along.

When electric wiring was first introduced to wood-frame house construction, the electrician drilled the two-by-fours to string wires through the walls, wire by wire, stud by stud. More than a century later, houses are still wired the same way. When steel studs were introduced in commercial construction, the studs were manufactured with knockouts ready for the wiring to be threaded through. The knockouts led to a modest improvement in efficiency, and they were necessary since drilling steel studs for every electrical cable isn't practical, but the electrician still unspools cable and weaves circuits through the building one strand at a time. If the electrician doesn't show up that day, everybody else waits. In industry, meanwhile, cable harnesses—bundles of wires cut, color-coded, and organized in advance according to a detailed circuit plan—have long been prefabricated by specialty suppliers. The cable harness is then rapidly installed by the manufacturer as a subcomponent of the final assembly.

The separation of thinking and planning from doing was the radical break of the industrial revolution. Henry Ford pioneered the isolation of processes into repetitive tasks performed by unskilled workers, which required that the task of organizing that work be turned over to skilled designers and engineers. In exchanging the autonomy of the craftsman for the more efficient separation of mind and hand, Ford achieved more productivity, to higher standards of quality, at lower cost. The benefits of this re-ordering of our way of making things are evident all around us in our cars, appliances, computers—the modern world with all its comforts and conveniences that we would be loath to give up.

In the 1970s, a new "post-industrial" order emerged, ushered in largely by changes in Japanese auto manufacturing. Sometimes referred to as Post-Fordism,[3] the new approach is characterized by "flexible specialization" and is made possible by advances in information technology. The replacement of mass-manufactured generic goods with a diversity of products geared to niche markets led to a greatly reduced but multi-skilled workforce able to manage digitally driven technologies, including Computer Numeric (CNC) milling, robotic welding, and soon, perhaps, large-scale 3D-printing. "Economies of scale" were supplemented by "economies of scope". A global network of supply chains has evolved in which pre-assembled components arrive at the assembly facility for the last steps in the manufacturing process.

Building construction is situated variously in the pre-industrial, the industrial, and the post-industrial worlds. The tendency for building technology to progress slowly and incrementally makes a wholesale reconsideration of systems difficult. Architecture firms, adhering to an atelier model of practice (and inhibited by their professional liability insurers), stay at arm's length from the means and methods of production.[4]

Wait! We build skyscrapers a half-mile high. Are you telling me that our building technology is backward? Well, yes, when you change focus from the result, which is indeed often extraordinary, and look instead at the process. Through that lens, it becomes clear that in certain crucial respects the industrial revolution has not yet arrived—or better stated, the past, present, and future in building technology are on separate and often conflicting trajectories.

Despite the future being already here in so many ways, the construction of buildings today remains rooted in the past, at the building site, as it has been for thousands of years. The assembly line that Henry Ford perfected a century ago, and which has advanced to the present day with just-in-time manufacturing and robotic welding, has yet to change the process of building. Most buildings are still built one at a time, piece by piece, from singular designs. While advances are made in aspects of prefabrication (facades, elevators, light fixtures, cabinetry, etc.), the construction industry has so far failed to apply efficient methods of manufacturing to the entire construction process.[5]

Building construction is fractionalized among many competing and often adversarial interests. Construction managers and general contractors farm out the work to myriad subcontractors, with added layers of sub-subcontractors, most of whom are working together for the first time and who have competing needs for time and space to perform their tasks. On a union project, the subcontractors themselves have limited control because the labor force owes loyalty to the union as well as to the subcontractor.

Each subcontractor is responsible for hundreds or thousands of bits and pieces of the building, some of those pieces field-constructed, like the wooden forms into which concrete is poured, and some factory-made and field-installed, like curtain wall facades. Factory-made curtain wall can be up to ten times more precise than a field-built steel frame to which it is attached.[6] A "loose-fit" mentality pervades. Only with very high budgets can precise joinery be achieved in the field.

Three-dimensional coordination of elaborate building systems—for example, the routing of ductwork and piping through a tightly packed space above a suspended ceiling—is done in the field under intense schedule pressure, and there is only one opportunity to get it right. To some extent, recent advances in digital design (Building Information Modeling, or BIM) have improved coordination, but last-minute adjustments that either sacrifice the quality of design and function or result in costly contract changes are still too often the rule rather than the exception. Each design is a one-off, with architects and engineers "re-inventing the wheel" on every new building. Even medium-size buildings can require hundreds of thousands of hours of design, coordination and negotiation among architects, engineers, consultants, code officials, and clients.

The Pursuit of Industrialized Building

The search for a better way to organize building construction, on a par with the automotive, aerospace, and shipbuilding industries, is the mythic quest of modern architecture. The modernist pioneers of the early 20th century believed that new building technologies in the hands of architects would be the solution to the housing problems of their era. Since that time, there have been attempts, some succeeding as a polemic,[7] and some succeeding as a prototype,[8] but none to date has succeeded in transforming housing construction.

Architects Stephen Kieran and James Timberlake made a cogent and compelling case for transforming how we build in their 2004 book *Refabricating Architecture*,[9] drawing a sharp contrast between the architect and the process engineer. In their argument, the architect is wedded to anachronistic notions about art, while the process engineer is dedicated to efficiency and "commodity". Architecture is fragmented, while industry is integrated. In manufacturing—unlike architecture and building construction—thinking and doing take place within one organization, fostering collaboration and coordination rather than disarray and conflict. The process engineer designs the relationships among the many parts and participants so that they merge seamlessly in a complex endeavor. The architect, on the other hand, is relegated to the comparatively narrow task of designing of a building.

Keiran and Timberlake studied modern supply chain manufacturing methods and compared those methods with traditional construction. They described how very large objects, like jumbo jets and ships, are built up from prefabricated assemblies comprised, in turn, of sub-assemblies and even sub-sub-assemblies. Only at the final stage are the largest "chunks" joined, which in manufacturing an airliner are entire sections of fuselage complete with systems and finishes. The various systems are then stitched together into a complete whole.

In shipbuilding, automotive, and aerospace manufacturing, the domain of the process engineer ends at the shipyard drydock, the factory gate, or the runway. Process engineering is an effective way to orchestrate the manufacture of large objects that exit the factory under their own power. So far, so good, but the vexing problem of assembling modular buildings, as opposed to a jetliner, is that what happens from the time that the module exits the factory to when it is assembled into a building is no longer integrated into the process.

Here is the crux of the matter: the problem of transportation logistics in modular building construction *is* the problem of modular building construction, and that problem has been overlooked.

This book builds on Keiran's and Timberlake's thesis. Like the modular approach they envision, our proposal falls broadly into the category of a "volumetric modular system", in which three-dimensional chunks of buildings are factory fabricated, and then moved some distance to the job site where they are aggregated into a completed building. Each module contains within it a small world of construction—the structural frame, wiring, plumbing, HVAC, fixtures, partitions, finishes; closets, cabinets, and appliances. Even the building façade can be attached before the construction crane carries the modules aloft.

Volumetric modular construction, a decades-old method primarily used for building wood-framed houses and low-cost temporary structures, has in recent years been adapted for high-rise urban housing. In 2016, a 32-story volumetric modular apartment building was completed in Brooklyn, NY. The developer set up a factory only a couple of miles from the building site, but challenging transportation logistics still hampered the construction process. The modules were oversize, hard to maneuver, and the city's Department of Transportation restricted transportation to night-time. Congested city streets meant that there was limited staging space at the job site. The factory produced modules at a fraction of the rate needed to keep the expensive construction crane operating at full capacity. There were other problems, including mismatched tolerances between site-built steel trusses and prefabricated modules that further contributed to delays and cost overruns. Eventually, the project was completed and occupied. Despite setbacks, it demonstrated that architecturally ambitious high-rise modular construction is feasible. Still, lessons remain to be learned.

The Legacy Modular Industry

In 2018, a total of 2,314 multi-family modular units were produced,[10] as reported by the Modular Building Institute (MBI).[11] Compare that to the total multi-family output of the U.S. construction industry, which reported 374,000 multi-family housing unit starts in 2018.[12] The legacy modular industry represented by the MBI is supplying an insignificant 0.06 percent—the majority of which is wood-frame modular—of the American multi-family housing market. Steel is the predominant structural material for mid- and high-rise[13] modular buildings in the U.S. The MBI doesn't track individual market sectors by wood or steel-frame construction, or by low-, mid-, or high-rise, but across all sectors and heights, steel frame accounts for about 30 percent of U.S. modular manufacturing capacity.[14] The modular industry's capacity for steel-frame manufacturing would therefore be about 0.02 percent of the total multi-family market.

The reason for this gap between the multi-family housing market and modular output is not simply lack of capacity. If that were the problem, the solution would be to just build more modular factories. But manufacturers are for the most part leery of overburdening themselves with debt and overhead, concerned that the next economic downturn would put them out of business.[15] The relatively small scale of the modular industry makes it unusually sensitive to economic downturns in regional markets. Unlike general contractors, who hire labor as demand fluctuates, and carry comparatively low overhead, modular manufacturers are heavily invested in plant, equipment, and employees. A fall-off in orders can quickly turn into a catastrophe. In 2011, amidst a construction slowdown, Kullman Industries, one of the oldest and largest steel-frame contract modular manufacturers, succumbed and filed for bankruptcy.[16] A manufacturer in New York, Capsys, shut down after their rent at the Brooklyn Navy Yard rose in 2015.[17] DeLuxe Building Systems, Inc., in Pennsylvania, closed in 2018[18] (now under new ownership as Deluxe Modular). These three represented about one-third of the steel-frame modular manufacturers east of the Mississippi.[19]

The underlying reason for the weak performance of the legacy industry is hidden in plain sight. The industry has not thrived in part because it has not adopted advanced industrial processes, but in equal part because it has not solved the problem of transportation logistics. And both failures are profoundly related.

At the risk of repetition: transportation is not only the problem that must be solved, but it is the problem that must be solved first, the prerequisite for a scalable system for manufacturing mid- and high-rise modular housing. The conventional wisdom in the legacy modular industry is that economy is achieved by building the largest possible modules that can be rolled down the highway and craned onto a foundation. The unquestioned assumption is that economy means the fewest number of trips from the factory to the job site, the fewest crane picks to hoist modules into place, and the fewest number of joints to close and finish in the field. The consequence of this commitment to super-size modules is that in order to be cost-effective and to compete with conventional construction, manufacturers must limit themselves to a 125-mile radius from the factory to the building site,[20] due to the cost of pilot cars,[21] overnight accommodations, fuel, special permits, insurance, etc.

Those few modular manufacturers who build steel-framed buildings for the commercial and multi-story market sell their approach as a time saver but not as a construction cost saver.[22] For some clients, the time-saving can be decisive—for example, a university putting up student housing that wants the work to be done over summer vacation—but the market remains, nevertheless, regionally bound due to limits on transportation.

PRINCIPLE #2 ECONOMICAL LONG-DISTANCE TRANSPORTATION

Large-scale industries require access to global markets. Large-scale markets are required to generate sufficient revenue to support R&D, investment in plant and equipment, and sophisticated marketing and sales. And the economical solution to long-distance transportation already exists: the intermodal containerized freight system.

Manufacturing Output and Crane Capacity

The idea behind saving time in modular construction is that modules can be manufactured while foundations are being excavated and poured. Modules will then start arriving at the job site for craning as soon as the foundation is ready.

The legacy manufacturers produce at a rate of two to three modules in a daily shift[23] with two lines running, if dimensions are repetitive and there is no unusual complexity. Production slows down as dimensional variation and complexity increases. A rate of two to three modules per day can work for a building of 150,000–175,000 square feet, when all modules are manufactured concurrently with foundations. But the time-saving argument starts to unravel when it comes to a large-scale urban high-rise. On larger buildings, once foundations are done, the rate at which modules are produced in the factory has to match the speed with which the crane can operate, or those time-savings quickly evaporate.

The following example, based on a repetitive 400-square-foot module,[24] will demonstrate that as scale increases, there is a natural limit on time-savings. A single crane can typically stack 8–12 modules a day, or up to four times the factory production rate. What happens when a large building—say 500,000 square feet, comprising about 1,250 modules—is being manufactured?

We'll assume that foundations will take six months. At the upper manufacturing rate of three modules a day, 390 modules or 156,000 square feet are in storage ready to start stacking when foundations are done in week 26. (It's worth noting that this will require about 7 acres of laydown space, allowing vehicular aisles between modules. Laydown space is another limiting factor.) The 860 modules needed to complete the remaining 344,000 square feet will take another 57 weeks to manufacture.

At a conservative craning rate of eight modules per day, that first batch, which has been waiting in storage, is set in place by week 36. Meanwhile, the factory is producing as fast as it can, but only five weeks later, by week 41, the crane has fully caught up with manufacturing output. Going forward that costly crane and operating engineer is limited to craning each day's manufacturing output of three modules a day and will be working at less than 40 percent efficiency. It will take another 42 weeks or so to manufacture and crane the rest of the modules. Stacking is done by week 83. It could have been completed by week 57, or 26 weeks earlier, if modules could have been manufactured at the rate that the crane can set them.

Stacking is done 19 months from the start of construction. Add, say, another five months of hook-ups and finishing after craning is finally done and the construction time comes to a total of 24 months, a timeframe comparable to a conventionally constructed building. The limiting factor when you start scaling up turns out to be the legacy industry's rate of factory production.[25]

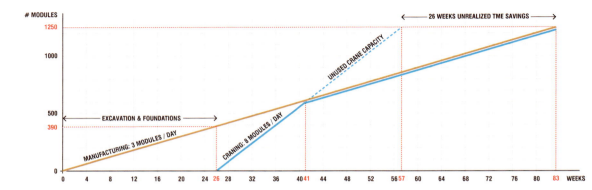

3.3
Manufacturing output vs. crane rate.

Now consider the legacy modular manufacturer's situation from a business point of view. The factory that undertakes a 500,000-square-foot building will be tied up for 19 months on that one project. This creates significant business risks. In addition to the potential for that one project to go badly and sink the company, all other sales opportunities must be passed up. By the time the manufacturer is finally ready to accept a new order, customers will have gone to the competition. To maintain marketing and sales momentum, project turnaround time cannot be much more than just a few months, and multiple projects need to be in production simultaneously to spread risk.

Large-scale projects require large-scale enterprises that operate in large-scale markets. Large-scale enterprises can afford large-scale facilities, investment in R&D, advanced manufacturing technology, and sophisticated marketing and sales. The 125-mile limit of transportation range has stunted the growth of the legacy modular industry and prevented it from operating on a national scale, and certainly not on a global scale.

Let's go back to 1947, when the Levitt family applied rational methods of manufacturing to the development of 17,400 houses on a Long Island potato field. The Levitt's achieved a peak daily production rate of over 30 houses at 750 square feet each,[26] or 22,500 square feet of housing per day. To achieve in multi-story modular manufacturing what the Levitts achieved in subdivision development would be the equivalent of 56 modules a day,[27] or 18 times the current legacy factory production rate. That would be enough to keep seven construction cranes busy.

Modular Systems Classified

To see a way forward to a scalable future, let's start with a taxonomy of the legacy modular industry. We'll classify the industry by the nature of the product and the market. We'll note the way architects interact with the manufacturer and the design flexibility associated with each category. For now, we'll include small buildings and single-family houses, and we'll include both steel and wood.

Relocatable Modular: Repetitive and Reusable. These are utilitarian buildings, made up of one or several modules, typically relocatable facilities like construction field offices. Relocatable buildings are the single largest segment of the U.S. legacy modular industry,[28] representing nearly half of its annual output. Relocatable modular buildings are leased or sold by a national or regional network of distributors, such as William Scotsman, Inc. or Design Space Modular Buildings. The distributors procure from regional manufacturers, who do production runs conforming to a standard specification.

Relocatable modular is standardized and inexpensive. Regional manufacturers have established relationships with the distributors, who provide factories with a reliable stream of revenue. The erroneous public perception that modular construction is inferior (which is starting to fade) is in part due to the utilitarian quality of relocatable modular.

3.4
Williams Scotsman relocatable offices.

Catalog Modular: Lots of Choice. The single-family residential modular industry offers a wide range of pre-designed as well as custom houses, comprised of one or more oversize wood-framed modules, with finishes and appointments that are indistinguishable from a site-built house. These houses are typically dressed in the usual period styles, and are planned and designed by in-house architects according to market research that tracks trends in buyer preferences. Catalog modular is based on a network of distributors who, in turn, procure from local manufacturers.

Like the old Sears Roebuck catalog house, these houses can be sold directly to home buyers. The advantage of catalog modular is that repetition of a basic type allows for incremental refinements and optimization in the manufacturing process and predictability in pricing. Of equal importance is the representation through photographs or computer simulations of exactly what the customer will get in the finished product.

A low-volume niche market has emerged for modular single-family homes targeted for a design-conscious demographic characterized by readers of *Dwell* magazine. Often founded by architects who oversee design, sometimes teaming with outside design firms, companies offering modern modular catalog houses include Connect Homes in California, Turkel Design in Massachusetts, and Simplex Homes in Pennsylvania.[29]

3.5
Dune Road House, designed by Resolution: 4 Architecture, manufactured by Simplex Homes (courtesy of Resolution: 4 Architecture).

Manufactured Homes: Industrial Scale. In the U.S., this is the generally accepted term for a home built in a factory setting to the federal specifications of the U.S. Department of Housing and Urban Development (HUD) and then transported in one or more sections to the home site. Manufactured homes are required to be built on a permanent steel chassis. The superstructure is likely to be wood framed with a large selection of options for interior and exterior finishes comparable to site-built homes. Upon arrival at the site, the house can be installed on either a permanent foundation or an alternative foundation system. A manufactured home built in compliance with HUD requirements will be inspected in the factory and given a certification label that indicates the home has been manufactured and inspected in accordance with federal standards and no further inspection within the walls of the module are required. New manufactured homes must be inspected in accordance with Federal Manufactured Home Installation Program and installed in accordance with the Manufactured Home Installation Standards. These programs are administrated either by the states or by HUD in the absence of a state program. While manufactured homes used to carry a stigma, the design distinctions between manufactured homes and catalog modular homes are blurring as manufacturers offer more and more choices and features, such as second stories, dormers, porches, and the like. Manufactured homes are produced on an industrial scale, are affordable, and represent a significant 6 percent of U.S. housing stock.[30]

3.6
Clayton Homes factory,
Athens, GA © 2020 CMH
Services, Inc.

Pod Modular: Standardized Room Types. There are a few firms, mainly European as well as Australian, who offer a standard series of steel framed modules that can be arranged in a variety of multi-story configurations, but each module itself is a standard room type with a fixed layout. Tempo, in the Netherlands, Polcom in Poland, and QuickSmart Homes in Australia are representative of this category. Tempo uses re-purposed shipping containers as the basic structural module, and Polcom uses a slightly larger module that works for pod hotels like the globally branded and design-savvy CitizenM chain. Fixed layouts and a standardized chassis improve production efficiency but pod modular offers limited variation, with layouts that are essentially cellular. Pod modular buildings are generally used in buildings that require repetitive one-room layouts, such as student housing and hotels.

3.7
CitizenM Bowery, New York
City. Pod hotel room being
craned (courtesy of Stephen
B. Jacobs Group).

Contract Modular: Built to Order. There are a handful of steel-frame modular manufacturers who operate like indoor general contractors to manufacture multi-story buildings. Contract modular manufacturers are usually hired by a client after a design has been drawn up by the architect, often with conventional construction in mind. Contract modular manufacturers will then work in consultation with the architect to adapt the design for modular manufacturing. (Architects who understand modular technology will avoid this step.) The manufacturer devises the modular breakdown and proposes any necessary modifications required to suit their manufacturing methods. Because no two building designs are the same, each project is comprised of modules that have idiosyncratic dimensions, often with multiple variations in one project.

Contract modular manufacturers often develop proprietary technical systems for the structural frame and connections. Each dimensional variation requires a new jig to build the structural frame, with multiple jigs if there are multiple module sizes in a project. Recent advances by Z-Modular, a manufacturer headquartered in Birmingham, Alabama, include the development of a standard cast-steel node and a flexible jig to accommodate varied frame dimensions. This has greatly improved manufacturing tolerances and interconnections between modules, but there doesn't seem to have been an appreciable impact on the overall rate of two to three modules per day.

The advantage of contract modular is the flexibility to accommodate many different building designs, but lack of standardization prevents a true industrial process. Each new project is of necessity a new production run.[31]

3.8
Contract Modular: Capsys Industries, Brooklyn Navy Yard.

Of these five existing approaches, some achieve design flexibility, some achieve production economy, and some achieve standardization of unit types. What has not yet been achieved is a true kit-of-parts system with extensive design variation and flexible planning, capable of mass-production within a set of standard dimensions, fully plug-and-play. Why not? It would seem to be the logical next step.

By default, developers and architects have turned to contract modular manufacturers for steel-framed multi-story urban housing. Because of their regional orientation, contract modular manufacturers tend to be provincial in thinking and slow to change. They don't do much business with the big national and international construction management firms, nor with the major architectural firms, further reinforcing an insular mentality. Big-city architects occasionally parachute into factories in Pennsylvania or Alabama. They typically find that the legacy manufacturers are unprepared for the design and detail standards to which architects are accustomed. Gluck+, the architects for The Stack, a seven-story modular apartment building in Manhattan, virtually camped out on the factory floor while the modules were being fabricated to provide continuous oversight and quality control.[32] This is not a scalable model.

Even with the recent resurgence of interest and investment in prefab and modular, the legacy modular industry in the U.S. remains bound—creatively, technically, and entrepreneurially—by the constraints imposed by oversize transportation. In the last several years, there have been a few exemplary mid-rise projects,[33] but these are more like demonstrations or prototypes than game-changers. It is also noteworthy that many of these have been "pod" hotels, which by their nature are based on small-size, easily transportable modules.[34]

Thinking outside the box, that well-worn cliché, is of no help here. The fixed idea that oversize modules are desirable has prevented the industry from simply thinking clearly *about* the box. To avoid the fate of dinosaurs, the modular industry will have to evolve. Oversize modules that weigh as much as 80,000 pounds are the architectural equivalent of those gargantuan beasts that eons ago went extinct. Building modules need to go on a diet. The only way to escape the 125-mile regional trap is to abandon the fixation on super-size loads. Right-sizing the building module leads to re-thinking the way modules are joined together, to greater design flexibility, and to a re-organization of the construction process. And sooner or later, when you follow the chain of logic, we will have to re-think the way housing is designed and by whom.

Here, again, is the basis of our solution: adopt the dimensions and freight handling standards long used for intermodal shipping as the standard for a building module, and from there develop a comprehensive and fully integrated system around that module. By adhering to the standards of intermodal transportation, the rules of the modular game will change.

The intermodal transportation system is designed for the global movement of goods by ship, rail, and truck, with seamless interchanges among modes. A sophisticated logistics industry manages container transport from source to destination for just-in-time delivery, orchestrating each leg of the trip and choosing the most economical route and mode available. The International Standards Organization (ISO) makes intermodal transport possible by regulating every feature of the system. Standardization is the essence of globalized shipping. While intermodal transportation is fundamentally the same as when it was introduced in the 1950s, technical standards are continually being updated. For example, radio frequency identification (RFID) now enables the logistics people to keep an eye on each container's location around the globe in real time.

By plugging into the existing intermodal transportation system, the costs and even the environmental impact of moving a module from the factory to the building site can be dramatically reduced. Modules can be trucked on the highway or through city streets without special permits. Laydown space is minimized because the intermodal logistics people are choreographing on-demand transportation. The relationship between a modular factory linked to the intermodal system and the market that it serves is no longer constrained by a 125-mile radius, and since the most economical leg is across blue water, a modular manufacturer using intermodal standards can operate economically on a global scale. Welcome to the club to which the rest of the world's manufacturing industries belong!

PRINCIPLE #3 INTERMODAL STANDARDS

It would be reasonable to ask how intermodal modular architecture is different from pod modular described a few pages back. Isn't it still limited by narrow, cellular room plans, fine for pod hotels but not much else? The short answer is that while the shipping container may be right-sized for transport, for a host of reasons, it is wrong for building construction. How we can design and engineer an intermodal module for high-rise housing with flexible layouts will be discussed in detail and illustrated in Chapter 6.

• • •

Conventional methods of construction are widely acknowledged to be anachronistic. There has been a steady stream of books, articles, and panel discussions devoted to the subject of productivity, prefabrication, new technologies, and so on. A legacy modular building industry has been operating on the margins for a generation or so, but self-limiting assumptions about module size have trapped that industry in small markets subject to economic volatility. Despite the occasional news-making project like the one in Brooklyn that overcame previous limitations on building height, modular construction has not yet transformed design and construction. We should aspire to make high-rise modular housing unexceptional, but in such a way that, as in our best manufactured products, the exceptional—in design, quality, functionality, and economy—is expected.

Modules geared to intermodal transport will become the building block of industrialized urban housing construction. Manufacturing is about moving materials in a carefully orchestrated flow through various processes in a controlled environment. By linking up with intermodal shipping, and by enlisting the logistics companies as the process engineers of transportation, the modular manufacturing process will flow through the factory gate to construction sites anywhere in the world.

Notes

1 Julia Vitullo-Martin and Hope Cohen, *Construction Labor Costs in New York City: A Moment of Opportunity*, report (New York: Regional Plan Association, June 2011), appendix, https://rpa.org/uploads/pdfs/RPA-CUI-Construction-Costs.pdf.
2 "Home," BTEA, accessed July 5, 2020, https://www.bteany.com/home/. See, for example, the *Handbook of the Building Trades Employers' Association of the City of New York*.
3 Attila Turi, Marian Mocan, Larisa Ivascu, Gilles Goncalves and Sorin Maistor, "From Fordism to Lean Management: Main Shifts in Automotive Industry Evolution within the Last Century," Managing Intellectual Capital and Innovation for Sustainable and Inclusive Society: Managing Intellectual Capital and Innovation (presentation, Proceedings of the MakeLearn and TIM Joint International Conference 2, Bari, Italy, May 27–29, 2015), http://www.toknowpress.net/ISBN/978-961-6914-13-0/papers/ML15-098.pdf.
4 The American Institute of Architects General Conditions of the Contract for Construction states: "The Architect will not have control over, charge of, or responsibility for, the construction means, methods, techniques, sequences or procedures, or for the safety precautions and programs in connection with the Work".
5 Paul Teicholz, "Labor-Productivity Declines in the Construction Industry: Causes and Remedies (Another Look)," AECbytes, March 14, 2013, http://www.aecbytes.com/viewpoint/2013/issue_67.html. Also see Chapter 8.
6 Erika Winters Downey and Jason Ericksen, "Tolerance Illustrated," *SteelWise*, October 2006, https://www.aisc.org/globalassets/modern-steel/steelwise/102006_30758_steelwise_tolerances.pdf. American Architectural Manufacturers Association AAMA MCWM-1-89 Metal Curtain Wall Manual, Par 3.03 Erection Tolerances.
7 Archigram, Japanese Metabolists.
8 Habitat '67 by Moshe Safdie and the Nakagin Capsule Tower were both polemics and prototypes. Neither could be replicated.
9 Stephen Kieran and James Timberlake, *Refabricating Architecture* (New York: McGraw-Hill, 2004), 11–15.
10 "Permanent Modular Construction Annual Report 2019," Modular Building Institute, 2019, https://www.modular.org/documents/public/images/2019-PMC-Report-reduced.pdf, 16.
11 The MBI represents the commercial segment of the modular industry, as distinct from the manufactured homes segment represented by the Manufactured Housing Institute (MHI). Multi-story projects are manufactured by commercial modular companies.
12 Jennifer Rudden, "Number of multifamily housing start in the U.S. 2000–2018," Statista, published June 29, 2020, https://www.statista.com/statistics/184845/multifamily-house-starts-in-the-united-states-since-2000/.

13   The International Building Code defines high-rise as "a building with an occupied floor located more than 75 feet (22,860 mm) above the lowest level of fire department vehicle access", generally 8 stories and above in housing. More stringent structural and life-safety requirements apply to high-rise construction.

14   Tom Hardiman (president, Modular Building Institute) in discussion with the author, December 19, 2019.

15   One exception is Z-Modular; a steel-frame manufacturer in Birmingham Alabama is building new plants in Ontario and Houston, which will add about 300,000 square feet to their current 96,000 square foot facility.

16   "Auction of Kullman Building Corp. Assets Set for Tuesday, Dec. 13 Under Direction of Alco Capital, Assignee for Benefit Creditors," Cision PR Newswire, published December 7, 2011, https://www.prnewswire.com/news-releases/auction-of-kullman-building-corp-assets-set-for-tuesday-dec-13-under-direction-of-alco-capital-assignee-for-benefit-of-creditors-135182808.html.

17   Hannah Frishberg, "Rising rents in Brooklyn Force Navy Yard Modular Factory Capsys to Close," Brownstoner, published October 20, 2015, https://www.brownstoner.com/real-estate-market/capsys-brooklyn-navy-yard-factory-closes-due-to-rising-rents/.

18   Daniel Urie, "Thousands laid off in 2017 at companies throughout Pa.," Penn Live Patriot-News, last modified May 22, 2019, https://www.pennlive.com/business/2018/01/warn.html.

19   The current roster serving the eastern seaboard includes: Deluxe Modular, Whitley Modular, Full Stack Modular, ModLogiq, Steel River Modular, Z-Modular, and in Canada, NRB (affiliated with ModLogiq) and RCM.

20   Ryan E. Smith, *Prefab Architecture: A Guide for Architects and Construction Professionals* (Hoboken, NJ: John Wiley & Sons, 2011), 205.

21   State-by-state transportation regulations vary, but generally require modules larger than 12 feet wide to be accompanied by pilot cars. Height limitations are generally 13 feet 6 inches.

22   Nick Bertram, Steffen Fuchs, Jan Mischke, Robert Palter, Gernot Strube and Jonathan Woetzel, "Modular Construction: From Projects to Products," McKinsey & Company, published June 18, 2019, https://www.mckinsey.com/industries/capital-projects-and-infrastructure/our-insights/modular-construction-from-projects-to-products#. States that "one of the fundamental benefits of a manufacturing approach in other industries is lower costs. But as yet there is no track record of consistent, game-changing cost savings among projects following this model".

23   Tom Hardiman (president, Modular Building Institute) in discussion with the author, December 19, 2019. Corroborated by conversations with factory personnel during visits to several modular manufacturers.

24   For purposes of discussion, we're assuming a fairly typical 12 × 34-foot module. To keep the numbers simple, we're calling it 400 square feet.

25   Norman Oder, "STV_8/15/14 With Highlights," Scribd (August, 2017), https://www.scribd.com/document/276397805/STV-8-15-14-With-Highlights. This is one of the problems that plagued the 32-story Brooklyn high-rise project. As excerpted from a Daily Construction Report filed on 8/15/2014, "Module Installation – 0 mods installed...297 mods installed out of 930 mods installed in 175 workdays since mod installation began = average of 1.7 mods per day. Complete through 10th floor".

26   Kenneth T. Jackson, *Crabgrass Frontier: The Suburbanization of America* (New York: Oxford University Press, 1985), 234.

27   Based on a 400 square foot module, 22,500 SF per day/400 SF = 56.25, i.e. the equivalent of about 56 modules per day.

28   Tom Hardiman (president, Modular Building Institute) in discussion with the author, July 1, 2020. Relocatable buildings represented 45 percent of the modular industry's output in 2019. The 55 percent representing permanent construction primarily comprises office/administrative at 50 percent, education at 25 percent, and multi-family at 9 percent, with the remainder consisting of hospitality, healthcare, and other building types.

29   "Modular Homes," Dwellito, accessed July 5, 2020, https://www.dwellito.com/modular-homes. Dwellito (no relation to *Dwell* magazine) is an aggregator of modern catalog modular house manufacturers.

30   "Facts about Manufactured Housing," Prosperity Now, published June 2019, https://prosperitynow.org/resources/facts-about-manufactured-housing-2019.

31   Gregg Pasquarelli and William Sharples (partners, SHoP Architects) in discussion with the author, April 2019. Embracing extensive dimensional variation as the primary goal, SHoP has established a modular enterprise, MODUS, based on a proprietary parametric design software platform.

32   Jeffrey M. Brown, "Edge of Construction: The Future of Modular" (panel discussion, AIA New York Center for Architecture, New York, February 2015).

33 To cite three exemplary projects: The Stack, designed by Gluck+ and manufactured by Deluxe Building Systems (subsequently closed and restructured as Deluxe Modular); Carmel Place, designed by nArchitects and manufactured by Capsys (out of business); Driggs Pod Hotel, designed by Garrison Architects and manufactured by Polcom.

34 See, for example, CitizenM Hotels, including the 21-story CitizenM New York Bowery. CitizenM's modules are manufactured by Polcom Modular in Gdansk, Poland. Due to their small size (at about 8 feet 6 inches, slightly larger than ISO standards), these can be shipped relatively economically to the U.S.

4 The Disruptive Advent of Intermodal Shipping

The drama of longshoreman Terry Molloy's awakening to his brother Charlie's exploitation of his talent as a prize fighter in the 1954 film "On the Waterfront" was taking place on the cusp of a revolution in overseas shipping. One wonders how the story would have played out if the protagonists had been aware that their familiar world, their struggles, their virtues and venalities, would soon be completely undone by a corrugated metal box with a pair of doors at one end and a hollowed out steel block welded to each corner.

In this chapter, we'll trace the decline of manual freight handling and the revolution in containerized shipping that began during the 1950s. Manufacturing as we know it today is based on global supply chains and just-in-time delivery made possible by intermodal transportation. Dock work, which once provided a livelihood for an army of semi-skilled laborers, is long gone, replaced by mechanized and automated processes. Like the vanished world of longshoremen, construction is a manual vocation that remains stubbornly resistant to change. The status quo, however, is unsustainable; construction is inefficient and must adopt new methods. The disruptive transition from manual dock work to containerization was managed equitably, with workers receiving a fair share of the gains from automated freight handling, suggesting a model for a similar transition in construction.

• • •

The Brooklyn docks where Terry Molloy grew up, and which were ruled with an iron hand by mob boss Johnny Friendly, have been converted to recreational use. The "shape", the time honored and often corrupt ritual in which longshoremen gathered at waterfronts and in hiring halls to vie for a day's work muscling freight, is consigned to history. A longshoreman today no longer brandishes a freight hook and is more likely to be jockeying a computer mouse or operating a crane from an air-conditioned cab than working out of doors in the heat and cold, snow and rain.

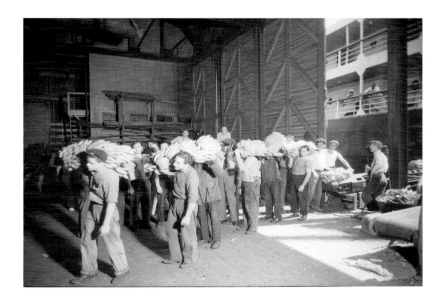

4.1
Longshoremen Unloading
Bananas, 1937.

During the pre-containerization era of "On the Waterfront", the powerful International Longshoremen's Association, the ILA, controlled the loading and unloading of freight along the eastern seaboard from Alabama to Boston. The ILA's west coast counterpart, the International Longshoremen's and Warehousemen's Union (ILWU), ran the ports from San Diego to Seattle. Freight arrived at the docks in every conceivable size and shape: bags, barrels, bales, crates, sacks, with all manner of goods comingled. It was up to the checker, a longshoreman, frequently older and unable to do physical work, to keep track of it all. Packaged goods were known as "break-bulk", as distinct from "bulk", which was loose material such as ore or grain that simply filled up the ship's hold. Break-bulk was lowered through hatches by block and tackle in rope nets, and longshoremen down in the hold stowed each piece using their judgment to best pack the available space with the minimum waste. They lashed the goods to the ships structure knowing that on a sea voyage the pitch and roll of the vessel could have catastrophic consequences if the freight was not properly secured. The work called for a strong back and a modicum of skill. It was dangerous work—a loss of balance or a misjudgment about the stability of a load could result in a crippling or fatal accident.[1]

4.2
Cargo Hold of a Liberty ship, 1946.

Before the Revolutionary War, when ships arrived in colonial ports with much needed cargo, workers were summoned to the docks with the cry "men along the shore!".[2] Initially voluntary and unpaid, by the 19th century, the work had become a newly arrived immigrant's occupation, a first rung on the ladder of economic betterment. The work would slow down between arrivals and departures, but when a ship could be seen entering the harbor and heading toward the dock, the hiring hall would be jammed with longshoremen anxious for the boss's attention. Corrupt bosses, as fictionalized in the character Johnny Friendly, often extracted a kickback in exchange for a job,[3] and such hiring practices were accepted with a shrug. Longshoremen were a tough, tight-knit fraternity who lived in insular neighborhoods within walking distance of the docks, and traditional codes of behavior maintained social order.

Employment on the docks was structured around ethnic and clan loyalty, in which a cousin or an uncle would introduce a newcomer "into the right gang".[4] Economic competition between rival groups was fierce. The Italians established themselves by coming in as strikebreakers in the 1890s to displace the Irish on the Brooklyn docks. The Irish maintained their grip over dock work on Manhattan's West Side.[5]

Longshoremen's unions emerged during the 19th century, out of fear that the shippers could always exploit the most recent immigrant arrivals and drive the cost of labor down for everyone. The first longshoremen's strike, in 1836, which began in New York and spread to Philadelphia, may have been the first organized labor action in the U.S. The strike of 1836 was put down by threat of armed military action.[6] The first longshoreman's union, the Longshoremen's Union Protective Association, or LUPA, was organized in New York in 1864.[7] Strikes in 1874, 1887, 1896, and 1907 stood out as historic benchmarks in the labor struggle on the docks.[8] The American Longshoremen's Union, formed in 1897, seemed to erase racial, religious, or national distinctions in the ALU motto "all men are brothers",[9] but Black longshoremen endured singular economic and social discrimination.[10] After an unsuccessful strike in 1907, the union on the eastern seaboard emerged in its modern form, adopting the name of the International Longshoremen's Association in 1908.[11]

Following the formation of the ILA, within the context of a highly regulated shipping industry, there was a long period of labor peace in New York. Then, with the end of World War II, labor actions became a regular occurrence with strikes in 1945, 1947, 1948, 1949, 1951, and 1954.[12] The unions protected inefficient labor practices, and there was pervasive theft and absenteeism. Dock operations by the 1950s had become the major component of shipping cost.[13] Once a freighter had cast off its lines and headed out to sea, the cost of sailing from point A to point B was comparatively low.

New York City at the end of World War II dominated export shipping in the U.S., handling one-third of all sea-going freight.[14] The geography of manufacturing for export in the era before the interstate highway system was of necessity urban and local. It made economic sense to locate factories in cities near the docks to minimize trucking and to have ready access to a pool of labor. Warehouses to store goods awaiting shipment or distribution inland similarly needed to be in proximity to both factories and docks. The garment district on Manhattan's West Side was a global manufacturing center, run with low-wage immigrant labor living in nearby tenements. Goods were produced in loft buildings that lined the streets and were warehoused and shipped from the Hudson River piers—a thrumming economic powerhouse bounded by a few city blocks, from 34th to 42nd Streets and from Seventh to Ninth Avenues.

Problems on the docks emerged regularly as a cause of concern among New York City public officials, who were anxious not to forgo the port's preeminent status and the economic power that went with it. In 1953, in an effort to smooth labor relations, the Waterfront Commission of New York Harbor took over Port of New York hiring in a move to eliminate corruption and to bring some degree of fairness and order to the shape.[15] Throughout the 1950s and even into the 1960s, under a succession of mayors, millions of dollars were poured into waterfront improvements,[16] new docks, and new warehouses, but the investments were for naught. Shipping, once a mainstay of New York's economy, was on its way out.

Malcom MacLean

Overseas shipping by the early 1950s was a stagnant industry, heavily regulated and subsidized by the federal government. The fleet of war-surplus Liberty and Freedom class ships were small and slow vessels, cheaply acquired. Shipping was a low-margin business, and the now defunct Interstate Commerce Commission (ICC) ensured that routes were not monopolized and that rates were maintained at sufficient levels to keep competing companies in business.[17] Foreign shippers were prohibited from coastwise (between ports along the same coast) shipping, and only U.S. flag vessels could transport military goods. In 1954, the executives of the shipping lines were conservative and tradition-bound,[18] comfortable within the regulated status quo and resistant, if not impervious, to change from the inside. Their insular world was capsized by an innovative trucking executive, Malcom Purcell McLean.

The image of a self-made man and a risk-taking entrepreneur, McLean's rise in the trucking business was an up-by-the-bootstraps story, with some help from FDR's New Deal. McLean started his trucking company at the age of 21, during the depths of the Depression, while working at a gas station and borrowing a pick-up truck to make extra money doing occasional deliveries. With family help, he acquired a used dump truck and soon won a federal contract funded by the Works Progress Administration. That contract afforded McLean an opportunity to purchase a new truck, hire a driver, and expand. McLean had a knack for business, and McLean Trucking grew steadily through the 1930s and 1940s, largely through a relentless focus on efficiency. By 1954, McLean had built his company into one of the largest and most profitable trucking concerns in the U.S. He was then 41 years old.

Coastwise shippers were positioned in the early 1950s to take business away from truckers along the eastern seaboard. Fearing competition, and frustrated by highway congestion—Interstate 95 was still years away from linking the entire coastal route from Maine to Florida—McLean hatched a scheme to drive truck trailers onto specially built ships and float them up and down the Atlantic coast. The trailers would then be reattached to tractors waiting dockside for a short highway leg to their destination. McLean was not looking for a solution to the notorious inefficiency of the ports. He was focused on his own trucking interests and the pursuit of greater profits.

An integrated business that owned both trucking and shipping operations, however, was novel, and it was illegal unless approved by the ICC. A guiding principle of the ICC was that no company could own more than one mode of freight transportation.[19] Intermodal transport was anathema.

The acquisition of a shipping line by McLean Trucking would be sure to raise red flags among the regulators. To work around ICC rules, McLean and his partners, through complex financial and legal legerdemain, placed McLean Trucking into a trust naming themselves beneficiaries, legally separating themselves from the company. They formed a new enterprise, McLean Industries, and proceeded to acquire the Pan Atlantic Steamship Company, and then the Waterman Steamship Company (which had earlier sold them Pan Atlantic) with highly leveraged financing. In short order, McLean Trucking was sold off, netting the partners a tidy sum.[20]

The union gave its blessing to McLean's "roll-on/roll-off" scheme— the Teamsters Union, that is, not the ILA.[21] The Teamsters were happy—they were expanding their trucking turf on McLean's coattails. The longshoremen, as time would tell, would have to make some adjustments.

The roll-on/roll-off enterprise, for which McLean initially envisioned seven specially designed ships that would each carry 288 trailers, would have cost in total 63 million dollars. It was to be financed by trading in his newly acquired fleet of converted surplus tankers under a government program that in exchange provided credit to pay for new ships.[22]

Plans were in still in flux, however, and after being widely reported in the press, the roll-on/roll-off concept and the expensive fleet of new ships was abandoned. The shortcomings of trailers with wheels had become apparent to McLean as he strove to maximize cargo carrying capacity. Trailers with wheels could not be stacked. To dispense with the wheels, McLean tried to separate trailer boxes from the trailer chassis, crane the boxes onto the ship, and then reverse the procedure for off-loading. Preliminary studies showed that this approach would cut the cost of shipping by 94 percent compared to traditional break-bulk. But like many things that sound simple, especially to impatient hard-driving executives, the design and engineering that would make the general concept of "lift-on / lift-off" into a reality was not so obvious.

McLean, now stymied by the difficulty of lift-on/lift-off, sought help from Keith Tantlinger, a mechanical engineer and vice-president of Brown Industries, a trailer manufacturer headquartered in Spokane, Washington. In 1949, he had worked out a design for a stackable 30-foot aluminum container. While that concept never caught on, Tantlinger had acquired a reputation as an expert in trailers and container concepts. He joined Pan Atlantic in 1955 as the director of research and development.

Tantlinger's contribution to containerization has been largely overlooked,[23] but it was seminal. While his tenure alongside McLean was a relatively brief three years, it was a critically important time during which containerization as we know it today was conceived and proven in operation. McLean supplied the entrepreneurial drive and was a business innovator, but he was not an engineer or an inventor.

Over the course of his career, Tantlinger acquired more than 70 patents on various aspects of containerization and other fields related to transportation. It is a testament to Tantinger's abilities that the design and engineering work he did more than 60 years ago has not been fundamentally improved upon. The patent record shows that Tantlinger was behind all the key innovations that turned McLean's business strategy into a scalable process.[24] Tantlinger is the sole named inventor on most of the Sea-Land patents. McLean's name is not to be found in any of the patent documents, and it seems unlikely that McLean made any technical contributions to the invention of mechanized shipping.

The general concept of containerization had been in use for several decades. Trailer ships had been operating on the Hudson River as early as 1937, and the Alaska Steamship Co. had started a version of container service in 1953.[25] Seatrain Lines had been running ships between New Orleans and Havana since 1929 with railroad boxcars, wheels attached, rolled along deck-mounted rails.[26] Seatrain used a gantry crane that straddled a railroad siding to load and unload the boxcars from freighters positioned parallel to the track,[27] establishing the intermodal choreography that was the precursor to modern containerization. After World War II, an intermodal container scheme of 10- and 20-foot boxes detachable from a truck chassis was proposed in detail by Higgins Industries, a New Orleans shipbuilding concern, but the idea was never adopted.[28] At around the same time, the Army Transportation Corps developed the Conex box (*Con*tainer *Ex*press), a small stackable steel container used to ship spare parts and other military items.[29]

Why, then, were none of these early forays transformative? McLean may have breached the regulatory barrier that separated trucking from shipping, but it is just as likely that his company would have remained a niche enterprise had Tantlinger not been involved. What did Tantlinger do that made such a difference?

The approach that McLean had been pursing when Tantlinger came aboard Pan Atlantic was to hoist his trailer boxes by manually attaching crane hooks to each of the container corners. This meant that four longshoremen had to clamber on top of the box, place the crane hooks while hand-signaling the crane operator, and then climb down before the box could be hoisted. Once in place on the ship, the process of unhooking had to be done in reverse, not all that much of an efficiency gain over traditional break-bulk handling using cargo nets and pallets. Also, each of McLean's proto-containers was designed with pedestals that fit into apertures in the ship's deck to lock the boxes into place. The limitation was that the protruding pedestal arrangement interfered with stacking, and no one had figured out a way to nest the pedestal of one box into the roof of another and secure it in a way that would be seaworthy. Finally, McLean's proto-containers were strengthened with external diagonal steel struts, which were cumbersome, structurally redundant, and made the boxes wider than the legal highway limit.[30]

To solve the problem of stacking, Tantlinger's team re-fitted the hold of a war-surplus C-2 freighter (one of six that McLean acquired) with a system of vertical angle iron rails positioned at the corners of a container stack, which would serve to guide the containers as they were lowered into the hold, like candy in a Pez dispenser. Cell guides, as the angle iron rails were called, had to allow for a loose fit, but not too loose—too much space would leave the containers free to bang around and even shift weight precariously; too little and the boxes wouldn't easily lower into position and could get stuck on the way out if the guides were forced out of line during a rough voyage. After some experiments, and using his best judgment, Tantlinger arrived at the final clearances: three-quarters inch cross-wise and one-and-a-half inches lengthwise. Just before the maiden voyage on October 7, 1957 of the "Gateway City", the first of Pan Atlantic's C-2 container ships, Tantlinger wedged thick strips of modeling clay into the gaps between the cell guides. Retrieving the clay afterward, he found that the pieces had only been slightly compressed.[31] The containers had barely shifted. With stacking now proven, the C-2 ships could carry 226 containers.

U.S. Patent No. 3,027,025, titled "Apparatus for Handling Freight in Transit", was filed on April 8, 1958, about six months after the maiden voyage of the "Gateway City". Keith Tantlinger is listed as the inventor, with the patent assigned to Sea-Land Service, Inc. (as Pan Atlantic had been renamed). Patent No. 3,027,025 embodies the key features of mechanized handling that are still the basis of modern intermodal shipping:

Automated Cranes. To automate the freight handling process, Tantlinger devised a rectangular steel frame, called a spreader, which matches the shape of a container roof. The spreader is fitted with four electrically operated rotating tapered lugs at each corner, which a crane operator can toggle back and forth with the flip of a switch. The spreader is lowered down by means of four sets of steel cable pulleys, and as the spreader approaches the container roof the tapered lugs self-align and plunge into specially designed corner fittings. The operator then throws the switch and the four lugs, operating in tandem, rotate and engage the container. The container is hoisted, and once placed into position, the crane operator releases the lugs and raises the spreader.

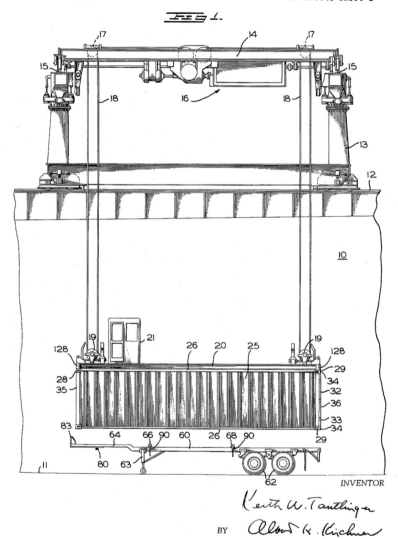

March 27, 1962   K. W. TANTLINGER   3,027,025

APPARATUS FOR HANDLING FREIGHT IN TRANSIT

Filed April 8, 1958

18 Sheets—Sheet 1

INVENTOR

Keith W. Tantlinger

BY *Albert K. Kirchner*

ATTORNEY

Corner fittings. The corners of the container needed a piece of hardware that would guide the lugs into position without manual assistance. Tantlinger developed the now ubiquitous corner fitting, a hollow cast steel block with oblong apertures in the top (and also in the sides for visual inspection and drainage). The top aperture receives the tapered lug. When the lug is electrically rotated it grips the inside of the hollow block.

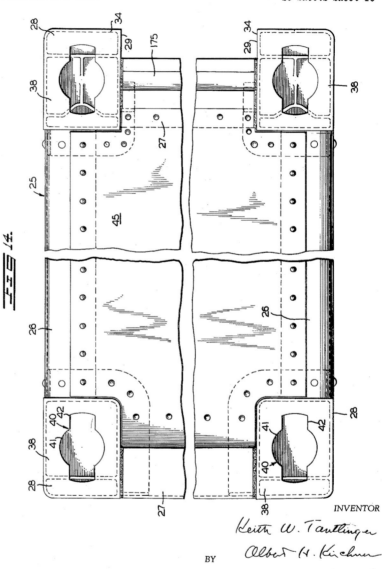

March 27, 1962   K. W. TANTLINGER   3,027,025

APPARATUS FOR HANDLING FREIGHT IN TRANSIT

Filed April 8, 1958   18 Sheets—Sheet 10

INVENTOR

Keith W. Tantlinger

BY   Albert H. Kirchner

ATTORNEY

Twist locks. A stack of shipping containers will quickly topple over at sea
if not for a device that secures the bottom corners of one box to the
top corners of the one below. Tantlinger invented a "twist lock" device,
which consists of a pair of tapered lugs—one facing up and one facing
down—that are manually operated by means of a lever. Twist locks are
inserted by a longshoreman into each of the four corner fittings of the

last container placed in the stack, and the bottom lugs are rotated to engage the hollow interior of the fitting. The next container is lowered into position and the upward facing lug guides the corner fittings of the descending box into alignment with the corner fittings below. The longshoreman operates the levers that lock the upper lugs into the corner fittings of the upper box. (Meanwhile the crane operator has disengaged the spreader and is moving it into position for the next pick.)

March 27, 1962   K. W. TANTLINGER   3,027,025

APPARATUS FOR HANDLING FREIGHT IN TRANSIT

Filed April 8, 1958   18 Sheets—Sheet 11

4.5
Twistlock Container
Connecting Device (U.S.
Patent Office).

Container Chassis. Tantlinger designed a special trailer equipped with its own twist lock devices to which a shipping container could rapidly be mounted and demounted. The trailers were equipped with standard hitches. Intermodal transport was born.

March 27, 1962   K. W. TANTLINGER   3,027,025

APPARATUS FOR HANDLING FREIGHT IN TRANSIT

Filed April 8, 1958   18 Sheets—Sheet 2

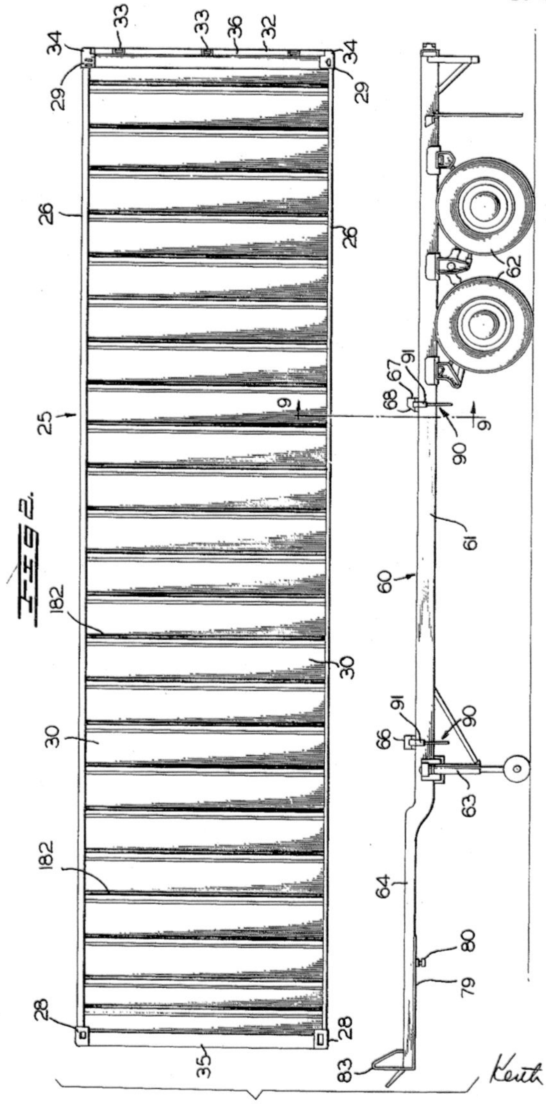

INVENTOR

Keith W. Tantlinger

BY *Albert K. Kirchner*

ATTORNEY

4.6
Container Chassis (U.S.
Patent Office).

The Emergence of Globalized Trade

By the early 1960s, Sea-Land was doing a good business. Containerized shipping had proven itself but was yet to be transformative. Then, with the escalation of the war in Vietnam in 1965, McLean had an opportunity to expand. 17,000 troops were arriving in Vietnam each month, presenting the military with a formidable logistics challenge. Traditional break-bulk shipping was plagued by delayed deliveries and pilferage. Substandard port facilities further exacerbated chronic shortages of critical supplies. Lack of both dock space and deep water meant that freighters had to wait offshore at anchor, becoming inaccessible floating warehouses cooking in the tropical heat.

In 1966, McLean was able to secure a two-year contract to make scheduled freight runs from San Francisco and Seattle to Vietnam with six Sea-Land container ships every 15 days.[32] McLean and the military chose deep water ports at Cam Ranh Bay and Da Nang, and converted them into container terminals using an innovative system of deployable floating wharfs.[33]

The shipments to Vietnam were lucrative, but the fact that empty containers were returning on the eastbound leg rankled McLean. He was free within the terms of his contract—a guaranteed schedule and payload for a lump sum payment—to do what he wanted on the return leg of the round trip.[34] McLean decided to load eastbound containers with Japanese consumer electronics and bring them to the U.S. In the autumn of 1968, Sea-Land ships began making stops in Yokohama on return from Cam Ranh Bay. This marked the beginning of globalized trade in the era of containerization. Between 1960 and 1970, Japan's exports grew more than 450 percent.[35]

4.7
Malcolm McLean, Port Newark, 1957.

Dimensional Standards

The Japanese had committed to an industrial policy of containerization in 1966[36] and had initially objected to McLean's 35-foot containers. They were unmanageable on most Japanese roads, and were incompatible with Japanese rail standards, which could not handle containers longer than 20 feet. Matson Navigation, which had been experimenting with 24-foot containers since the late 1950s, was a few weeks ahead of McLean in setting up service from Japan. Even their 24-footers were too long.[37] Containers were being manufactured in other odd sizes, including 17- and 27-foot boxes.[38] The lack of dimensional standards for shipping containers was becoming a critical issue.

It was evident that without standards containerization would soon reach a growth limit. The potential efficiency of intermodal transport would be limited by the incompatibility of crane spreaders, rail flatcars, and truck chassis with multiple container dimensions. There could be no common carriers of independently owned containers. All this was fine as far as Sea-Land and Matson were concerned. They were doing a good business with their own ships and their own idiosyncratic containers and related equipment, but success and a bias against regulation[39] were blinders that kept McLean from seeing the broader picture.

It was essential that containers function as interchangeable parts if intermodal transportation were to realize its full potential. The task of setting standards for containerization was a contentious process, with various governmental and commercial interests pushing and pulling. Each container length that was already in use had its own rationale. Sea-Land had chosen a 35-foot box because at the time that was the longest trailer allowed on east coast highways.[40]

The American Standards Association (the ASA, later renamed the American National Standards Institute, or ANSI, in 1969) performs the critical job of setting standards for "products, services, processes, systems, and personnel"... in other words, for just about anything technical that might bear on a commercial transaction. The ASA's MH-5 committee (MH for materials handling) made up of industry representatives was formed in 1958 to study and come to consensus on standards for containerization.[41]

The standard 8-foot[42] width to which all shipping containers still conform had been established without much argument. The question of height was determined by highway bridge clearances. Eight-foot and eight-foot-six-inch were adopted initially, and then, as bridge clearances increased, 9-foot-6-inch ("hi-cube" in shipping container argot) was added. The debate over length, however, was described by Kieth Tantlinger as a "dogfight".[43] The existing fleets of 24-foot (Matson) and 35-foot (Sea-Land) boxes were a starting point. However, the railroad flatcar had been standardized at 85 feet, and neither 24- or 35-foot containers optimized the use of a flatcar. For that reason, among others, ASA stakeholders coalesced around 20-foot and 40-foot boxes.[44]

McLean's Sea-Land Service stuck with 35-foot boxes until well into the 1980s, amassing what was then the single largest holding of shipping containers in the world.[45] McLean had created a lucrative business in intermodal freight, but his disregard for standardization suggests little interest in the globalization of shipping. Tantlinger, who seems to have appreciated the full potential of automation and standards, approached McLean toward the end of 1962 and persuaded him to release Sea-Land's patents. It took five more years before the International Standards Organization, headquartered in Geneva, would adopt Tantlinger's system as the draft international standard for intermodal shipping. It took another two years before the first ISO handbook on intermodal standards was published in 1970.[46]

It's difficult here to understand McLean's thinking. Perhaps he didn't foresee that technical standardization would lead inevitably to dimensional standardization. Stacking containers atop one another required that the corner posts line up. Container cells on ships had to match container dimensions. The spreader frames for craning had to match the positions of the corner fittings. It was an *integrated* system. Perhaps McLean believed that his massive inventory of 35-foot boxes would shield him from competition, but when Congress not unreasonably considered writing the ASA dimensions into law as a requirement for doing business with the Defense Department, McLean complained in Congressional testimony that the other shipping lines had formed a "conspiracy to destroy competition".[47] In fact, standardization had opened container shipping to robust competition, and by refusing to adopt those standards the hard-headed businessman had inflicted injury on himself.

Today, the ISO Standards Handbook for Freight Containers is the industry bible. Standard container lengths have grown to include 45-, 48-, and 53-footers (these longer containers have intermediate posts and fittings located at the 40-foot position in order to stack. The remainder of the box is cantilevered). The Tantlinger corner fitting remains unchanged. The handbook covers specialized containers, refrigerated containers, containers with tanks for liquids and gases, open-sided containers, and more. The last section of the Fourth Edition deals with electronic security seals, a matter of serious concern in the era of international terrorism.

The volume of container traffic in global ports grew from 225 million TEUs in 2000 (TEU is the industry standard term for container capacity, representing "Twenty Foot Equivalent Units"; a 40-foot container equals two TEUs) to 793 million TEUs in 2018.[48] The growth of containerships seems not to have stopped, although a theoretical limit has been suggested. The first generation of converted tankers in the late 1950s were 650 feet long and carried up to 800 TEUs. Today's largest containership, the Triple E (for economy of scale, energy-efficient, and environmentally improved), barely squeezes through the Straits of Malacca, between Malaysia and Indonesia, with a load of 18,000 TEUs.[49] These giants are a quarter-mile long.

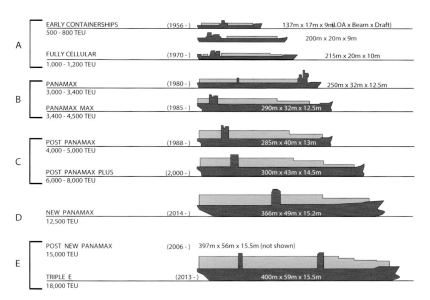

4.8
Size and Capacity
of Containerships,
1956-present.
Source: OECD International
Transport Forum.

Mechanization and Modernization

While it is not within the scope of this book to go into an extended discourse on the broader topic of "globalization and its discontents", the book's subject matter compels at least a passing mention. Globalization disrupts employment, exerts downward pressure on American wages, and exports low-skilled jobs (and some high-skilled jobs) overseas. The ILU workers on the east coast and the ILWU workers on the west coast who witnessed the advent of the shipping container were on the front lines of globalization, a few decades before American factory workers. For the longshoremen, a strong union and a willingness to fight for their jobs ensured that the transition to automated freight handling would be equitable.

Technological change can be met with resistance or it can be managed strategically. Harry Bridges, the head of the ILWU on the west coast, was an effective labor leader who negotiated the landmark 1960 Mechanization and Modernization Agreement on behalf of his union, saying "we should accept mechanization and start making it work for us, not against us".[50] The union struck bargains to keep more workers on the job than containerization required, phasing out those jobs through attrition, and providing excellent pensions and medical benefits for retirement.[51] Meanwhile, a greatly reduced younger workforce learned the new skills required to operate a modern container terminal. The transition from manual to automated shipping is a model for the management of disruptive change, a topic that we will return to in Chapter 8. It's worth quoting Arthur Donovan, a maritime historian, here:

> Perhaps the most distinctive feature of the container revolution regarding longshore work was that during the period in which its originators were capturing an ever-increasing share of the breakbulk market, the returns they realized were so much greater than their operating costs that they were able to cover the capital costs of building container systems while also providing full pay for redundant longshoremen and high wages and benefits for those actually working on the docks. It was the profits flowing from an enormous increase in efficiency, when compared to the earlier system of breakbulk shipping, that enabled the operators to revolutionize the waterfront while giving labor its due.[52]

• • •

Lewis Mumford, in *Technics and Civilization*, locates the deepest source of technology in an innate human "will to order".[53] Mumford identifies the mastery of time as the fundamental ordering system without which technology cannot exist. He writes: "If the mechanical clock did not appear until the cities of the thirteenth century demanded an orderly routine, the habit of order itself and the earnest regulation of time-sequences had become almost second nature in the monastery". He goes on: "the clock is not merely a means of keeping track of the hours, but of synchronizing the actions of men". Synchronization is the root of technology—again, Mumford: "the clock, not the steam engine, is the key-machine of the modern industrial age".[54]

Keith Tantlinger's "Apparatus for Handling Freight in Transit" is an integrated system for transferring containers to and from a ship, a tractor-trailer rig, and the flatbed car of a freight train. With sea-lanes strapping the globe as a worldwide conveyor belt, container ships and their land-side terminals, along with railroads and expressways, have merged into a virtual global-scale factory process.

In mechanizing the handling of freight, McLean and Tantlinger irrevocably altered the worldwide flow of goods, with synchronized automated freight handling. Just-in-time manufacturing, organized around precisely scheduled shipments, could not have been conceived in the era of manual freight handling. Intermodal transport expanded the seamless flow not just of products, but of the *components* of products to encompass an entire global supply chain. Roughly half of all imports to the U.S. consist of unfinished parts, components, pieces, or raw materials intended for assembly into finished goods here, or are forwarded elsewhere for final processing.[55] Global supply chains are the basis of our modern economy, and many of our construction products are already sourced globally. The logical next step is to embed global supply chains in a modular system geared to intermodal transport.

PRINCIPLE #4 GLOBAL SUPPLY CHAINS

• • •

Upon reading Mumford: "as with all instruments of multiplication the critical question is as to the function and quality of the object one is multiplying"[56] one thinks: sounds reasonable enough. But globalization is an "instrument of multiplication" that Mumford, writing more than 80 years ago, could not have foreseen. Confronted by a landscape of strip malls and big box stores, stocked with our post-panamax overabundance of stuff, it's no surprise that we might find ourselves averse to the global reality.

This book applies the lessons learned from the advent of intermodal transportation to the problem of multi-story urban housing. Intermodal modular architecture has the potential to foster a livable, equitable, and sustainable urbanism at all income levels, but it means embracing globalization. We can duck our heads, or we can climb aboard these sheer-hulled flotillas of gross domestic product and re-shape the box itself to a human purpose.

Notes

1 Charles B. Barnes, *The Longshoremen* (New York: Russell Sages Foundation, 1915), 51–54.
2 "The ILWU Story," ILWU, accessed July 9, 2020, https://www.ilwu.org/history/the-ilwu-story/.
3 "History," Waterfront Commission of New York Harbor, accessed July 9, 2020, http://www.wcnyh.gov/history.htm.
4 Collins J. Davis, "'Shape or Fight?': New York's Black Longshoremen, 1945–1961," *International Labor and Working-Class History* 62, no. 1 (2002): 148, accessed July 2, 2020, www.jstor.org/stable/27672812.
5 Davis, 147.
6 Barnes, 93.
7 Barnes, 95.
8 Barnes, 95.
9 Barnes, 111.
10 Davis, 143–146.
11 Barnes, 123.

12 "WLB Orders Strike Ended," *New York Times*, April 28, 1945. George Horne, "4,000 Pier Workers in Wildcat Strike Delay 11 Sailings," *New York Times*, August 21, 1947. "Pier Strike Terms Reached; Pay Increased by 13 Cents; Union to Vote on Saturday," *New York Times*, November 25, 1948. "Wildcat Strikers Make 15 Piers Idle," *New York Times*, October 16, 1951. A.H. Raskin, "I.L.A. Leaders Ask Pact Acceptance," *New York Times*, December 31, 1954.

13 Marc Levinson, *The Box: How the Shipping Container Made the World Smaller and the World Economy Bigger* (Princeton, NJ: Princeton University press, 2006), 21.

14 Levinson, 80.

15 Levinson, 23.

16 Levinson, 88–90.

17 "Interstate Commerce Commission," U.S. Government Manual, July 1, 1995, 597–599, https://www.govinfo.gov/content/pkg/GOVMAN-1995-07-01/pdf/GOVMAN-1995-07-01-Pg596.pdf.

18 Maritime Transportation Research Board, *Case Studies in Maritime Innovation* (Washington, DC: National Academy of Sciences, 1978), 23.

19 Arthur Donovan and Joseph Bonney, *The Box That Changed The World: Fifty Years of Container Shipping – An Illustrated History* (East Windsor, NJ: Commonwealth Business Media, 2006), 25–26.

20 Levinson, 44–47. Levinson gives a fascinating account of the financial innovations that McLean pioneered, along with Walter Wriston, president of National City Bank, later Citibank.

21 A. H. Raskin, "Union Head Backs 'Sea-Land' Trucks: Beck Approves A Coastwise Trailer-Transport Service to Help the Industry," *New York Times*, February 17, 1954.

22 "7 Ships Proposed to Take Trailers," *New York Times*, June 17, 1955.

23 David Leonhardt, "Keith W. Tantlinger, b. 1919," The Lives They Lived, *New York Times Magazine*, December 22, 2011.

24 "Number Search," USPTO Patent Full-Text and Image Database, accessed July 11, 2020, http://patft.uspto.gov/netahtml/PTO/srchnum.htm.

25 Donovan and Bonney, 5.

26 Donovan and Bonney, 6.

27 Donovan and Bonney, 32.

28 Donovan and Bonney, 35.

29 Donovan and Bonney, 118.

30 Levinson, 50.

31 Donovan and Bonney, 68.

32 Donovan and Bonney, 119–120.

33 Donovan and Bonney, 118–119.

34 Levinson, 172–188; Donovan and Bonney, 115–119.

35 Trade Statistics of Japan. Ministry of Finance, Yearly total Value of Exports and Imports -Fixed base (Unit: 1000YEN) "Total Value of Exports and Imports (1950-) – Trade Statistics of Japan," Trade Statistics of Japan, accessed July 9, 2020, https://www.customs.go.jp/toukei/suii/html/nenbet_e.htm.

36 Levinson, 186.

37 Levinson, 187.

38 Donovan and Bonney, 121.

39 Donovan and Bonney, 120.

40 Donovan and Bonney, 121.

41 Hans van Ham, J. C. van Ham and Joan Rijsenbrij, *Development of Containerization: Success through Vision, Drive and Technology* (Amsterdam: IOS Press, 2012), 45.

42 Imperial dimensions are still the international container standard, a leftover from the post-war era of American hegemony.

43 van Ham and Rijsenbrij, 44.

44 Hearings before the Subcommittee on Merchant Marine and Fisheries of the Committee on Commerce, United States Senate, Ninetieth Congress, July 13, 14 and 17, 1967, Serial No. 90-31, 326.

45 Donovan and Bonney, 121.

46 van Ham and Rijsenbrij, 45–46.

47 Donovan and Bonney, 120.

48 "Container Port Traffic (TEU: 20 foot equivalent units)," The World Bank, accessed July 9, 2020, https://data.worldbank.org/indicator/IS.SHP.GOOD.TU.

49 "Triple-E Class Container Ship, Denmark," Ship Technology, accessed July 9, 2020, https://www.ship-technology.com/projects/triple-e-class-container-ship/. "Malaccamax," Maritime Connector, accessed July 9, 2020, http://maritime-connector.com/wiki/malaccamax/.

50 "America on the Move, Transforming the Waterfront," National Museum of American History Behring Center, accessed July 9, 2020, https://americanhistory.si.edu/america-on-the-move/transforming-waterfront.

51 Arthur Donovan, "Longshoremen and Mechanization," *Journal for Maritime Research* 1, no. 1 (1999): 66–75.

52 Donovan, 73.

53 Lewis Mumford, *Technics and Civilization* (New York: Harcourt Brace & Company, 1934), 3.

54 Mumford, 14.

55 Douglas A. Irwin, "The False Promise of Protectionism," *Foreign Affairs*, May/June 2017, https://www.foreignaffairs.com/articles/united-states/2017-04-17/false-promise-protectionism.

56 Mumford, 241.

5　Promises of Progress
Four Case Histories

William Levitt and Sons set the standard in 1947 for commercial success in production housing. Their approach, while not modular, utilized pre-cut lumber and Taylorized the construction process.[1] The system perfected by Levitt was predicated on the availability of large expanses of flat land in which the building site could almost replicate a factory floor, but with materials, machinery, and workers moving down the earthen assembly line rather than the product itself. Levittown was manufactured.

The four case histories in prefabrication in this chapter pre-date as well as post-date Levitt. In each, we can see how research and development, design, manufacturing, and marketing were integrated activities. Volumetric modular systems are not included because there is no relevant history of modular, let alone multi-story modular, that we can look to for the kinds of lessons that we want to learn. There have indeed been proposals for multi-story modular construction systems, and some projects of significant architectural or technical interest have been realized,[2] but we don't have examples of commercially marketed systems that give us a model for a successful enterprise.[3] The case histories that follow offer such examples, and the lessons are transferable.

Three of the four cases—the Sears catalog house, the Lustron Corporation, and Techbuilt—concern mass production of the single-family house. The fourth, the School Construction Systems Development (SCSD) project, employed an ingenious design approach to achieve economies of scale through supply chain procurement. In all four, price, market, and cultural acceptance were critical factors. Each enterprise reckoned with constraints such as production capacity, distribution, and financing.

Running alongside the history of prefabrication as a commercial enterprise is what we might call an "aspirational" history of industrialized housing. This history of aspirations, mainly a series of interesting but commercially unrealizable propositions,[4] lives a parallel life in architectural literature. From the early 20th century through the 1960s, architects were advocating for an industrial solution to the problem of mass housing, but polemics[5] overshadowed matters of production economy, commercial viability, and mass appeal. It seems odd that architects would so casually engage in a field in which the very nature of what is possible is conditioned by the rationality of manufacturing and the remorseless logic of business. Avant-garde rhetoric has had a value in calling attention to critical failures of modern housing but has never proposed a plausible alternative to site-built construction.

Denise Scott Brown, writing in 1968, captured the disconnect between avant-garde rhetoric and the economics of high-volume production:

> Someone in Archigram should find out why the prefabrication of housing in America has been a failure in spite of massive inputs of government money... the prefabs, since their savings were related to only half the cost of the house (almost half the house cost in a single house goes into site-work), were not able to bring about significant cost reductions. Levitt, by owning or controlling enough components of the building industry to ensure rationalization of the construction process from manufacture of the elements to delivery and erection, was able, without going to car bodies or plastic capsules, to produce the best value housing in America.[6]

From the start, the pioneers of the modern movement declared that their mission in large part was to solve the problem of housing masses of newly urbanized factory workers, and more broadly, to re-think the nature of habitation in an industrialized and mechanized world. The early modernists' rejection of tradition and their promulgation of industrialized housing was part of a cohesive world view that wove technology and aesthetics together with social concerns. The pioneering generation of the 1920s failed to transform the means of production, however, despite the promise of compelling prototypes. The white, taut, abstract forms of the early International Style that characterized the 1927 Weissenhof Housing Exhibition may have exemplified utopian social ideals, but prefabrication remained aspirational.[7]

Following World War II, a new generation took on the problem of mass housing, and during the 1950s, design proposals put forward by leading architects continued to reflect utopian ambitions.[8] Public housing in the U.S. during that era did provide improved living conditions for large numbers of people but retained only the husk of a utopian dream. By the 1960s, a new generation of architects and critics had largely abandoned the social agenda.[9] The industrial transformation of housing remained as distant as ever. Academics like Colin Rowe succeeded in propagating modernist aesthetics stripped of a social program, and building technology became a handmaid to formalism.[10] Meanwhile, architectural polemicists—Archigram, Superstudio, the Metabolists— proposed notions that bore little likelihood of realization[11] (if that was ever the intention), while highlighting with wit, irony, and perhaps despair the failure of the architectural establishment. Habitat 67, designed by Moshe Safdie for the 1967 World Exposition in Montreal, seemed to herald, finally, the arrival of the future. In fact, it signaled the beginning of a 30-year fallow period during which modular architecture was largely forgotten. Post-modernism was ascending in the 1970s, and critics like Charles Jencks applauded the dynamiting of the Pruitt-Igoe towers in St. Louis,[12] the emblem, it seemed, of all that had gone wrong with modernism.[13] The ideals on which the modern movement was founded, which included engagement with the social task of housing and the espousal of a marriage between industry and architecture, were abandoned.

Thus, we can trace two paths that have barely intersected over the history of modular and prefab. There is a history of architectural aspirations, and a commercial history. The architects for prefab commercial enterprises remain mostly in the background. The design aesthetic has ranged from historical eclecticism with popular appeal, to a middle-of-the-road modernism intended for a design-conscious middle class. One purpose of these commercial ventures in prefabrication and modular manufacturing has always been, of course, to generate profits or to realize cost savings on behalf of public agencies.

The following case histories will show how commercial enterprises have used modern techniques, methods of organization, marketing, and distribution to manufacture and sell houses and to build schools. In addition to examining those techniques and methods, the case histories embody a through line that will illustrate our next principle.

PRINCIPLE # 5   LEVERAGE EXISTING INFRASTRUCTURES

In this context, the term "existing infrastructures" is used broadly, to include transportation systems, supply chains, existing industrial products and processes, brand recognition, and even government procurement policies. As will be seen, each of the enterprises that we look at leveraged one or more existing infrastructures resourcefully.

Each case history contributes to our understanding of how a contemporary solution might work. Sears Roebuck's savvy branding and marketing underpinned their Modern Homes success; the Lustron Corporation, in emulating the vertically integrated automobile industry of its era, created a housing production line of unprecedented scale; the Techbuilt house achieved construction economy through hard-minded design rigor while elevating popular taste; and SCSD, by creating an innovative rules-based kit of parts for school construction, turned existing methods of project delivery upside down.

Case 1: Sears Roebuck

"Modern Home No. 146" reads the caption under a rendering of a 2,200-square-foot two-story Victorian-style home in the Sears Roebuck catalog of 1908, proclaiming further that "This house can be built on a lot 46 feet wide", with the pre-cut kit going for about $1,600, or, adjusted for inflation,[14] about $105,248 today.

5.1
Sears, Roebuck & Co.
Modern Home No. 146, 1908.

Although this at first sounds like an extraordinarily low price, materials are only one component of the cost of a home. When all the costs are factored in,[15] then the total cost of that house in 1908 would have been $4,111, and today would be on the order of $270,400,[16] or about $123 per square foot. While such comparisons can only be approximate, it would appear likely that a Sears kit home was in the range, in 2020 dollars, of today's cost for a conventional builder's house.[17] This suggests that the Sears home buyer may not have been motivated by price alone, and other factors must have been at work. If price was not driving sales, how did the Sears Roebuck catalog house achieve its success? What can we learn about marketing prefab and modular housing from the Sears Modern Homes Program?

First, there was an existing marketing infrastructure. Sears had already amassed prodigious marketing and branding know-how that it had perfected in moving its retail wares. The success of the Sears Roebuck houses demonstrated that a consumer catalog company could sell houses, much as they could sell other merchandise. A new Sears home was also a sales channel for other Sears goods: new homes needed new appliances, new furniture, and so on. A catalog entry doesn't try to disguise Sears' eagerness: "We want to help you furnish that home, when you are ready for new furnishings. We want to sell you the thousands of things that you and your family need from day to day".[18]

Second, the Sears Modern Homes program reduced the unknowns. The catalog presented an attractive and accurate rendering or photograph of the house.[19] The various detail elements, down to the molding profiles, were carefully illustrated and specified. Prospective buyers could see homes built by other customers,[20] and may have visited a relative or friend who lived in a catalog house—a tangible and reassuring example of what they would soon be acquiring.

Third, Sears' reputation and the success of its national catalog offering reflected well on the Modern Homes program. This is evidenced by a promotional history written in 1918, which proclaimed that "the customer must be satisfied for lifetime for every house we sell is a standing advertisement for Sears Roebuck & Company".[21] Seen from another perspective, Sears had attained widespread brand recognition and a home purchaser no doubt would have had successful dealings with Sears on other items, which surely spurred home sales. There would have been a tacit recognition that Sears would strive to protect its brand and would not stoop to selling shoddy merchandise.

Fourth, by selling pre-cut materials at a fixed price, Sears removed financial risk, helping the potential buyer to overcome doubt and anxiety. Still, during the early years of the program, the home buyer would need to engage a local contractor for foundations and to assemble the kit, so some financial risk remained. It was not unheard of for an intrepid buyer to build a Sears house themselves.[22]

Sears Roebuck's house program came into existence sometime between 1906 and 1908, when an unsung merchandising genius named Frank W. Kushel had an epiphany. We don't know much about Frank Kushel, but in addition to being astute, he must have been a risk-taker and a persuasive salesman. In 1906, he had been re-assigned within the ranks of Sears' middle-management, moving from the china department to the building supplies department with instructions to shut it down.[23] The company had been selling lumber, hardware, roofing, etc., as a regular catalog offering since 1895, but that line of business had proven unprofitable. Ignoring his mission, Kushel instead came up with a plan for shipping pre-cut materials on order direct from the mill to the site, eliminating the cost of maintaining warehouse inventory. By 1908, the first catalog-order houses were available,[24] inaugurating one of Sears' most successful ventures. Within a couple of years, Kushel had turned the money-losing division around.

Ready-to-go house plans were the hook that drew customers away from the local building supply yards, and Kushel clearly had a firm grasp of the marketing power of design and customer service. Over the course of its existence, the Sears Roebuck Modern Home department offered 447 different numbered or named house designs,[25] not counting unrecorded minor modifications that were made to suit an individual buyer's taste. The houses ranged from small summer bungalows to elaborate Tudors ("The Pennsgrove"), Southern Colonials ("The Jefferson"), and other period-style residences. They were broadly grouped according to three price levels, called "Simplex Sectional", "Standard Built", and "Honor Built", reflecting differences in size, quality of materials, and appointments.[26] Altogether more than 70,000 houses were sold over the Modern Homes' 32-year run.[27]

The pre-cut framing lumber, siding, windows, flooring, cabinetry, pre-hung doors, and finish trim were produced at various millwork factories across the U.S. and were then crated and shipped direct to the customer. The largest of these operations was a 40-acre lumber plant in Cairo, Illinois, located strategically along a primary freight rail line.[28] All Sears houses were transported by rail, with crates timed to arrive according to the construction sequence.[29] Building sites needed to be within reasonable distance of a freight depot. The heyday of the Sears house coincided with the development of the first rings of metropolitan commuter suburbs, which were planned in proximity to train lines.

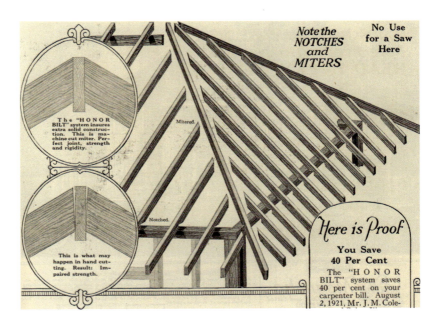

5.2
In the early 20th century, hand-held machine tools were a rarity, and the advantages of factory-cut lumber made good advertising copy.

A skilled contractor could complete a Sears house to the required quality standard in about 352 hours, compared to over 580 hours for a conventional house of that era.[30] In 1930, Sears took over construction supervision, either performing the work with their own forces or subcontracting it.[31] Controlling construction quality would protect Modern Homes, and by association, Sears Roebuck, from brand damage.

In 1929, at the peak of the Modern Homes program, there were 48 sales offices around the country staffed by 350 salesmen,[32] achieving $12 million in sales[33] in the year that marked the start of the Great Depression.

Mortgages were first offered in 1911 and by 1918 had become central to Sears' sales and marketing strategy. In providing financing for the kits it sold, Sears discovered a marketing opportunity as well as a profit center. The company even offered money up front to purchase a building lot, and financed foundations and site work as well.[34] By 1929, sales had reached a peak of $12,050,000, with loans accounting for $5,622,000 of that total.[35]

The Depression eventually inflicted damage on the company, which it passed on to its customers who could not carry their mortgage payments. By 1930, Sears was left holding half its loans, and in 1934 the company liquidated $11 million in mortgages.[36] Mortgage financing was discontinued the following year. Despite the Depression, however, sales for the remainder of the 1930s remained relatively strong, ranging from $2 million to $3.5 million a year.[37]

Sears Roebuck & Company knew their market and focused their sales strategy on consumer choice. Sears understood their customer base for houses the same way they understood it for the full range of catalog merchandise. They offered reliable homes with traditional styling and familiar layouts. But even if outward appearance was traditional, Sears' Architectural Division was continually introducing behind-the-scenes innovations in the use of materials and technology. Central heating, the substitution of drywall for plaster, and asphalt roof shingles were among Sears Roebuck's early innovations.[38] For the 1934 Century of Progress World's Fair in Chicago, Sears displayed a prototype steel-framed house that incorporated central air conditioning.[39] Steel framing in house construction appeared to be the wave of the future.

Despite continuing sales, with customer financing now arranged through the Federal Housing Agency, the Modern Homes department shut down in 1940 due to loan defaults and material shortages on the eve of World War II.[40]

Case 2: Lustron

On the heels of the Allied victory in 1945, the federal government in Washington began unwinding its enormous military build-up and set about returning the U.S. to a peacetime economy. As the military demobilized, soldiers by the hundreds of thousands returned from Europe and the Pacific and began to re-enter civilian life. Families, separated for the duration of the war, re-united; young couples married and started new families. The world of 1945 looked very different from the world of 1940, and the veterans of World War II were eager to reap the rewards of victory and settle down to live a good life. The stage was set for Carl Strandlund, a correspondence-educated engineer, to establish the Lustron Corporation and pioneer the mass production of porcelain-enameled steel houses.

Strandlund had a knack for manufacturing, possessed enormous energy and had, by all accounts, personal magnetism.[41] He had achieved early career success during the 1920s as the president of the Oliver Farm Equipment Company. His technical improvements to the firm's agricultural machinery and production line led sales to grow from $20 million to $120 million over five years,[42] making him a wealthy man along the way.

At the beginning of World War II, the nation's industrial sector was commandeered to defeat the Axis powers. The government ordered the Chicago Vitreous Enamel Product Company, a manufacturer of porcelain-enameled sheet steel[43] to re-tool its factory for military purposes. In 1942, Strandlund, who had earned a reputation as a savvy businessman and technical innovator, joined Chicago Vit (as the company was nicknamed) to lead their wartime effort. He rose to vice-president and general manager the following year after dramatically increasing the output of armor plate for the war and profits for the company.[44]

During the war, the government maintained tight control over critical materials. Steel was strictly reserved for military needs, and rationing continued even after the war. In 1946, Strandlund went to Washington to plead the case for sheet steel that would enable Chicago Vit to win a contract for 500 porcelain-enameled Standard Oil gas stations.[45] To his disappointment, the Civilian Production Administration (formerly the War Production Board) summarily rejected the request. In an odd twist of events, however, Strandlund seems to have drawn rapt attention from federal officials when he off-handedly mentioned the possible use of porcelain-steel for house construction.[46]

The nation was facing a severe housing crisis, with far too few homes available within the financial reach of returning veterans. Young families frequently doubled up in cramped quarters; parents and children moved in with grandparents; and couples searched in vain for affordable housing. The U.S. Senate estimated that homes were needed for 500,000 new households a year, while at the same time, millions of urban dwellings were considered sub-standard and in need of "slum clearance" and replacement. Overall, the government projected the need to build a total of at least three million new homes between 1946 and 1948 to stem a severe housing shortage. Federal officials were under pressure to rapidly mount an effective housing program.[47]

Strandlund's offhand remark found a receptive audience in a progressive New Dealer named Wilson Wyatt, the director of the Office of the Housing Expeditor under the National Housing Administration (NHA). True to his job title, Wyatt smoothed the way: steel would be released to Chicago Vit—lots of it—if it were to be used for the manufacture of housing instead of gas stations. Strandlund's charm and charisma no doubt helped close the deal, but behind the charm was a capable mind that must have already been focused on the technical challenges that lay ahead. Manufacturing porcelain-steel houses, as it turned out, was a comparatively straightforward problem. Strandlund failed to foresee less tangible but hazardous political pitfalls in his relationship with Washington.

The new company formed by Chicago Vit to manufacture houses was named Lustron. In the standard company history, the name was compounded from "Lusterlite" (Chicago Vit's tradename for its porcelain panel product) and the application of "luster on" steel.[48] This prosaic official explanation, however, doesn't do justice to the branding genius—conscious or unconscious—of Lustron. It was a one-word poem, with overtones of desire fused with the techno-futurist sounding "tron" (electron! cyclotron! cosmotron!).

Strandlund and his team commissioned architects Roy Burton Blass and Morris Beckman to sketch up the first Lustron house for manufacture. Blass and Beckmann were competent architects but unremarkable designers. Blass had remodeled a few Chicago movie theaters that featured porcelain-steel panels manufactured by Chicago Vit and came to the company through that connection.[49] Beckmann was an MIT graduate and a former chief draftsman for the Chicago-based corporate architecture firm Skidmore, Owings and Merrill.[50]

Blass and Beckmann's first model, the "Esquire", was a 1,025-square-foot two-bedroom ranch, which Lustron intended to sell for $8,000 (land not included). While on the expensive side, it was highly rated by Consumer Reports and considered good value for its durability, ease of maintenance, and mechanical systems.[51]

The federal government had promised Strandlund that they would order in bulk, tens of thousands of houses at a time. On that basis, in the fall of 1946, the Lustron Corporation took over an idled Curtiss-Wright Aircraft plant in Columbus, Ohio.[52] The empty factory still needed machines, and workers to operate them, and Strandlund needed money for both—$22 million (about $290 million in today's dollars)[53] by his initial estimate. He secured a loan from the Reconstruction Finance Corporation (RFC), a New Deal agency.

The public was ready for the porcelain-steel Lustron house, as can be gleaned from contemporary reports. In April 1948, a model house, furnished with Eames plywood chairs and Kurt Versen lamps, was erected and opened for

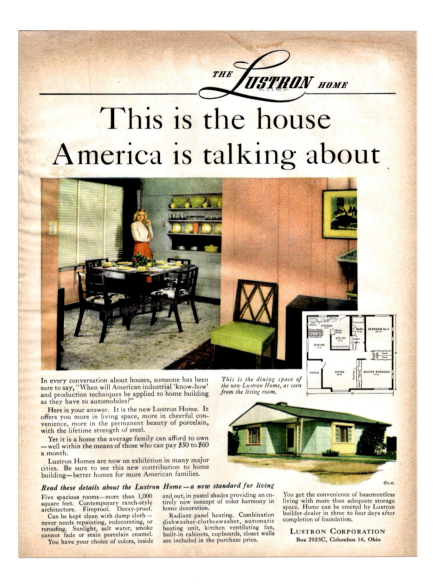

5.3
Advertisement for Lustron
Esquire Model.

tours on the corner of 52nd Street and Sixth Avenue in Manhattan.[54] The
buzz that the house created generated lines of visitors stretching around
the block.[55] Radio personality Norman Brokenshire gushed: "Young man,
you are standing in the greatest single development in housing since they
put one stone on top of another!".[56] Sales were climbing two years after
the first houses were offered despite the failure of the government and
the military to follow through on promised bulk purchases. A two-page
advertising spread in *Life* magazine elicited 150,000 inquiries, with similar
ads in other journals generating another 55,000.[57] A house finished inside
and out in porcelain-steel was hardly conventional, but potential home
buyers were open-minded enough to see the value of a steel home, and
they were able to envision themselves living comfortably in one.

As Lustron headed into the second year of production, the company was partway up the learning curve. Exclusive of land, the cost of the initial models was coming in at $10,000, which was well beyond the reach of most American wage earners.[58] As production slowly ramped up, sales prices dropped a bit, and were estimated at $8,000–$9,000 for a two-bedroom model.[59] By 1949, there were 234 franchised dealer-builders in 35 states ready to do business,[60] but the factory was having difficulty delivering enough homes to keep crews busy. Strandlund acknowledged start-up problems, but he stated unequivocally at the end of 1949 that the factory was fully tooled and ready to produce at full capacity.[61] In July of that year, 48 houses were turned out in one day, well on the path to full production, and far beyond Levitt's output. Strandlund was confident that, despite "growing pains [Lustron was] emerging as a strong, healthy company".[62]

Recognizing that the models in production were over-priced, Strandlund engaged a new architect, Carl Koch, as a design consultant to come up with a more affordable house with a new look. While Lustron's innovations in manufacturing were cutting edge, Strandlund understood that he needed higher-caliber design talent. Koch, who had been educated at MIT and Harvard, was keenly interested in prefabrication and took on his assignment with enthusiasm. In turning to Koch for help, Strandlund demonstrated that he was capable of learning and adapting.

Part of the cost problem was the sheer number of parts that had to be assembled on-site. The time estimated for site assembly, nevertheless, was only 350 hours (the same as for a Sears house). Not surprisingly, the first few houses took far longer, clocking in at more than 1,200 hours, but with a few houses under their belt, the distributors were able to get assembly time down, with one dealer reporting 436 hours on the tenth house.[63] With further experience, along with improvements recommended by Koch, 350 hours appears to have been within reach.

When Koch & Associates arrived in Columbus they met immediate resistance from Lustron's in-house design department. Most of Lustron's design staff had migrated from the auto industry, and were accustomed to acting as stylists, leaving technical matters to the engineers and production people. Koch was expected to simply re-style the product and leave it to the engineers to figure out how to manufacture it. Instead, taking an analytical approach, he insisted on gaining a thorough understanding of the production process[64] before drawing a single line. Koch also ruffled feathers when he found fault with some of the stodgy details of the existing models—the bow window, the somewhat mannered exterior corner post, and especially with the excessive number of porcelain-steel panel joints. In re-conceiving the system, Koch pushed for more pre-assembly in the factory,[65] intending to whittle the number of separate components shipped to the site from 3,000 to 37.[66] Koch also took advantage of a newly acquired metal stamping press, which could produce 8-foot-long self-supporting panels instead of the 2×2-foot panels that had been the size limit up to that point.

The new design, which never came to market, reflected Koch's modernist education at Harvard under Walter Gropius and Marcel Breuer, as well as his apprenticeship to Swedish architect Sven Markelius. Elements were organized by an underlying geometric grid, proportions were harmonious, and the layout was based on modern open plan principles geared to contemporary living. Adhering to a modular approach, panels with doors, with windows, or with none were interchangeable, leading to greater design flexibility. As Koch put it, "the law of combinations is one of the pleasant mathematical secrets of modular [design]".[67]

One notable drawback of Lustron's use of porcelain-steel was the difficulty of introducing variety in components and making design updates, Koch's modular innovations notwithstanding. A pre-cut lumber operation is flexible and involves little set-up time. Houses made of steel plate require heavy factory machinery to cut, punch, bend, and enamel, which means significant set-up time. Design changes required expensive re-tooling. Lustron, hampered by the relative inflexibility of steel fabrication, could at first offer only two models, a five-room and a six-room house (subsequently two more models of the five-room and one of the six-room were added).[68] There were also difficulties obtaining sufficient quantities of steel. Each Lustron house consumed about 10 tons of steel. (Steel was a limited resource, and Lustron had done studies showing that the use of plywood and other materials could reduce steel content to 4 tons.)[69]

Even if Carl Koch's re-vamped design had been introduced, and if Lustron had gone on to bring out further variations, it seems unlikely that they could have achieved anywhere near the number of options offered by Sears. But the novelty and technical sophistication of Lustron houses did resonate with American post-war optimism. Porcelain-steel had the advantages of being fireproof, easy to maintain, and durable. The subtle pitch was to a homeowner's desire for an affordable smart status object. Carl Strandlund knew that there was a certain stigma associated with prefab, and the brilliant public relations stunt of building the demonstration house in mid-town Manhattan (as well as a hundred other demonstration models in cities across the U.S.) helped to free Lustron from down-market associations.

What Strandlund got almost entirely right was the scale and sophistication of Lustron's manufacturing operation. In the various chronicles of the day-to-day dealings and demise of the company, perhaps not enough emphasis is given to his technical achievements. Strandlund transformed the frame, cladding and fit-out of the single-family home to suit the methods of mass production. He devised innovative ways to use porcelain-steel for every component, inside and out. He thought through manufacturing, transportation, and assembly at the job site as a single, integrated process.

Here is a partial list of Lustron's equipment inventory, excerpted from a Senate Subcommittee on Banking and Currency hearing regarding the disposition of Lustron's assets after liquidation,[70] which gives a sense of the extraordinary scale of the factory.

1. 161 presses, ranging from 20 tons to 180 tons, mechanically operated.
2. 19 bit shears for cutting material.
3. 19 big rollers equipped with cut-off press on each machine.
4. 201 welders, portable electric.
5. 31 storage tanks with agitators.
6. 27 ball-mill operators.
7. 48 Arc-Nelson steel welders.
8. 11 gas and electric furnaces.
9. 40,000 lineal feet of conveyors, miscellaneous lengths.
10. 67 spray booths.
11. 28 scooter and motor cars for plant transportation.
12. 65 lathes, presses, tools, and miscellaneous equipment.
13. 16 fixed dust collectors.
14. 32 gas or electric lift trucks.
15. 3 pickering machines.
16. 1 water-cooling tower.
17. Miscellaneous pumps.
18. 1,000,000 square feet of floor space.

The former Curtiss-Wright plant contained three million square feet of high bay, long span factory floor area. Only one-third of the factory was utilized; the company expected to grow into the remainder. There was a special welding machine for roof trusses that could produce 168 spot welds in two seconds.[71] There was a three-story high bathtub press, the first of its kind, that could produce 75 bathtubs an hour.[72] Rails were installed in the floor to guide specially made Freihof trailers down the line, where components were finished and loaded on the trailers in a reverse order of the on-site construction sequence—i.e. last component loaded first, first component loaded last. The trailers were of standard width and length, so there were no burdensome transportation costs, enabling Lustron (in theory) to sell anywhere in the country.

Strandlund's factory was capable of manufacturing 20,000 houses a year,[73] or an average of 77[74] per day, with a maximum output of 100 houses per day.[75] Conveyor belts moved houses down the line at 20 feet per minute.[76] While output was still below capacity in 1950 when the company shut down, there is no evident reason why full capacity couldn't have been achieved. Strandlund's proven ability as a production engineer shines through in the logic and thoroughness of his vertically integrated and rationalized approach.

5.4
Transporting Lustron house components on one of the specially designed Freihof trailers (courtesy of KDN Films).

As the decade of the 1940s wore on, the RFC's loans, which ultimately totaled $37.5 million (or roughly $400 million in today's dollars[77]), drew increasing attention. A series of congressional hearings put Lustron, and Carl Strandlund personally, under mounting pressure. Strandlund, forced to spend long periods of time in Washington defending the company against the political onslaught, was diverted from the essential task of leading the effort in Columbus. Lustron, still in its early stages, was spending a million dollars a month,[78] making an easy political bull's-eye. Excessive executive salaries, including Strandlund's, didn't help appearances. Without re-tracing the history of those hearings,[79] the nasty tenor is captured in contemporary magazine titles such as "The House That Lots of Jack Built" (*Collier's*) and "That Lustron Affair" (*Fortune*).[80] By May of 1950, scarcely two years into production, the RFC recalled its loans and sent the Lustron Corporation into receivership. It had lasted a mere four years, from 1946 to 1950, which included two years of initial financing, design, prototyping, and tooling, and barely two years of production.

Years later, Carl Koch eloquently summed it up:

> When I leaf back through the records – plans, brochures, contracts, the transcript of Congressional autopsies – I admit to a confusion of feelings between the way we regarded it then... and the way it turned out to be. Seldom has there occurred a like mixture of idealism, greed, efficiency, stupidity, potential social good, and political evil. Seldom, surely, has a good idea come so close to realization, and been so decisively slugged.[81]

The Lustron experiment, had it been allowed to continue, might well have transformed American housing.

Case 3: Techbuilt

Good Design, that post-war amalgam of practicality, optimism, and "intelligent living" expressed in the form of everyday objects, was the hallmark of what is now known as Mid-century Modern. While today's home furnishings industry may find the Mid-century label useful, the creation of a period style couldn't have been further from the minds of the great designers of that era, such as Charles and Ray Eames, George Nelson, and Harry Bertoia, to name only a few. For that generation, style was the residual artifact of a vibrant discussion about what really mattered to live well in the modern technological world.[82]

Perhaps no residential design achievement of the 1950s had greater popular impact than the Techbuilt house, conceived by Carl Koch and put into production three years after Lustron's demise. The Techbuilt was a stage on which the daily rituals of mid-century family life could be enacted, with the Nelson lampshades, Lenor-Larsen textiles, and Saarinen chairs as stage props. The images of those interior ensembles in photographs and memory are redolent of a particular time and place in America.

In developing the Techbuilt, Koch drew on all the earlier lessons, frustrations, and downright failures with which he had up to that time been associated. He had learned to suppress the impulse to design for the magazine pages, remarking on his architectural style with characteristic irony: "my own, I grieve to say, is sometimes given as 'modern but not too modern'".[83] At the same time, he was able to tap into the zeitgeist, aligning his aesthetic predisposition with that of a certain class of culturally adventurous, liberally educated professionals. The Techbuilt, nestled among clusters of river birches and rhododendrons, embodied the image of an Edenic shelter that a generation of war-weary veterans found compelling. Techbuilt made modernism safe with a recognizable gabled form, and yet was entirely unencumbered by historical pastiche, a remarkable achievement for a house designed for the popular market, or at least for a significant segment of it.[84]

Koch had for some time been experimenting with prefabrication before his brief involvement with Lustron. The Acorn house,[85] an innovative approach to the modular transportation conundrum, consisted of an 8-foot-wide core module containing kitchen and bath, flanked by hinged stressed-skin wall panels and likewise hinged roof panels, all of which were accordion-folded flat against the kitchen/bath module for transport. The stressed-skin panel was the key to the hinging concept, because it was light, yet strong and stiff.

The principles of structural statics tell us that most of the stress in a structural member occurs in its outer fibers, and the rest is there primarily to maintain the separation between those outer layers. By bonding a thin plywood skin to each side of a honeycomb made of paper strips, the maximum use of the outer fibers is attained. The rest is mostly air. In a nutshell, stressed-skin panels are a high-strength and light-weight composite.

Stressed-skin was to Koch as the sex questionnaire was to Kinsey: it led to liberating new possibilities, but it infuriated the guardians of the existing order. Local building officials did not understand the stressed-skin panel, and therefore did not tolerate it. In 1949, residential building codes were rigidly prescriptive (and still are). Getting the building inspector to recognize an innovative approach that was performatively equal to or better than standard 2×4 studs was an uphill battle. Much back and forth ensued between architect and inspector. After Koch submitted detailed engineering calculations (and then patiently explained them), the building permit was finally granted.[86]

Koch devised a highly economical foundation system for the Acorn house that capitalized on the light weight of the superstructure. The foundation comprised slender precast concrete posts that could be lifted and placed without heavy machinery. As each post was suspended in position over an excavated pit, concrete was poured into the pit up to the bottom of the post.[87] No expensive formwork was needed. The kitchen/bath module was placed on the post foundations, and the walls were bellowed open and anchored to outlying foundation posts—instant rooms! Finally, the roof panels were unfolded and fastened down. The Acorn house could be set up and ready for occupancy in a day.

5.5
Acorn House prototype unfolding, 1948 © Ezra Stoller/Esto.

Koch was a tinkerer, and he attracted a group of like-minded hands-on associates who loved making things. Having approached and failed to interest aircraft manufacturers to make the Acorn stressed-skin panels, they decided to build their own panel-pressing machinery. The merry band scrounged together a manufacturing operation financed out of their own pockets.

In 1949, Koch put up a demonstration model of the first Acorn in Concord, Massachusetts. *Life* magazine sent Ezra Stoller, the well-known architectural photographer, to shoot a feature that would show the house spreading its wings, so to speak. In his book "At Home with Tomorrow", Koch recounts a situation in which Stoller went up in a helicopter to take aerial views. The roof had already been buttoned down, so they ordered the crew to lift it back up and re-enact installation for the camera. At just that moment, the wind started to gust, and the roof panels became unmanageable. Picture the scene: the crew on the roof struggling, Stoller circling aloft waiting impatiently for a photo opportunity, and Koch on the ground photographing the chaos for his own amusement, a near-catastrophe that he later fashioned into a droll anecdote.

A spread in *Life* (sans aerial pictures) and a lot of public notice notwithstanding, the Acorn project proved resistant to financial backing. Several more were built, but the enterprise was soon abandoned for lack of funding. Koch & Associates went on to consult for Lustron, but again, failure.

In 1951, Koch joined two similarly forward-thinking types, a builder and a land developer, to spearhead a cooperative housing development near Concord. They called the development Conantum, drawing on a local Native American place name, and conceived it as a kind of anti-Levittown, designed to respond to the existing topography rather than to flatten it into a housing tract. Conantum was one of many similar cooperative endeavors going on around the country during the late 1940s,[88] a kind of modernist back-to-nature movement.

Conantum involved some 70 owners,[89] each fronting a portion of the money to acquire land. Koch and his team designed all the houses as variations based on a standard model: a three-story gabled "barn" with a compact footprint, in which the lowest level was a walk-out basement nestled into a slope.

The architects acted as construction superintendents, overseeing several different general contractors and stepping well outside of the conventional arms-length role of the architect. Conantum's houses were not prefabricated, but they were dimensioned to minimize the cutting and waste of material. That made them a challenge to build for contractors who were unwilling to pay close attention to the drawings and details. Ultimately, the three original partners lost money, mainly because they

5.6
Conantum house, with
three-story fully glazed end
walls © Ezra Stoller/Esto.

had been obliged to offer the owners a fixed price before they had a firm grasp on construction costs.

Despite the financial loss, Koch took pride in Conantum's social achievement, which was to "provide a start to participation, involvement and improvisation".[90] The active involvement by the owners in the process of planning and building led to strong community bonds, evidenced by many long-staying residents, including Koch and his family.[91] The sense of community was also manifested in ongoing stewardship of common spaces, a notable outgrowth of community building as a shared endeavor.

Gamely risking further punishment, the architects went back to the drawing board with hard-earned lessons, searching for a prefabricated solution that would prove out in the marketplace. In their quest for a winning formula, Koch and his team wrung all the inefficiency and redundancy out of the Conantum model. They sought economy by reducing the house from three to two stories, in which the partially excavated walk-out basement became the lower level, and the "attic" under the gently sloped roof became the upper level. Because the slab on grade and the roof were essential elements, living space could, in a sense, be captured "free" in

5.7
Carl Koch © Ezra Stoller/
Esto.

the basement and attic.[92] The Conantum middle level was dispatched as being uneconomical.

The new house was planned on a 4×4-foot module, based on the width of a sheet of plywood. The post-and-beam frame supported stressed-skin panels for the walls, the second floor, and the roof. The two-story glazed end wall was prefabricated as a single unit. Four timber beams running the length of the house supported the second floor and roof. (You can distinguish a Techbuilt from a builder's imitation because Techbuilt has no ridge beam. Two beams flank the ridge on either side to allow the roof panels to create an efficient balanced cantilever.) Non-load bearing interior partitions gave each owner the opportunity to choose their layout and allowed easy modification as needs changed over time. Costs were estimated at $7.50 per square foot in 1953 dollars, about three-quarters the cost of a standard builder's house.[93] One truckload delivered the kit to the jobsite. Four carpenters could complete the shell in two days.[94]

In 1953, Koch and company pooled their remaining resources and built a spec house, sold it, then built a few more, and sold them. What happened next could not better prove Branch Rickey's theorem that "luck is the residue of design". Television came calling. In those days, reality TV wasn't even a distant gleam in a producer's eye, but just as good (if not in fact better) was a two-part educational show funded by the Ford Foundation,[95] hosted by Alastair Cooke and narrated by Burgess Meredith, that followed the construction of a Techbuilt from empty site to finished product. In today's jargon, the show got 20 million hits—viewers, of course—and over the next three weekends, there were five-mile traffic jams from every direction as people flocked to see a Techbuilt house for themselves.[96] Orders started to pour in.

Concord 480   24′ x 48′; 1152 sq. ft.
Designed for convenience, the compact plan offers all the amenities of a larger house. The full basement accommodates storage, utilities, hobbies, and living space if desired.

5.8
Pages from Techbuilt brochure, c. 1958 (courtesy of David Meerman Scott).

Entrepreneurs like to use the shape of a hockey stick laid sideways as a metaphor for rapid business growth, where the handle represents the time before an investment pays off, and the payoff is the upward-cocked blade. In Techbuilt's case, the growth chart was all blade and no handle. Of course, the years invested in Acorn, Lustron, and Conantum represented a long fallow period during which Koch realized no return, but eight months after the TV show aired on February 14, 1954, the newly incorporated Techbuilt Homes, Inc. made a public offering and sold 120,000 shares of common stock at $2.50 per share.[97]

How to meet this instant demand for Techbuilt houses was the next question. Deliberately forgetting everything they had learned about vertical integration from Lustron and giving up the soul-satisfaction of hands-on construction, Koch and his team set about developing a supply chain. They quickly established strategic partnerships with four existing prefab manufacturers: Acorn Houses, Inc.,[98] Acton Ma; Bush Prefabricated Structures, Inc., Huntington, Long Island; Creative Buildings Inc., Urbana IL; and Structural Prefabricators, Whittier, CA. The four manufacturers would make the post-and-beam and stressed-skin panel kit for the house shell according to Techbuilt's specifications. Other items, such as readily available pre-hung doors and windows, were purchased by Techbuilt at bulk prices and shipped directly to each job site, timed for arrival with the shell. In Koch's words, "Techbuilt came, not so much as a 'package' [but] as a system of converging components".[99]

Techbuilt emulated Lustron's distribution network, franchising 21 builder-dealers throughout the country. The builder-dealers took responsibility for everything but the Techbuilt kit—land, utilities, exterior materials, and interior finish and fit-out, plumbing and heating, etc. (Later, Techbuilt began including some of these items.) In all, over roughly a decade, more than 3,000 Techbuilt houses were constructed. Eventually, there were more than 90 builder-dealers and 22 Techbuilt models.[100]

Techbuilts gracefully accommodated variations and accessories like carports, breezeways, and canopies. Balconies could be cantilevered from extended second floor beams. The "Techbuilt Spacemaking Furniture System"—modular wardrobe, storage, shelving, and media units, dimensionally keyed to the 4×4 planning module—was added to the line of products offered.

In tempering the architect's instinctive urge to take virtuoso flight, Koch achieved what no other architect before or since has accomplished, namely, to introduce design excellence into a commercially successful production house.[101] Techbuilt, by selling over 3,000 units and inspiring countless builders' knock-offs, shaped a generation's understanding of modern domestic architecture. Koch:

> we are actually responding in a traditional way when we build houses that are consistent with our national temperament and technological progress. There is all the opportunity in the world to make a modern house reflect good living and a happy approach to life. But it requires spending some time with matters of the mind and spirit.[102]

Koch understood that the construction of a Techbuilt house was not an end, but rather, it was a beginning, "meant to provide the generous basis for a number of things, not the least of which is intelligent living".[103]

Case 4: The School Construction Systems Development Project

If the post-World War II housing crisis lit the fuse for a boom in suburban home construction, the fecundity of returning veterans and their spouses set off another explosion about six years later—a boom in public school construction. The skyrocketing cost of school construction became an issue of national concern, with the annual construction of 15,000 classrooms in California alone costing $300 million in 1961 dollars.[104] Suburban schools, a community's dearest capital investment, are generally financed with bonds that must be approved by an often-contentious popular vote. School construction bonds are paid for with property taxes, and the battles over a bond for a new school, or even a new roof on an old school, can be epic, pitting parents of young children against retirees on fixed incomes, neighbor against neighbor. School bond battles invariably invoke age-old political divisions over the proper role of government in the provision of public goods. Self-appointed watchdogs of government waste see to it that every dollar expended is scrutinized, and where a dollar can be cut it will be. The construction budgets for most public schools, save for a handful of very affluent communities, are razor thin.

The SCSD project was an experiment during the 1960s that aimed to reduce costs and increase the supply of school buildings by designing a kit of pre-engineered construction components. In an unprecedented policy maneuver, a consortium of 13 California school districts[105] pooled resources to pre-purchase SCSD components in bulk, enabling economies of scale. Architects then designed schools for each district by creating an arrangement of those components, which could be assembled in varied configurations. The project was far more than a technical exercise—it drew on the thinking of progressive educators who were keen on introducing flexibility into the design of educational environments. Systems-based design and flexible educational environments were thus interdependent. It's hard to overstate how innovative a pairing of concepts that was.

Architects responded to the new ideas about education that were in the air with new ideas about the kind of spaces that foster learning. An understanding of and appreciation for the experience of young children in school environments led architects to shun the monumentality characteristic of pre-war school architecture, and instead emphasize appropriate scale, daylight, and connections to the outdoors, playing fields, and the landscape. The standard classroom for one teacher and thirty students, repeated along a corridor (what school architects call the eggcrate plan) was increasingly regarded as anachronistic. Progressive private schools founded on the theories of John Dewey were having an influence on public education. New teaching methods might involve the rearrangement of the classroom from regimented desks to clusters for small group work, or the joining of classrooms for team-teaching a large group, or the provision of resources for hands-on learning within the classroom that were previously housed in functionally separate spaces. The uncertainty about space needs while ideas about education were undergoing rapid change made flexibility a new driver in the design of school buildings.[106]

Systems analysis, which grew out of World War II "operations research", was a rational approach to problem-solving "in which each step of the decision-making process is made explicit whenever possible"[107] to balance desired objectives against cost.[108] Systems analysis was as fresh and crisp as the sea of buzz cuts and starched white short-sleeved shirts at Mission Control in Houston. Any problem could be solved if you could restate it as a series of logical propositions, grounded in objective criteria. The pre-Vietnam era of the Kennedy presidency, when "Organization Man" was in his prime, was marked by faith in rationality—a curiously self-contradictory faith. The unwinnable and tragic war in Vietnam was about to destroy that faith, of course, but for a few years in the early 1960s, there was a certain innocence and optimism.

The groundwork for SCSD was laid in 1954, when a young architect, Ezra Ehrenkrantz, returned from an inspirational Fulbright year in England.[109] Ehrenkranz had studied systems architecture in the U.K., which had been developed in response to shortages of labor and materials after World War II. British architects had demonstrated that prefabricated systems for school construction could be used to design elegant and economical buildings. The floor plan of a systems school was based on a standard module, which coordinated the dimensions and placement of structural and space dividing elements. The module was a constant no matter where the building site was located. Since the components were engineered and coordinated in advance, architects could focus on planning and design with a high degree of certainty about cost. Ehrenkrantz was impressed by what he saw and returned to the U.S. intending to plant the systems design seed in American soil. He became a fervent advocate for systems design in the U.S. that a decade later became the basis for the SCSD project.

Unlike the systems schools in Great Britain, which were typically urban and multi-story, schools in mid-century American suburbs were rarely higher than two stories and more often were one story. That distinction gave Ehrenkrantz a point of departure to develop a homegrown solution[110] that played to the strengths of American industry and market competition.

In 1958, the Ford Foundation set up a new educational think tank, the Educational Facilities Laboratories (EFL).[111] EFL was the brainchild of two senior Ford Foundation executives, Alvin C. Eurich (later the president of the Aspen Institute) and Clarence H. Faust, who had been working on issues in education. Eurich and Faust believed that the path to innovation in education was through innovation in school design, and that new teaching methods would emerge in response to changes in the school environment. They aimed to rid "the education establishment of its attachment to forms and methods that were impediments to the teaching-learning process" on the premise that it would be "easier to change buildings and what went into them than to change people".[112]

The year that EFL was founded, Ehrenkrantz submitted a report on his experience in England and the potential application of the systems approach to the construction of American schools. Eurich and Faust judged the idea promising but not in synch with the staid Eisenhower era. It took seven more years before Ehrenkrantz saw his ideas first realized.

The catalyst for the establishment of the SCSD project was a national conference in 1961[113] on the problem of school construction sponsored by Architectural Forum (a now-defunct architectural journal) and EFL. The conference was attended by a delegation of school officials from various states, as well as a deputy secretary from the U.K. Ministry of Education. Ehrenkranz and other architects along with representatives from industry had seats at the table.[114] As might be expected, there were simplistic proposals for standardized school plans. Ehrenkrantz and his allies at EFL argued persuasively that a systems approach, following the British model, could give architects the flexibility to design schools for the particular needs of a community while achieving economies of scale through the use of standardized components.

Under the administration of the Stanford University School Planning Laboratory[115] and in consultation with educators, the design team developed detailed performance specifications. Ehrenkranz and his colleagues established seven system categories. The first four, the structure, the integrated ceiling and lighting system, HVAC, and flexible partitions, comprised the basic building. The other three systems—lockers, casework, and fixed lab equipment—comprised interior fit-out.[116]

Completely departing from the standard division of building trades, the systems would be bid as integrated packages. The technical make-up of the components was not specified. Instead, "the components were bid on the basis of performance specifications which prescribed what the products must do, instead of the usual specifications and drawings, which describe what the products should be".[117] Further departing from convention, the system components were bid *before* a design of a school had been drawn up.

Each system manufacturer was required to coordinate with the others to ensure, for example, that structure, HVAC, lighting, ceilings, and partitions would all meet seamlessly at the construction site.[118] "The [SCSD] performance specifications spelled out criteria for... the individual components, pressing for a level of coordination at which components would begin to assume functions other than their own".[119] As Ehrenkranz put it, "confronting industry with... performance specifications was a reversal of the process by which its process and customs had grown up over the centuries".[120] Coordination among manufacturers didn't come naturally, though. The design team had to "arrange some marriages"[121] before the final systems contracts were awarded.

SCSD schools were planned on a 5×5-foot grid. Columns were spaced on 60-foot centers—double the standard school column spacing—for planning flexibility. Thirty-six-inch deep trusses for 60-foot roof spans (60-inch trusses were used for the gymnasium and other longer-span spaces) supported a light-weight metal deck.[122] An integrated ceiling system designed on the 5-foot module housed lighting, acoustically absorbent panels, air supply grilles, and partition attachment points. A non-load bearing moveable partition system comprised of prefabricated panels allowed for flexibility to reconfigure space virtually overnight.[123] Folding doors integrated into the partitions allowed teachers to quickly join or separate classrooms during the school day. Flexible HVAC ductwork, along with a variety of interchangeable light fixtures and other environmental systems housed within the "service sandwich" were designed for reconfiguration along with changes in partition layouts. Microzones for HVAC control ensured comfort as spaces were reconfigured.[124]

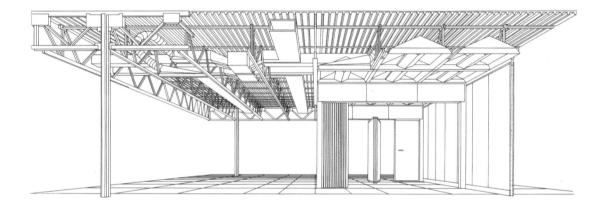

5.9
SCSD section perspective showing system components © McGraw Hill, *Architectural Systems: A Needs, Resource and Design Approach* by Ezra Ehrenkrantz.

Each school architect was responsible for planning and component selection within the rules of the system and the available options. Architects had complete latitude when it came to the design of facades, which could range from floor to ceiling glass to conventional hand-laid brick.

Vendors had considerable autonomy when it came to engineering and detailing—even the choice of structural materials—as long as they complied with dimensional parameters and performance requirements, and coordinated with other systems. The SCSD negotiated with the vendors to establish the amount of business they would need committed in advance to justify the cost of full technical development. After nearly a year of technical development, a 3,600-square-foot prototype was erected to demonstrate the validity of the awarded component bids.[125]

In this way, the structural system, the HVAC system, the ceiling system, the partition system, and so on were optimized and coordinated by the manufacturers, reducing the burden on the architect to prepare detailed working drawings and specifications. A combination of competitive pressure and precise performance specifications ensured quality control. SCSD "centralized industrial production of components of buildings and de-centralized the ways in which they were assembled".[126] As a colleague put it, Ehrenkranz "was intent on twisting the tail of industry"[127] by using the principles of "standardized but versatile components and a large, guaranteed market for them"[128] to achieve the SCSD's goals. "Manufacturers were forced by the nature of the project to work together in teams to integrate their products for the benefit of the client".[129]

In all, 13 SCSD schools were built in 1966 and 1967[130] before the experiment ended. While the SCSD project did not achieve the anticipated 20 percent cost savings[131] (costs were in the range of conventional construction),[132] the buildings were well regarded.[133] SCSD had achieved proof of principle.

As the sixties wore on, well, the times they had a-changed, to paraphrase Bob Dylan. Organization Man was getting old; NASA had sent men to the moon, but when iconic images of the Earth were beamed back from space, a new environmental consciousness dawned and technology lost its luster. Assassinations, Vietnam, race riots, Woodstock, and then Altamont marked the close of the decade. Slide rule rationality saw its irrational side reflected back in the face of youth counter-culture, and the Whole Earth Catalog eclipsed systems thinking.

The cultural changes of the sixties led, in New York City, to school decentralization and community control, a trend that was soon followed elsewhere around the country. This marked the death knell for systems-based school design. Community involvement in new school planning and design meant that architects could not even give the appearance of imposing a systems solution. Much later, in 1979, a member of the SCSD team observed that "racial conflicts were still only nascent in the early 1960's, and had not been accepted as a major focus of school planning".[134]

The irony is that the abandonment of an economical method of school delivery occurred just as double-digit inflation arrived in the 1970s, which ate away the purchasing power of school board budgets. The further irony is that the cultural rejection of systems thinking in school design was accompanied by a reactionary return to traditional eggcrate school design and classroom-style instruction. The progressive ideal of the open and flexible classroom pioneered by Ehrenkrantz and SCSD should have been in alignment with the Whole Earth Catalog idea, right there along with the methane generators and yurt kits, but SCSD was tagged as Establishment architecture, think-tank architecture, with all of the toxic associations to Cold War bastions like the Rand Corporation or Herman Kahn's Hudson Institute.

If the SCSD experiment had continued, it might have led to a widespread transformation of American construction practices. SCSD has been criticized, perhaps fairly, as overly restricting the architect's design freedom.[135] Given time it might have evolved into an open-source prefab ecosystem with a wide range of options and accessories. Maybe it was an idea ahead of its time, an idea that would have flourished in millennial culture, the era of the revolution in information technology. Let's hold that thought.

Notes

1 Kenneth T. Jackson, *Crabgrass Frontier: The Suburbanization of the United States* (New York: Oxford University Press, 1985), 235. The Levitt's divided the construction process into 27 distinct steps, each carried out by a separate crew.
2 Habitat 67 designed by Moshe Safdie, or the Nakagin Capsule Tower designed by Kisho Kurokawa are notable multi-story modular buildings.
3 Kathryn Brenzel and David Jeans, "Warped Lumber, Failed Projects: TRD Investigates Katerra, SoftBank's $4B Construction Startup," *The Real Deal*, December 16, 2019, https://therealdeal.com/2019/12/16/softbank-funded-construction-startup-katerra-promised-a-tech-revolution-its-struggling-to-deliver/. Katerra, a recently founded vertically integrated construction company, hopes to bring a flat pack mass timber structural system to market on a large scale. The company has experienced growing pains and it is too early to know whether their approach will prove successful.
4 "General Panel System House, Los Angeles, CA (1949–1950)," PCAD, accessed July 12, 2020, http://pcad.lib.washington.edu/building/6938/. Walter Gropius and Konrad Wachsmann's system for the General Panel Corporation (1941–1948), based on a technically advanced structural joint, was a serious attempt to commercialize a prefab system but only about 200 houses were completed.
5 Twentieth-century architects who advocated for industrialization but who stayed arm's length from commercial industry include le Corbusier (with the exception of an ill-fated building materials venture), the Metabolists, Archigram, and Moshe Safdie, to name several.
6 Simon Sadler, *Archigram: Architecture without Architecture* (Cambridge, MA: MIT Press, 2005), 189.
7 Construction photographs of Le Corbusier's villas, for example, reveal crude masonry infill behind the pristine white stucco skin. Le Corbusier was more interested in the *idea* of industrialized construction than in its actualization.
8 Daniel Weiss, Gregor Harbusch and Bruno Maurer, "CIAM 4 and the 'Unanimous' Origins of Modernist Urban Planning," ArchDaily, published February 7, 2015, https://www.archdaily.com/596081/ciam-4-and-the-unanimous-origins-of-modernist-urban-planning. For example, the Congrès Internationaux d'Architecture Moderne (CIAM) in its heyday espoused "the four functions": housing, working, recreation and traffic, and "their strict and schematic spatial separation", setting the stage for Jane Jacobs to advocate for the complete opposite in "The Death and Life of the Great American City".
9 Eric Paul Mumford, *The CIAM Discourse on Urbanism, 1928–1960* (Cambridge, MA: MIT Press, 2002), 268. CIAM dissolved in part due to the reaction of some members against modernist planning principles as realized in a built form. It had become, "by the 1960's... the shared negative symbol of the failures of modern architecture".
10 Colin Rowe and Robert Slutzky, "Transparency: Literal and Phenomenal," *Perspecta* 8 (1963): 45–54. This seminal essay influenced a generation of architects and students (including this author) and was central to a shift toward formalism in modern architecture.
11 Marie Doezema, "Time Is Running Out for Tokyo's Nagakin Capsule Tower," *Bloomberg*, August 26, 2019, https://www.bloomberg.com/news/articles/2019-08-26/tokyo-s-famous-capsule-tower-may-not-be-doomed. The Nakagin Capsule Tower (1972) by Kisho Kurokawa is an exception that proves the rule. The architect claimed that the capsule-like apartment units were designed for replacement every

20 years but there was never a practical way to do this. The units deteriorated to the point of being unlivable. The fate of the tower is now in the balance as plans for demolition are being drawn up. Architectural aficionados hope to see it restored as a monument to the Metabolist movement.

12 As a student at Cooper Union, I attended a lecture by Jencks in which he used an image of the towers imploding to drive his point across. I recall one of my professors, Richard Stein, calling the demolition "one of the great moral failures". He understood that the real story at Pruitt-Igoe was racial and political.

13 *The Pruitt-Igoe Myth*, directed by Chad Freidrichs (St. Louis, MO: Unicorn Stencil, 2011), DVD. For a balanced assessment of what went wrong, see "The Pruitt-Igoe Myth," a documentary film by Chad Fredrichs.

14 "Measuring Worth Is a Complicated Question," MeasuringWorth.com, accessed July 12, 2020, https://www.measuringworth.com/. For this calculation, we used the "household purchasing power" approach.

15 Carmel Ford, "Cost of Constructing a Home," NAHB Economics and Housing Policy Group, published December 1, 2017, https://www.nahbclassic.org/fileUpload_details .aspx?contentTypeID=3&contentID=260013&subContentID=707961. The National Association of Home Builders (NAHB) publishes an annual survey of home building costs with seven components of total sales cost broken out by percentage: construction cost, finished lot cost, financing cost, overhead & general expenses, marketing cost, sales commission, and profit. For purposes of comparison, we are assuming that the same percentage ratios applied in 1908. The conversion to 2020 dollars assigns a relatively low labor component to the construction cost (30 percent) to account for pre-cut lumber.

16 "Measuring Worth Is a Complicated Question." For this calculation, we again used the "household purchasing power" approach.

17 "How Much Cost It Cost to Build a House?" HomeGuide, accessed July 12, 2020, https://homeguide.com/costs/cost-to-build-a-house. According to HomeGuide. com, based on 2017 Census data, the national average was $100 to $155 per square foot, with the northeast at the high end of the range.

18 Katherine H. Stevenson and H. Ward Jandl, *Houses by Mail: A Guide to Houses from Sears, Roebuck and Company* (Washington, DC: Preservation Press, 1986), 36.

19 Stevenson and Jandl, 36.

20 Stevenson and Jandl, 29.

21 Stevenson and Jandl, 19.

22 Stevenson and Jandl, 30.

23 Stevenson and Jandl, 20.

24 Stevenson and Jandl, 20.

25 "What is a Sears Modern Home," Sears Archives, last modified March 21, 2012, http://www.searsarchives.com/homes/.

26 What is a Sears Modern Home, 2012.

27 What is a Sears Modern Home, 2012.

28 Stevenson and Jandl, 20.

29 Stevenson and Jandl, 30.

30 Stevenson and Jandl, 30.

31 Stevenson and Jandl, 22.

32 "Chronology of the Sears Modern Homes Program," Sears Archives, last modified March 21, 2012, http://www.searsarchives.com/homes/chronology.htm.

33 Chronology of the Sears Modern Homes Program, 2012.

34 Stevenson and Jandl, 20–21.

35 Stevenson and Jandl, 22.

36 Stevenson and Jandl, 22.

37 Stevenson and Jandl, 23.

38 What is a Sears Modern Home, 2012.

39 Chronology of the Sears Modern Homes Program, 2012.

40 Regina Cole, "The Sears House was the American Dream that Came in a Box," *Forbes*, October 23, 2018, https://www.forbes.com/sites/reginacole/2018/10/23/the-sears-house-was-the-american-dream-that-came-in-a-box/#7defaad9731b.

41 Douglas Knerr, *Suburban Steel: The Magnificent Failure of the Lustron Corporation, 1945–1951* (Columbus, OH: Ohio State University Press, 2004), 70–71.

42 Thomas T. Fetters and Vincent Kohler, *The Lustron Home: The History of a Postwar Prefabricated Housing Experiment* (Jefferson, NC: McFarland, 2002), 11.

43 Porcelain-enameled steel, first used in kitchen appliances, and then to clad commercial building facades, is strong, durable, and corrosion-resistant. It has an attractive finish that can be rendered in a variety of colors and is still used today for appliances and as a building cladding material.

44 Fetters and Kohler, 12.

45 Fetters and Kohler, 15.
46 Knerr, 76.
47 "Post-war Housing Crisis," Ohio History Collection, accessed July 12, 2020, https://www.ohiohistory.org/visit/exhibits/ohio-history-center-exhibits/1950s-building-the-american-dream/lustron-about/help-for-lustrons/meet-the-lustrons/meet-history/meet-history-post-war-housing-crisis.
48 Knerr, 77.
49 Fetters and Kohler, 18.
50 Knerr, 78.
51 Fetters and Kohler, 27.
52 Coincidentally, the city of Columbus had another porcelain-steel manufacturer, the Porcelain Steel Building Company, a subsidiary of White Castle, which was established in 1934 to manufacture panels for the White Castle burger stands that still dot American highways.
53 "Measuring Worth Is a Complicated Question". For this calculation, we used the "Consumer Price Index" method.
54 "Steel House Goes on Display Here," *New York Times*, April 14, 1948.
55 Douglas Knerr, *Suburban Steel: The Magnificent Failure of the Lustron Corporation, 1945–1952* (Columbus, OH: Ohio State University Press, 2004), 104.
56 Fetters and Kohler, 47.
57 Fetters and Kohler, 48.
58 Fetters and Kohler, 28.
59 Comparative Costs of Lustron 2-bedroom House Model 02. Cost data supplied by Lustron dealers, as reprinted in Fetters and Kohler, Appendix E. Variations in price reflected variations in transportation costs and local costs of foundations and erection.
60 Fact sheet accompanying press letter from Carl Strandlund, as reprinted in Fetters and Kohler, Appendix A.
61 Press release letter from Carl Strandlund, as reprinted in Fetters and Kohler, Appendix A.
62 Press release letter from Carl Strandlund, as reprinted in Fetters and Kohler, Appendix A.
63 Knerr, 147.
64 Fetters and Kohler, 116–117.
65 Fetters and Kohler, 119.
66 Carl Koch and Roger K. Lewis, *Roadblocks to Innovation in the Housing Industry: A Report to the National Commission on Urban Problems* (Washington, DC: National Commission on Urban Problems, 1969), 22.
67 Carl Koch, *At Home with Tomorrow* (New York: Rinehart, 1958), 119.
68 *Hearing Before a Subcommittee on Banking and Currency, First Session on the Proposed Disposition of the Lustron Corp. Prefabricated Housing Plant at Columbus, Ohio*, 82nd Cong., 5 (1951) (statement of Carl Strandlund, president, Lustron Corp.).
69 *Hearing Before a Subcommittee on Banking and Currency, First Session on the Proposed Disposition of the Lustron Corp. Prefabricated Housing Plant at Columbus, Ohio*, 82nd Cong., 17 (1951) (statement of Richard Dyas, Chief, Housing Branch, Reconstruction Finance Corp.).
70 *Hearing Before a Subcommittee on Banking and Currency, First Session on the Proposed Disposition of the Lustron Corp. Prefabricated Housing Plant at Columbus, Ohio*, 82nd Cong., 39 (1951) (letter from Arthur H. Padula to C.Y. Dodds, September 11, 1950).
71 *Hearing Before a Subcommittee on Banking and Currency, First Session on the Proposed Disposition of the Lustron Corp. Prefabricated Housing Plant at Columbus, Ohio*, 82nd Cong., 6 (1951) (statement of Antonio Montagno, engineer, Lustron Corp.).
72 *Hearing Before a Subcommittee on Banking and Currency, First Session on the Proposed Disposition of the Lustron Corp. Prefabricated Housing Plant at Columbus, Ohio*, 82nd Cong., 6 (1951) (statement of Carl Strandlund, president, Lustron Corp.). Lustron invested in the bathtub press because they could not obtain tubs in sufficient quantity to meet their production goals. In a rare but costly mistake, the press was engineered to produce a non-standard tub of 61.5 inches in length (60 inches is standard) which precluded selling bathtubs as a side business to amortize the investment in tooling.
73 *Hearing Before a Subcommittee on Banking and Currency, First Session on the Proposed Disposition of the Lustron Corp. Prefabricated Housing Plant at Columbus, Ohio*, 82nd Cong., 5 (1951) (statement of Carl Strandlund, president, Lustron Corp.).
74 *Hearing Before a Subcommittee on Banking and Currency, First Session on the Proposed Disposition of the Lustron Corp. Prefabricated Housing Plant at Columbus,*

Ohio, 82nd Cong., 17 (1951) (statement of Richard Dyas, Chief, Housing Branch, Reconstruction Finance Corp.).

75 Koch and Lewis, 19.
76 Koch and Lewis, 19.
77 Measuring Worth Is a Complicated Question. For this calculation we used the "Consumer Price Index" method.
78 Fetters and Kohler, 85.
79 See Fetters; Knerr.
80 "Meet Carl Strandlund," Ohio History Collection, accessed July 12, 2020, https://www.ohiohistory.org/visit/exhibits/ohio-history-center-exhibits/1950s-building-the-american-dream/lustron-about/help-for-lustrons/meet-the-lustrons/meet-history/meet-carl-strandlund.
81 Koch, 111.
82 Don Wallance, *Shaping America's Products* (New York: Reinhold Publishing Corporation, 1956). A contemporaneous survey of mid-century design from the practitioners viewpoint. (The late industrial designer Don Wallance was the author's father.)
83 Koch, 66.
84 Betty Pepis, "The People's Choice," *New York Times*, January 2, 1955.
85 Not to be confused with Acorn Houses (subsequently Empyrean), a later and separate prefab branch of the Acorn experiment.
86 Koch.
87 Koch.
88 For example, Crestwood Hills Mutual Housing Association (California 1950) designed by Cory Buckner; Mar Vista, California (California 1948) designed by Gregory Ain with landscape planning and design by Garrett Eckbo; Moon Hill (Massachusetts 1948–1950), designed by the Architects Collaborative (Walter Gropius and his partners).
89 Koch.
90 Koch.
91 "Albert Carl Koch and NC Techbuilt Houses," NCModernist, accessed July 12, 2020, https://ncmodernist.org/techbuilt.htm.
92 Ford Foundation TV Radio Workshop, "Excursion," aired on February 14, 1954. Featuring the first Techbuilt house being constructed.
93 *Omnibus*, "Ford Foundation's TV Radio Workshop Techbuilt Show" (1954; Ford Foundation), internet resource, https://thetechbuilthouse.com/.
94 Ford Foundation TV Radio Workshop, 1954.
95 Ford Foundation's TV Radio Workshop Techbuilt Show, 1954.
96 Koch, 159.
97 "New Techbuilt Shares to Finance Expansion," *Democrat and Chronicle* (Rochester, NY), September 8, 1954, 25.
98 Koch was not affiliated with Acorn Houses, Inc., which was an outgrowth of the folding Acorn House experiment.
99 Koch, 162.
100 "Progress Report: The Work of Carl Koch & Associates," *Progressive Architecture*, December 1958, 112.
101 Koch won AIA design awards for both the Acorn and Techbuilt houses.
102 Sarah Lueck, "Case Study: Mid-Century Modern Deck Houses," *Aamodt/Plumb* (blog), n.d., https://aamodtplumb.com/case-study-mid-century-modern-deck-houses/.
103 Koch, 174.
104 James Benet, Christopher Arnold, Jonathan King, James W. Robertson, *SCSD: The Project and the Schools, a Report from the Educational Facilities Labratories* (New York: Educational Facilities Laboratories, 1967), 16.
105 Benet, Arnold, King and Robertson, 19. The First California Commission on School Systems.
106 Judy Marks, "A History of Educational Facilities Laboratories (EFL)," National Clearinghouse for Educational Facilities, last modified 2009, https://files.eric.ed.gov/fulltext/ED508011.pdf.
107 Malcolm W. Hoag, "An Introduction to Systems Analysis" (Santa Monica, CA: RAND Corporation, 1956), 1.
108 Hoag, 2.
109 Benet, Arnold, King and Robertson, 16.
110 Ezra Ehrenkranz, "What's Happening to SCSD and Why," *Nation's Schools* 83, no. 4 (1969): 57.
111 Marks, 2009. EFL's board came from the highest levels of the American corporate and political world: Winthrop Rockefeller, governor of Arkansas; Milton Mumford, chairman of Lever Brothers; Henry Dreyfuss, the renowned industrial designer;

Clay Bedford, president of Kaiser Aerospace; and a handful of other apostles of the "Establishment".

112 James W. Armsey, "A Commentary on a Series of Grants by the Ford Foundation to the Educational Facilities Laboratories, Inc. 1958-1975, 1976 Sept. (Reports 012263)," 1976, Box 587, Ford Foundation Records, Catalogued Reports, Reports 11775-13948 (FA739E), Rockefeller Archive Center, Sleepy Hollow NY.

113 Benet, Arnold, King and Robertson, 16.

114 Benet, Arnold, King and Robertson, 16.

115 Benet, Arnold, King and Robertson, 18.

116 Educational Facilities Laboratories, *SCSD, An Interim Report* (New York: Educational Facilities Laboratories, 1965), 11–12.

117 Educational Facilities Laboratories, 9.

118 Benet, Arnold, King and Robertson, 18.

119 Educational Facilities Laboratories, 9.

120 John Boice, *School Construction Systems Development Project* (publisher unknown; reproduced by the U.S. Office of Health Education and Welfare, Office of Education, 1965), 66.

121 Benet, Arnold, King and Robertson, 19.

122 Educational Facilities Laboratories, 9.

123 Benet, Arnold, King and Robertson, 20.

124 Benet, Arnold, King and Robertson, 19.

125 Benet, Arnold, King and Robertson, 19.

126 George Rand and Chris Arnold, "Evaluation: A Look Back at the 60's Sexiest System," *AIA Journal* 68, no. 4 (1979): 52.

127 Rand and Arnold, 52.

128 Educational Facilities Laboratories, 7.

129 Educational Facilities Laboratories, 13.

130 Joshua David Lee, "Questioning Modern Approaches to Flexibility: 50 Years of Learning from the School Construction Systems Development (SCSD) Project" (Ph.D. dissertation, University of Texas at Austin, 2016), 97.

131 Lee, 97.

132 Benet, Arnold, King and Robertson, 14.

133 Lee, 97; Benet, Arnold, King and Robertson, 9.

134 Rand and Arnold, 55.

135 Ehrenkranz, 57.

Part 2

6   The Intermodal Modular System

My decision in the autumn of 2005 to leave the safe harbor of an internationally recognized firm and sail off into an unknown future seems, in hindsight, a quixotic and maybe even reckless adventure. During the previous summer, I'd been introduced to two New York real estate developers, Alex Abrams and Eldon Scott, who had set out to manufacture modular buildings from used shipping containers. Abrams, a lawyer by training and former tech entrepreneur, and Scott, a businessman with experience in building retail stores and restaurants from shipping containers, were searching for a new approach that would bring predictability to construction cost. Their quest was born of frustration with the high-risk development process in New York, where they had been doing downtown residential loft conversions. They had just formed a company, soon to be named Global Building Modules, Inc., or GBM, and had raised funds to get the company started. Abrams and Scott invited me to join their venture to head up design and R&D.[1] Unaware, of course, of the 2008 financial storm that was at that moment brewing but whose fury would not be unleashed for two more years, I was game to pursue a new endeavor with freedom to innovate and change the way housing is designed and built.

I was excited about the prospect. What shape would our new modular system take? Shipping container reuse was the starting point, but where it would lead was up to us to decide. In this chapter, I will show how—and more important, why—our approach evolved from the reuse of existing shipping containers to the invention of the Volumetric Unit of Construction

(VUC). The VUC, as we refer to it, shares the same intermodal transportation system as the shipping container, but in every other respect has been completely redesigned and reengineered for architecture. The VUC enabled us to think about intermodal modular architecture as a "delivery system"[2] for urban housing that would foster open-source design and a global housing supply chain.

When we first met to discuss my joining their fledgling enterprise, Abrams and Scott had just entered into an agreement with a British outfit, Urban Space Management (USM), to use their method for converting shipping containers into building modules. Eric Reynolds, USM's founder, presides over a large expanse of water frontage on the Docklands side of the Thames River, where he has put up a series of live/work rental units, five stories high and made of recycled containers with porthole windows. The first such structure was erected in 1998, followed by several more. Reynold's hands-on experiments with shipping containers were done out of a small manufacturing operation that he'd set up at Container City, as the Docklands property is known. Those early projects demonstrated that living spaces could be constructed from varied arrangements of modified 8×40-foot shipping containers.

The Beta Project

I joined GBM in November of 2005 and started work. Our twin goals were to design and construct a modular building, our "beta" project, on Lafayette Street in downtown Manhattan (property that Abrams and Scott controlled), and to develop an integrated system of modular construction suited for manufacturing on a global scale—to invent, in effect, not just a modular system, but an entirely new modular industry.

Our staff soon numbered six architects and a construction manager working within the company. I drew on my network of professional relationships to bring in a team of capable technical consultants. My first phone call was to a top-flight structural engineer, Dan Sesil, who is a partner with LERA, the distinguished engineering firm responsible for the Shanghai World Financial Center, the Clinton Presidential Library, and other high-profile projects. One of Sesil's many strengths as an engineer is his clarity of thought at the conceptual stage, which enables him to synthesize integrated and elegant solutions. Sesil was interested in working with us, and eventually we assembled a group of technical consultants as one would normally find on a building project, but in addition to engineers our consulting team also included a patent law firm, a market research firm, and an overseas procurement consultant.

The Lafayette Street project, located in a landmarked historic district, was slated to go before the New York City Landmarks Commission. The Commission had a reputation for enforcing contextual design and an antipathy to non-traditional solutions. We intended to demonstrate that a modern building comprised of repurposed shipping containers could have an architectural "conversation" with the 19th-century industrial architecture of the surrounding neighborhood. We would emphasize the tough, no-nonsense character of shipping containers.

In fact, shipping container imagery was exactly the opposite of what we had in mind as GBM's brand identity. In our first brainstorming sessions, we decided that the shipping container sent the wrong message. Architects and artists were already working with that idea, designing pop-up buildings and houses which played off the notion of the shipping container as an evocative industrial artifact. And of course, USM in London had built its identity around shipping containers fitted with oversize portholes. The shipping container image works for creating buzz as a running shoe boutique or a sidewalk cafe, but as a housing system, we wanted the building image to be flexible. It was ironic that to clear the landmark hurdle, our first project, 372 Lafayette Street, would look like shipping container architecture.

The small trapezoidal site made it awkward to fit rectilinear modules. Our solution was a hybrid building that included a conventional steel frame to fill in leftover space, which is where we put the stair/elevator core and public corridors. While a tight, irregular site was not ideal for modular architecture, it was a proving ground where we could work through myriad technical issues.

The apartment floors comprised twelve 8×20-foot modules. The modules were 11-foot high (the tallest that we could transport without a special permit), which enabled us to have 9-foot-10-inch ceilings. One challenge, critical for intermodal modular architecture, is how to obtain usable room

6.1
372 Lafayette Street, fifth floor plan with mate-lines indicated in red.

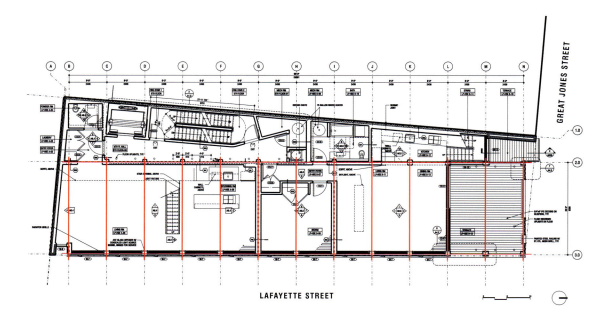

dimensions from 8-foot-wide modules. We'll get to our structural solution for that later in this chapter.

The exterior of the building clearly identified the distinction between modular and conventional elements. The modular stack, painted a vibrant red, rested on a charcoal-gray steel-framed base. A shallow canopy ran the length of the storefront, punctuated at one end by a red entrance marquee. A precast concrete lot line wall provided the code-required fire separation. On the north side, a series of projecting "Juliet" balconies served to articulate the modular stack as a discreet volume. Because Lafayette Street and Great Jones meet at an oblique angle, this articulation resolved the awkward problem created by placing orthogonal modules in a non-orthogonal street wall context.

We strove to pare the architectural expression of the window frames facing Lafayette Street down to the slimmest possible profile, and to crisply define the joints between modules by devising an extruded aluminum "boundary frame" around the windows. The boundary frame, pre-attached to each module, would allow us to make standardized, weathertight connections between modules. The top two floors of the building were to be duplexes, with outdoor terraces defined by empty frames, to express the idea of a plug-and-play system. Energy-efficient design considerations meant that we could not leave the thermally conductive corrugated container shell exposed to the weather, so we designed a properly insulated corrugated metal rain screen[3] for the

6.2
372 Lafayette Street, perspective rendering.

façade facing Great Jones Street. Compounding the irony of shipping container imagery, our corrugated metal façade was a visual proxy for the actual corrugated shell underneath.

After months of preparation, we went before the Commission in a public hearing to present our design. While I spoke, the Commissioners sat, with impassive expressions, and I had no idea whether things were going well or badly. When the time came for discussion, the Commissioners remarks were surprisingly enthusiastic, including: "very inventive and elegant"; "quite well thought through and very elegantly designed and proportioned"; "a very rich composition. I think it would be great"; and "it takes a really unusual fabric, material, and turns it into a very intelligent design while still letting us see what has been done".[4] The vote was unanimous in favor of approval.

6.3
372 Lafayette Street, rendered elevation of building top.

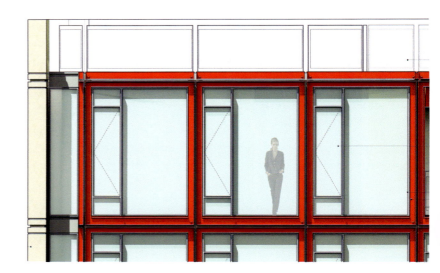

6.4
372 Lafayette Street, rendered elevation of building base.

China

In March of 2006, Scott, Reynolds, and I traveled to China to tour various factories that might manufacture GBM's modules or be component suppliers. At that stage, we had not settled on a strategy for manufacturing. We were considering a number of approaches, including: (1) engage a Chinese shipping container manufacturer to fit out containers at a facility in the Shanghai or Guangdong region; (2) engage a Chinese ship builder to procure containers and fit them out; or (3) lease a manufacturing space of our own and oversee the manufacturing process, with labor subcontracted to local Chinese construction firms.

We started out each morning on an itinerary of factory visits, returning at night to our base in Hong Kong, and then later in the trip, Shanghai. From Hong Kong, we made trips to nearby Shenzen and across the Pearl River on a ferry to Guangdong, a major industrial region with factories scattered throughout a forlorn landscape. My impression of China in 2006 was of industrial activity buzzing at every scale. China as the world's workshop is a well-worn cliché, but what came across to my eye at the ground level was the constant stream of people bicycling along the highway carrying all manner of goods. Sidewalk artisans at outdoor workbenches repaired those well-used bicycles, as well as household appliances and other sundry items. The entire country seemed to be engaged in some form of manufacturing. A 24/7 convoy of trucks on the highway and barges on the Pearl River were hauling goods, mostly to intermodal ports for export. It was all made possible by Malcolm McLean's transformation of global shipping through containerization.

We visited a shipping container factory in Jiangmen City in Guangdong province, a state-owned behemoth operated by China International Marine Containers Ltd. (CIMC). With 11 plants spread across China, CIMC is capable of manufacturing two million TEUs[5] each year, accounting for more than half of the world's supply of shipping containers.[6] CIMC's Guangdong plant pumps out the ubiquitous steel boxes at a rate of one every three minutes, mostly general-purpose containers that come in a range of ISO-conforming sizes. CIMC also makes a variety of special purpose containers: refrigerated containers for produce; extra-long containers for carrying wind turbine blades; and "flat racks" configured like a four-poster bed for carrying heavy equipment. They will make any type of container if handed a specification. At the time of our trip, there were about 35 types of specialty containers being manufactured, totaling 15,000 specialty units a year.

We entered CIMC's main shop, a vast hall the length of two football fields, and were greeted by an earsplitting din and the acrid smell of welding fumes. (The air outside wasn't much cleaner than inside—we barely caught a glimpse of the sun through the eye-stinging smog during our entire ten-day visit.) Overhead industrial skylights admitted weak shafts of daylight that barely penetrated the gloom.

From raw material to finished product, the manufacture of shipping containers at CIMC is a vertically integrated process done under one roof. We saw an army of workers operating heavy machinery for steel fabrication: hydraulic presses, shearing machines, roll-forming machines, gantries, and the like. Steel coil (steel plate in the form of massive rolls that can weigh up to 30 tons)[7] entered at one end and went down the line through a series of shearing, bending, machining, jigging, welding, and painting processes. CIMC even manufactures its own marine-grade plywood for container floors, starting with hardwood logs, which were rotary-peeled into veneer and glued up into panels. About the only items not made at the Guangdong plant were Keith Tantlinger's cast steel corner blocks. At the end of the assembly line, finished containers were certified as conforming to ISO standards, and out popped a shiny new container emblazoned with Maersk, Cosco, Hapag-Lloyd, and all the other logos familiar to anyone who gazes out of the window while driving past Exit 13 on the New Jersey Turnpike. Take the ramp, turn left for IKEA.

What we learned during our 10-day tour is that manufacturers in China will gladly make anything for you. They may have no experience with what you are asking them to make, and if you care about quality, or conformance to a specification, be prepared. Unless your representative is on the factory floor overseeing the work, quality will suffer. Do not expect drawings or specifications to be followed unless a figure in authority insists on following them. China is a hierarchical relationship society. Contracts matter less than contacts; lawyers matter less than lunch—which we took family style in company dining rooms, with a variety of small dishes turning on a lazy Susan.

Intellectual property protection in China is a well-known hazard. Our CIMC tour included a visit to a section of the plant where shipping containers were being fitted out for student housing. To our amazement, we were given an up-close look at the competition's product. It was unsettling to think that another company was already working with CIMC on a modular project.[8] We were disturbed by the casual way we were allowed access to another firm's presumably confidential IP. This experience confirmed doubts about whether CIMC, or any Chinese company for that matter, could be a reliable assembly partner. That may have been the most salient lesson of our trip.

Writing the Code

Modular architecture lacks theory.[9] Despite occasional technical improvements, we don't have a conceptual framework. The legacy manufacturers are not to blame for this—it is not their responsibility to do architects' thinking for us. We, architects, have for the most part been absent from the discussion of modular architecture as a distinct discipline. Architects who work with modular systems generally rely on manufacturers to tell them how to adapt their design for modular technology. This will not lead to transformative change. To use a historical comparison, when steel and concrete revolutionized building construction in the late 19th century, modern architecture emerged only through the work of architects who understood and embraced the broader implications of the new technology.[10] Modular architecture is at a similar threshold today.

During our two years of research at GBM, we strove not only to develop technical solutions but also to develop a theory of modular architecture geared to scalable manufacturing and commercial enterprise. Because we were simultaneously working on the Lafayette Street beta project, our exploration of theory was grounded in real-world problem-solving.

Our research began with basic stacking studies, to come up with a rules-based approach for defining the different types of modules located in specific positions within a modular stack. For example, a "simple stack" has the following 12 distinctly different module positions (not accounting for mirroring).

top corner	top middle	top end	top interior
middle corner	middle middle	middle end	middle interior
bottom corner	bottom middle	bottom end	bottom interior

For each of those positions in a simple stack, one can then define a series of surface variations in the six faces of a module. In the examples illustrated here, the four vertical faces are either fully open or fully opaque (more complex subdivisions would come later). Our studies were done "by hand" in 2006 using CAD. Today, this exercise would be done using parametric design software.

6.5
Example of face permutations: Simple Stack/ Middle-Corner.

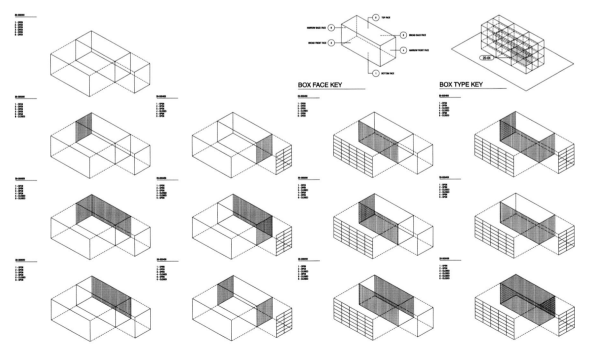

Add a cantilevered module at any location within the stack and you get another series of permutations.

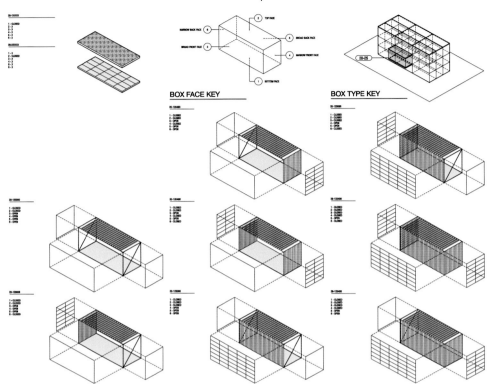

BOX FACE KEY

BOX TYPE KEY

Another series follows when you create a recess, or void, where a module would otherwise exist within the stack.

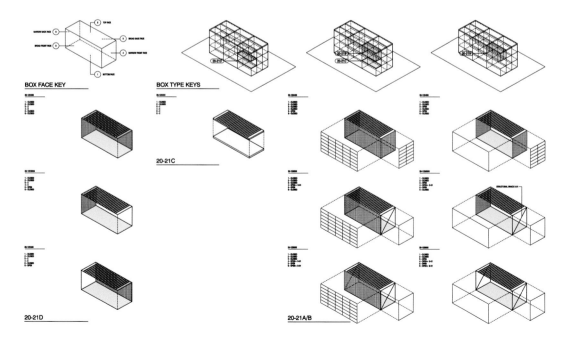

BOX FACE KEY

BOX TYPE KEYS

20-21C

20-21D

20-21A/B

Further permutations are possible with eccentric stacking, using an internal truss that directs loads to the corner posts.

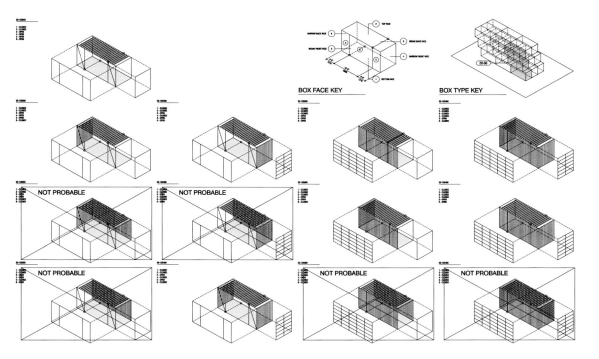

6.6 (opposite, top) Example of face permutations: Cantilevered Modules/Middle-Middle.

6.7 (opposite, bottom) Example of face permutations: Void Modules/Middle-Corner.

6.8 (above) Examples of face permutations: eccentric stacking.

With simple stacking, cantilevered modules, void modules, and eccentric stacking, one can create an endless series of compositions, all derived from a known number of module types and face permutations. In all cases, we adhered to structural principles, making sure that loads were directed to foundations either vertically through posts, or in special cases, eccentrically through diagonals. From there, we went on to develop standardized technical solutions. We also began working on the rules to govern façade composition and interior layouts. Within a rules-based system using a standard module, we saw a rich design vocabulary emerge.

Abandon Shipping Containers!

After our return from China, in the spring of 2006, we started preparing the technical drawings to manufacture and construct the beta project. We hung on to the notion that the millions of unused shipping containers piled up in our ports could be repurposed as construction modules. As we drilled deeper into the details, however, it became increasingly apparent that we were struggling to overcome some inherent technical and logistical limitations.

While recycling shipping containers seemed at first to be resource-smart and environmentally virtuous, a realistic look at the problem of repurposing used shipping containers showed how unfeasible that approach is for any but the smallest buildings. 372 Lafayette Street, a relatively small project, required only 60 modules. To build a modest 100,000-square-foot building would take about 300 modules. To get to a truly industrial scale, millions of square feet, would entail tens of thousands of repurposed containers a year.

Imagine driving your container handler into a holding yard at the Port of Newark where empty shipping containers are piled. You pick the first one from the stack, lower it down, and give it a visual once-over. It is too dented. You put it aside (if you can find the space) and go on to the second one. It is too corroded. You stack that one on top of the first discarded container, and examine the third one, which appears undamaged but needs to be measured to be sure it hasn't been knocked out of square. You make it through the first stack, pick three possible good ones, and then put the three discards back in place. The problem is clear: culling through stacks of used containers turns out to be unworkable from a quality control, logistics, and large-scale manufacturing standpoint.

We then decided to buy new shipping containers from CIMC (there aren't any shipping container manufacturers in the U.S.) and have them delivered to our facility in Newark. Most shipping container buildings that you might occasionally see or read about, in fact, are constructed with new containers. For a while, we thought we could justify freshly minted containers by using them to ship goods from China to the U.S., but you give up schedule control to the broker who arranges to fill your container with merchandise. There is no way to know if your container would leave port this month or next. We settled, at that point in our progress, on purchasing new containers, shipped empty to our Newark facility.

Upon arrival at our assembly plant, we would then have to remove the doors, to be sold for scrap. Next, we would have to saw or torch off the parts of the corrugated container sides that interfere with the layout and sell those for scrap too. By now, more than half of the steel shell would have been removed, representing significant waste material. We would need to reinforce the thin edge beams ("rails" in container-lingo), which had been weakened by removing the corrugated shell, by welding on an additional steel bar.

There was still one more problem. The floor of a typical shipping container is made of plywood. The New York City Building Code for our six-story building called for fireproof construction, and in that type of construction, the load-bearing floor must be a non-combustible material. Plywood does not meet the code. We scoured the internet for a non-combustible panel material with sufficient strength that could be used instead of plywood. We couldn't find anything with both the required structural properties that could also stand up to the soaking that it could get during a sea voyage. We looked at treating the plywood with fire retardant, but that was still not code compliant. We explored removing the plywood and replacing it with concrete once the container had arrived in Newark. During a trip to Container City in London, we examined the screws that fasten the plywood to steel framing and discovered that they are difficult, almost impossible, to remove. There was yet another problem. To make the plywood floor waterproof, the underside of a standard shipping container is coated with a thick, sticky bituminous coating. In addition to making the wood floor more flammable, it's not good for indoor air quality. Shipping container plywood is also typically treated with pesticide, another possible contaminant.

We explored pouring a reinforced concrete slab over the plywood deck to make a new, non-combustible structural floor, but that would eat up several inches of valuable ceiling height. We thought, why not turn the container upside down, and pour concrete into the underside using the plywood floor as formwork? That would encapsulate the bituminous coating and we wouldn't lose ceiling height. We pursued this idea for a while, and even filed a patent. But expensive machinery would be needed to flip the containers over, and they would have to stay upside down for several days while the concrete cured.

We saw nothing but dead ends in every direction. The shipping container would have to go. It was a liberating moment.

6.9
The shipping container is encumbered by doors, unneeded corrugated sides, and plywood floors. All unnecessary features of the shipping container have been eliminated.

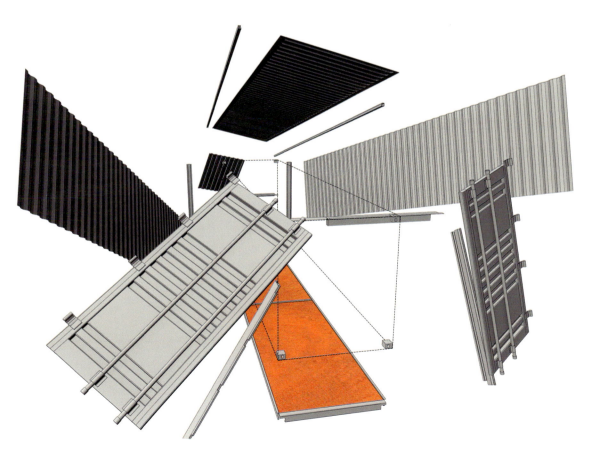

The Volumetric Unit of Construction

Shipping containers are designed for shipping, not for building—an apparently self-evident fact that was obscured by our well-intentioned efforts to salvage existing containers. Once we freed ourselves from the limitations of containers, the development of a new type of module seemed almost easy compared to the technical challenges of our beta project. Our new module, the Volumetric Unit of Construction, or VUC, would retain the one essential property of a shipping container that mattered—its ability to be transported intermodally. To do that, we would keep the eight standard corner blocks (or nodes) that allow automated handling, and we would use standard ISO container dimensions. Everything else would be up to us.

PRINCIPLE #6 **USE INTERMODAL STANDARDS, BUT DON'T USE SHIPPING CONTAINERS**

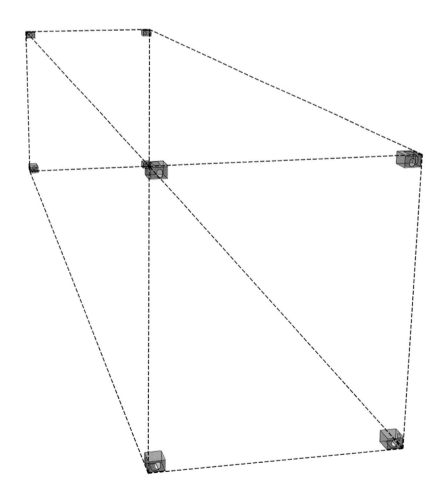

6.10
The Volumetric Unit of Construction (VUC) begins as a stripped-down wire frame with eight ISO standard cast steel corner nodes.

One of our goals was a lightweight structure that would pay off indirectly by reducing the cost of foundations. Light weight would also reduce transportation greenhouse gas impact, which we will explore in depth in the next chapter. An all-steel structure, with a steel plate floor, was the answer. It would eliminate concrete curing time, a production choke point. We wanted our modules to move through the assembly process with the efficiency and economy of an automotive plant.

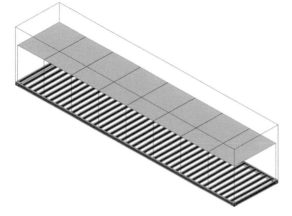

6.11
The all-steel VUC floor assembly.

The VUC's lightweight steel structure presented acoustical and vibration challenges, which in conventional concrete structures are much easier to manage. There are three factors that contribute to our sense of the construction quality of a floor. First, if the floor is designed to be stiff enough (i.e. low "deflection"), it will feel sturdy underfoot. Second, it is important that the floor be designed to not resonate like a tuning fork with vibrations induced by footsteps. Structural engineers talk about floor vibration terms of "micro-inches per second" (mips) and generally want to tune the structure to keep that number low. This is where mass helps and is why concrete floors are easier to design. Damping is the third factor. For example, by adding a layer of cork or rubber underneath a wood or tile

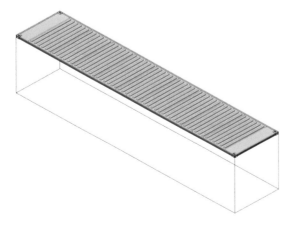

6.12
The press-formed VUC roof assembly.

floor, damping can reduce the vibration energy transmitted by footsteps. Through a combination of stiffness, tuning, and damping, our floor assembly produced results that well exceeded code-required acoustical requirements and met the standards of high-quality condominium construction.

We used press-formed sheet steel, a standard shipping container material, to give the roof enough stiffness to support the weight of workers standing on top during construction. The press-formed roof is fully welded, watertight, and allows rainwater to drain off.

Corrugated sides are still useful, but instead of sawing away corrugated steel, we add it only where needed.

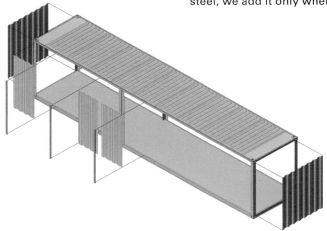

6.13
VUC corrugated side panels.

With standard dimensions, a ready supply of floors, roofs, corner posts, and corrugated panels can be stored flatpack for rapid, on-demand assembly of VUCs.

6.14
Flat-packed VUC floor and roof components can be shipped intermodally.

Temporary Protection

Because much of the VUC frame is open-sided, interior materials and finishes must be protected from the elements during transportation. Modular, reusable protection panels are installed prior to shipping, and after removal at the job site, those panels are sent back to the factory for reuse. The protection panels add stiffness for transportation and are air- and watertight.

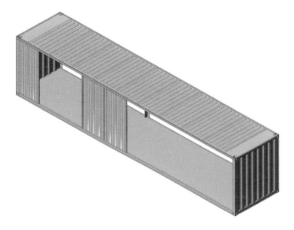

6.15
Unprotected VUC openings.

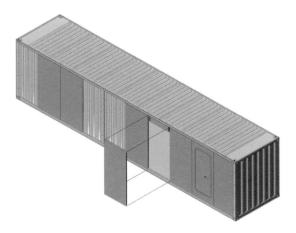

6.16
Temporary protection panels.

Beam Stitching

One of the frequently cited drawbacks of modular architecture is the doubling up of structure that occurs when you stack modules, each with its own independent frame. This wastes resources and adds floor thickness, with associated penalties. Transportation height limitations mean that every extra inch of redundant structure must be subtracted from interior ceiling height. In high-rise construction, there is also a penalty paid when extra structural depth causes a building to lose stories to meet zoning height limits. As we worked on our structural system, we sought to make the floor as slim as possible by taking full advantage of both the floor and the roof of adjoining stacked VUCs. Because the stiffness of a beam is proportional to the square of its depth, by combining floor and roof members to nearly double the effective beam depth, we gained almost four times the stiffness with no sacrifice in ceiling height.

The technical challenge was how to marry the floor and roof structures. Insights that we gleaned from our trip to China led to our next breakthrough. At CIMC's factory, we saw that the edge supports of shipping containers (the rails) are made by bending, or "cold-forming", a piece of steel plate into a 40-foot-long structural profile. Unlike "hot-rolled" structural steel used in buildings (e.g. I-beams), which are only available as standard catalog profiles, cold-forming gave us the freedom to shape a rail exactly the way we wanted it. We used that freedom to devise profiles that would facilitate bolting the top rail of a VUC to the bottom rail of a VUC stacked above, thereby creating a composite beam. The total structural depth of a VUC, just shy of 11 inches, is able to span up to 24 feet. "Beam stitching" is the name we gave to our method of interconnecting the floor and roof rails.

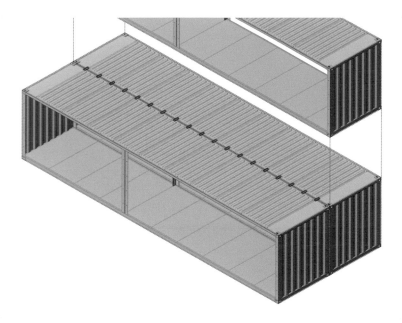

6.17
VUC beam stitching spacer blocks.

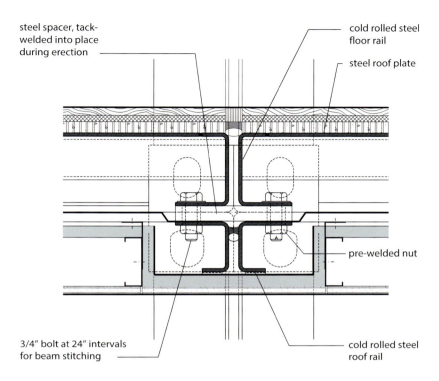

steel spacer, tack-
welded into place
during erection

cold rolled steel
floor rail

steel roof plate

pre-welded nut

3/4" bolt at 24" intervals
for beam stitching

cold rolled steel
roof rail

6.18
Beam stitching detail.

Beam stitching also helps interconnected VUCs resist wind loads by unifying an entire floor of VUCs into what structural engineers call a "diaphragm". A diaphragm is a stiff plate that efficiently distributes wind loads to vertical trusses or shear walls that keep the building from falling over. The taller a building gets, the more important diaphragms become.

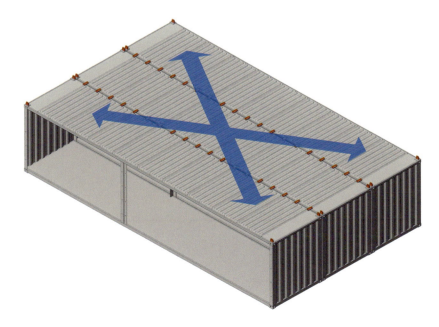

6.19
Beam stitching engages
adjacent VUCs to create a
diaphragm.

Post-tensioning

When we were designing 372 Lafayette Street, we encountered difficulty with the bolts that join modules from one floor to the next at the corners. These corner connections are another part of the "lateral-load" system that prevents a structure from toppling. The cast steel node was a logical place to locate bolts, but the hollow node only had room for one bolt. Sesil wanted two bolts in each corner for redundancy in case one was improperly tightened during field erection. We neatly sidestepped that problem by turning to a solution called "post-tensioning" instead of bolting. In post-tensioning VUCs, a half-inch diameter steel cable is threaded through each corner from the top to the bottom of the modular stack. Each cable is then stretched tight with a hydraulic jack and locked off at 20,000 pounds of force.[11] In combination with the rigid corrugated shell, the post-tensioned cables provide the necessary resistance to wind and seismic loads.

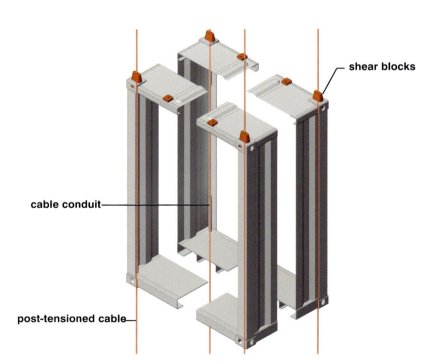

shear blocks

cable conduit

post-tensioned cable

6.20
Post-tensioned lateral load
system components.

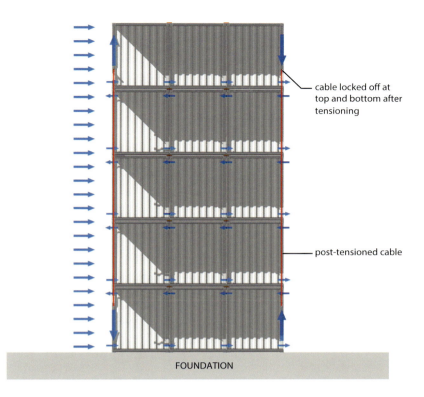

cable locked off at
top and bottom after
tensioning

post-tensioned cable

FOUNDATION

6.21
Post-tensioned lateral load
system: free-body diagram.

High-Rise

Post-tensioning is an efficient wind bracing system for mid-rise buildings up to six stories but is not suitable for taller buildings. We had an opportunity in 2009 to explore a high-rise solution when an east-coast urban university asked my firm[12] to study the feasibility of the VUC system for a 17-story student housing project. Working with Sesil and his team, we came up with an approach in which each VUC contains the individual diagonal members of a multi-story wind truss. When VUCs are then stacked and connected, the diagonals combine to create a complete wind-resisting system.[13] The integrated VUC trusses, as shown in the illustrations, are located "off-node" in the demising walls between dormitory units.

• • •

The VUC wastes no steel. There are no cargo doors to be discarded, no corrugated sides to be sawn off. The VUC starts with standard floors, roofs, and posts, and corrugated steel sides are only added where needed to suit a specific building design. The VUC is an open frame, not a closed box. When aggregated together as a building, the posts form a grid, not unlike the structural grid of a steel or concrete building. We are so accustomed to gridded structures, in fact, that we often forget that until the advent of modern architecture in the early 20th century, rooms were defined by load-bearing walls. With the advent of steel and concrete frames, rooms could be divided by freely located non-load-bearing partitions.

Beam stitching enables the VUC to span up to 24 feet without loss of ceiling height, and it makes flexible room layouts possible. There is

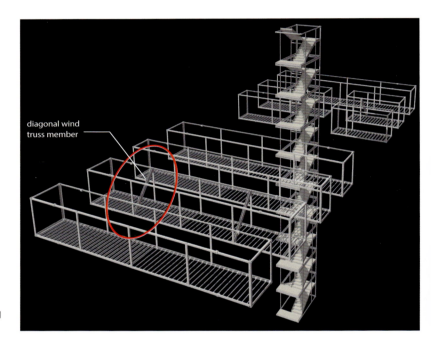

diagonal wind
truss member

6.22
VUC frames with integrated diagonal members of a wind truss.

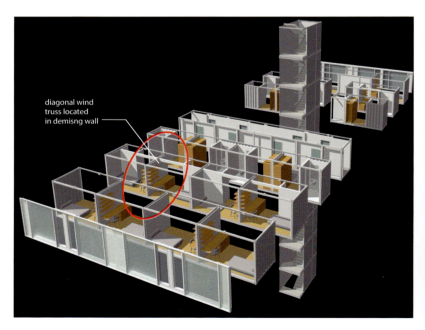

diagonal wind
truss located
in demisng wall

6.23
Diagonal members are located within demising partitions.

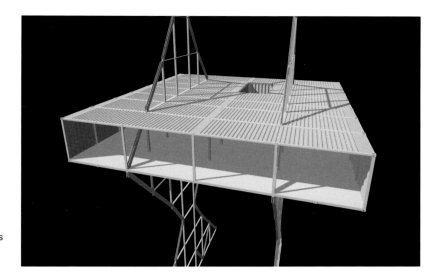

6.24
When VUCs stack, diagonals combine to create a wind truss.

no need to lay out one room in each module. As will be shown in the illustrations that follow, rooms can, and mostly will, straddle modules, allowing for substantial variation in layouts. The VUC is thus "spatially indeterminate", in contrast to other modular systems in which room dimensions are defined by the box, i.e. "spatially determinate". Much like Le Corbusier's concept of the free plan where space-enclosing partitions are independent of structural columns, spatially indeterminate planning is unrestricted by the dimensions of the VUC.

PRINCIPLE #7   SPATIALLY INDETERMINATE MODULAR PLANNING

Spatially indeterminate planning led to another breakthrough. It lets us organize VUCs parallel to the long axis of a building rather than perpendicular as in conventional modular construction. The primary façade of an intermodal modular building does not need to appear cellular as modular buildings so often do. This fundamentally changes the design expression of modular facades, which will be evident in our next study.

Philadelphia Mixed-Use Project

In 2014, a developer asked my firm[14] to do a feasibility study for a large mixed-use development on an irregularly shaped site in northern Philadelphia. Like the Lafayette Street project, but on a bigger scale, the non-orthogonal site challenged us to use orthogonal VUCs in an inventive way. The developer's master plan called for townhouses, mid-rise blocks, and high-rise housing over a ground floor retail podium.

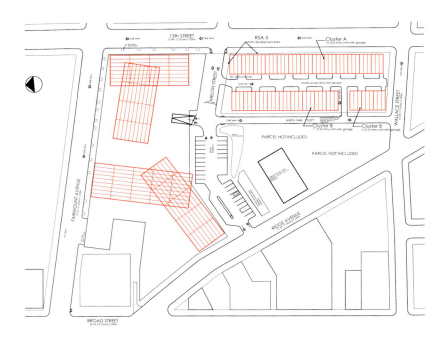

6.25
Philadelphia Mixed-Use
Project, site plan with VUC
grids.

As at Lafayette Street, we wanted to respect the urban street wall context. By superimposing stacks of standard 8×40-foot VUCs at varied angles determined by the street geometry, we were able to achieve that goal without introducing odd-shaped modules.

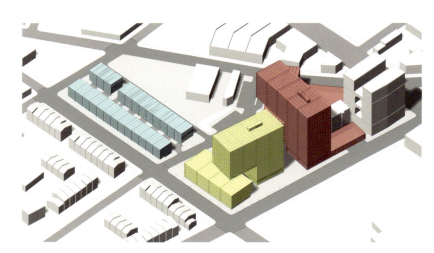

6.26
Philadelphia Mixed-Use
Project, axonometric
diagram.

By lifting one stack above another, we preserved the orthogonal integrity of each. We resolved the load paths between stacks with an interstitial transfer truss. A curvilinear stair maintained the continuity of the fire stair through that interstitial zone. These two elements were among very few concessions we made to non-modular construction. The apartment floors themselves comprised 1,640 standard 8×40-foot VUCs.

The Intermodal Modular System

6.27
Philadelphia Mixed-Use
Project, transfer truss
concept.

6.28
Philadelphia Mixed-Use
Project. Aerial view showing
varied building typologies
ranging from row housing
to towers. Modular towers
are constructed over a
conventional ground floor
podium with retail and
building lobbies; within
the interstitial spaces at
the transfer trusses and
curvilinear stair isa green
roof. The curvilinear stair
is sheathed in translucent
glass.

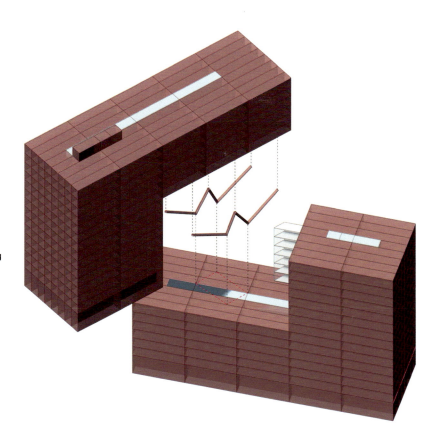

1 Bedroom Apartment

Studio Apart

ONE-BEDROOM / ALCOVE STUDIO UNITS

6.29 (above)
One-bedroom/Alcove
Studio, isometric.

6.30 (opposite, top)
One-bedroom/Alcove
Studio, exploded isometric.

6.31 (opposite, bottom)
One-bedroom/Alcove
Studio, plan.

ONE-BEDROOM / STUDIO UNITS AT CORE

6.32 (above)
One-bedroom/Studio at
core, isometric.

6.33 (opposite, top)
One-bedroom/Studio at
core, exploded isometric.

6.34 (opposite, bottom)
One-bedroom/Studio at
core, plan.

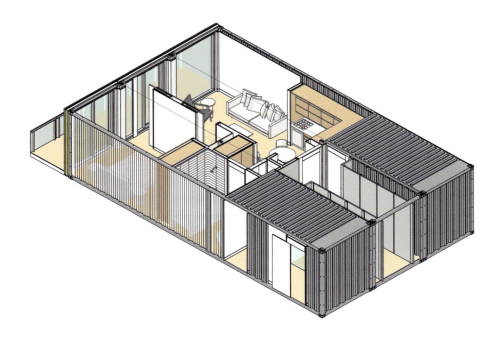

ONE-BEDROOM END UNIT

6.35 (above)
One-bedroom end unit,
isometric.

6.36 (opposite, top)
One-bedroom end unit,
exploded isometric.

6.37 (opposite, bottom)
One-bedroom end unit, plan.

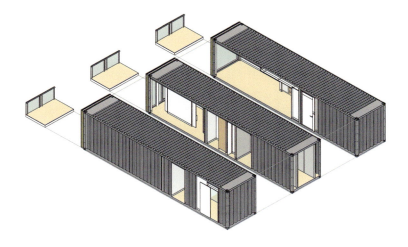

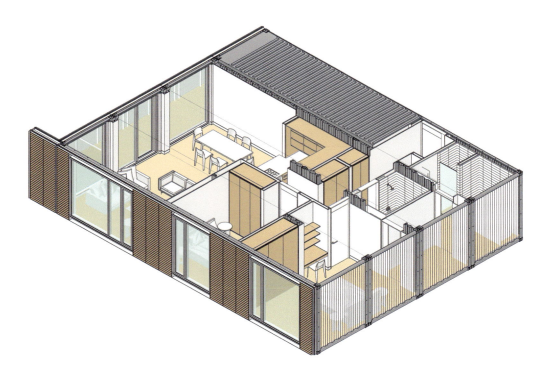

TWO-BEDROOM UNIT

6.38 (above)
Two-bedroom end unit,
isometric.

6.39 (opposite, top)
Two-bedroom end unit,
exploded isometric.

6.40 (opposite, bottom)
Two-bedroom end unit,
plan.

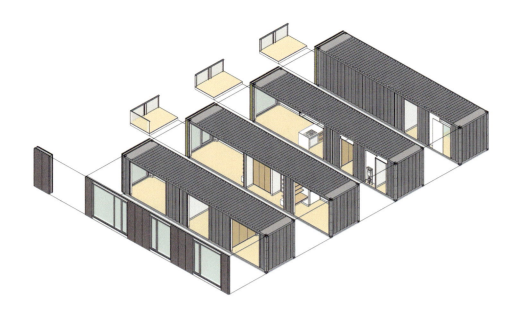

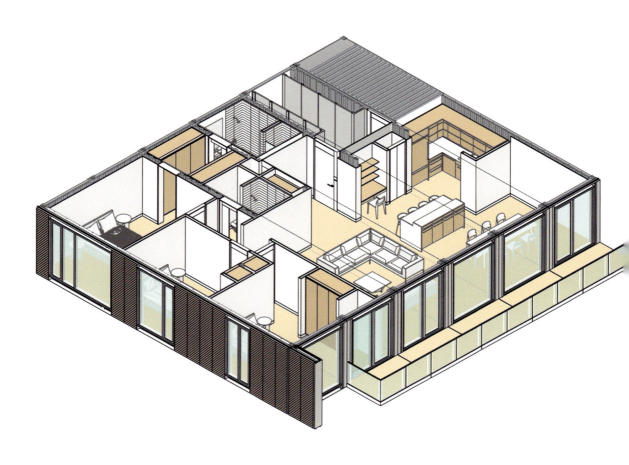

THREE-BEDROOM UNIT

6.41 (above)
Three-bedroom end unit,
isometric.

6.42 (opposite, top)
Three-bedroom end unit,
exploded isometric.

6.43 (opposite, bottom)
Three-bedroom end unit,
plan.

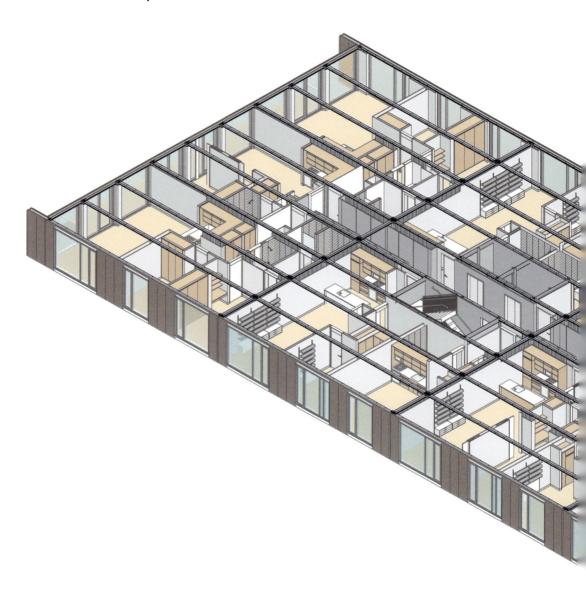

6.44
Typical high-rise floor,
composite isometric.

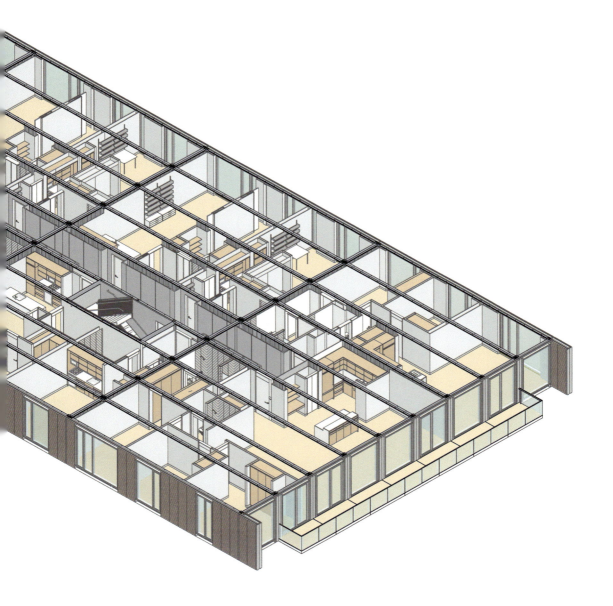

As illustrated, the project included a mix of unit types from studios to three-bedroom apartments. Like the automotive industry, the same underlying chassis supports a wide range of models from affordable to luxury. Aside from apartment size, the difference in price points is mainly a matter of features and options. This has benefits for "inclusionary housing", where developers are offered incentives such as added floor area for including a percentage of affordable units in a project. In practice, inclusionary housing often results in a separate, stripped-down building for affordable units on the same or nearby site as the luxury building, meeting the letter of inclusionary requirements, while expressing an architecture of exclusion. By virtue of economics and versatility, the VUC can foster true inclusionary housing where affordable and luxury units are mixed within the same building.

Facades

Energy efficiency—the overall resistance to thermal transfer—is a critical factor in façade design. Since 2012, energy codes in the U.S.[15] have required what is referred to as "continuous insulation" for colder climate zones, in which a layer of insulation must wrap the thermally conductive elements of a building to create an uninterrupted thermal envelope. "Thermal bridging", the term for heat transfer through non-insulated structural members, must be carefully avoided. Care must even be taken in detailing the various girts, clips, and brackets that attach the facade to the structure, as these intermittent penetrations through the insulation layer can be significant thermal bridges.

Recognizing the severe shortcomings of corrugated steel shipping containers from an energy standpoint, we made rain screen facades with continuous insulation a basic feature of the VUC. Rain screens (briefly mentioned earlier in connection with 372 Lafayette Street) consist of open-jointed cladding mounted in front of a well-drained and ventilated cavity. Continuous insulation is put in the cavity, where it wraps the building shell like a blanket, and behind the insulation is a waterproof

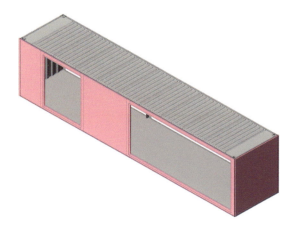

6.45
Continuous insulation.

and airtight barrier. In summer, the inch or so of air space between the cladding and the insulation allows the façade to breathe like a light cotton shirt, ventilating hot air through the open joints. In winter, the thermal wrapper keeps the steel structure warm.

Open-jointed, breathable walls have technical and aesthetic advantages. Open joints avoid the maintenance problems associated with, for example,

6.46
Philadelphia Mixed-Use Project, rain screen material studies. From top: terra cotta, fiber-cement, varied sine-wave anodized aluminum, pre-weathered zinc.

brick walls—no need to repoint mortar or replace failed sealant joints. Modern high-rise buildings are designed to sway in strong winds, and thin, lightweight cladding materials with open joints easily accommodate that movement. Finally, technical advantages aside, rain screen facades introduce a new design freedom. Just about any material can be used—metal, terra cotta, stone, cement board, composites, ceramics, wood, and so on.

We associate the modern curtain wall with sleek buildings sheathed entirely in glass, but for the sake of energy efficiency, we must wean ourselves away from corner-to-corner, floor-to-ceiling glass facades and embrace a mix of glass with opaque, insulated surfaces. Rain screens can be integrated with glass into prefabricated "unitized" curtain wall panels, mounted outside the building frame.

Prefabricated unitized facades are among the most technically sophisticated building systems, with intricately designed gaskets and chambers around the edges of each facade unit that keep the weather out, even under hurricane conditions. Methods have evolved that allow workers to install curtain wall façades while standing safely within the building, and on high-rise buildings this translates into time and cost savings. As each unit is installed, its gaskets interlock with the gaskets of adjacent units to create a weathertight seal. There is no need to drop an expensive scaffolding to laboriously apply seals from the outside of the building.

In conventional construction, facades are installed while the building is still an unfinished frame, but modular construction presents a new set of challenges. Installing facades from the finished interior is not feasible—there is too little space to work and too much potential for damage. Installing facades from the outside after modules have been erected is of course possible, but expensive. If high-rise intermodal modular is to fulfill its promise, facades must arrive at the job site pre-attached to VUCs, ready to crane into place. After craning, unitized façade panels should engage and self-seal in the same way as in a conventional unitized facade.

The main issue that must be addressed in pre-installed unitized modular facades is the tendency for relatively fragile gaskets to be damaged as modules are craned into position.[16] To work properly, gaskets must be protected from contact during craning but must press against adjoining units to make a tight seal. These would appear to be irreconcilable goals.

I had the opportunity in 2019 to work on this problem in a grant-funded course and research project, The Prefabricator's Workshop,[17] that I co-taught at Pratt Institute in Brooklyn. In our approach, the unitized façade is delivered to the jobsite mounted on the module but raised a few inches above its final position to guard the horizontal joint from damage during craning. After the module is craned into position, the façade unit is lowered into position by turning adjustment screws until it has engaged its counterpart in the module below.

At vertical joints, a 1-inch space is maintained and temporarily protected during craning to guard the vertical edges from damage. After craning, opposing gaskets are brought into contact by means of a spring mechanism. As in all contemporary façade design, there are redundant seals to ensure water and air tightness.

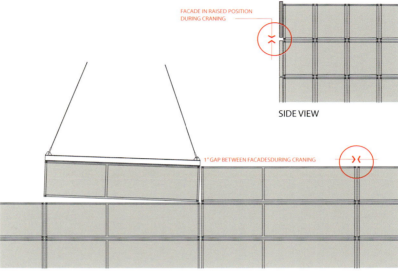

FACADE IN RAISED POSITION DURING CRANING

SIDE VIEW

1" GAP BETWEEN FACADES DURING CRANING

FRONT VIEW

6.47
Facade Craning Tolerance
Above: raising the façade during craning prevents damage to horizontal joints. Below: maintaining a gap during craning prevents damage to vertical joints.

In conventional construction, the widely varying tolerances between a steel or concrete structural frame and a curtain wall necessitate as much as 2 inches of adjustability in any direction. VUCs can be manufactured and erected to the same tolerance as a curtain wall, and facade mounting brackets need only be designed for micro-adjustments, measured in eighths of an inch.

Façade Accessories

Balconies, loggias, sun-shading systems, monitors, canopies and awnings, penthouses, trellises, and other such additive components make buildings environmentally responsive and enrich what might otherwise be non-descript boxes. Accessories can regulate daylight, block solar heat, and provide access to the outdoors. Accessories articulate and inflect the expression of architectural form. Accessories are often a stylistic signature, and variations in the design of accessories are virtually limitless.

Think of the VUC, with its standard dimensions and connections, as an operating system analogous to an iPhone. Think of accessories as apps. With apps, the intermodal modular system can be as performative, expressive, and varied as talent and creativity will allow.

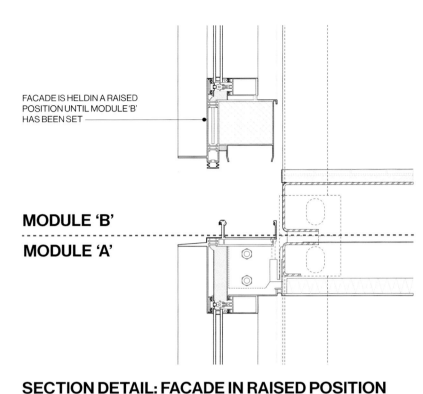

FACADE IS HELD IN A RAISED
POSITION UNTIL MODULE 'B'
HAS BEEN SET

MODULE 'B'
- - - - - - - - - - - - - - -
MODULE 'A'

SECTION DETAIL: FACADE IN RAISED POSITION

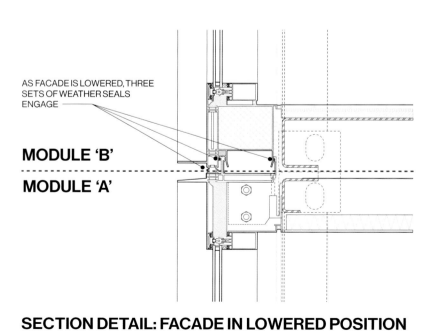

AS FACADE IS LOWERED, THREE
SETS OF WEATHER SEALS
ENGAGE

MODULE 'B'
- - - - - - - - - - - - - - -
MODULE 'A'

6.48
Above: detail of stack joint in
raised position. Below: after
the VUC is set, the façade
is lowered in a controlled
movement.

SECTION DETAIL: FACADE IN LOWERED POSITION

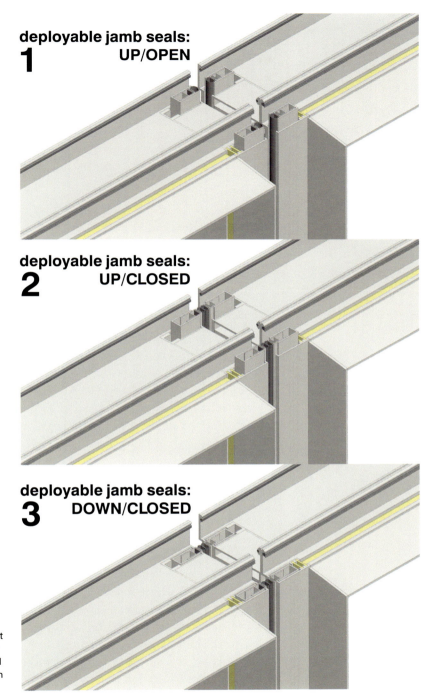

deployable jamb seals:
1 **UP/OPEN**

deployable jamb seals:
2 **UP/CLOSED**

deployable jamb seals:
3 **DOWN/CLOSED**

6.49
Above: detail of vertical joint in open position with 1-inch gap. Below: detail of vertical joint after gaskets have been actuated.

6.50
Examples of VUC façade
accessories.

Fire Protection

When temperatures in a fire reach 575 degrees Fahrenheit, steel starts to lose strength, and increasingly loses strength as temperature rises. At 1,500 degrees, 90 percent of the strength is gone, and steel beams will sag like taffy. At that point, a steel structure will fail with tragic consequences. As a fundamental matter of public safety, steel frame construction and fire protection go together like hand and glove.

Despite common use of the term "fireproofing", there is no such thing as truly fireproof construction, only fire-resistive construction. Eventually, the structure will weaken if a fire burns long and hot enough to raise the temperature of steel above 575 degrees. The question is how long the steel columns, girders, and beams can be kept below that temperature, and the fire be compartmentalized, so that the structure will not fail before occupants can get safely out of the building. Fire-resistance ratings of structural members range from one to four hours as determined by the building height, floor area, use, as well as the structural importance of the member or assembly being protected.

There are two broadly categorized types of fire protection systems: membrane fire protection systems and direct-applied fire protection. Membrane systems comprise a fire-resistant wrapper, often gypsum board, that encloses hollow construction such as joist-supported floors, or stud walls. Direct-applied fire protection comprises a fire-resistant material, typically cement leavened with minerals such as perlite and vermiculite, that is sprayed on or troweled directly to steel. Depending on how long the steel must be protected from fire, conventional sprayed fireproofing can be up to 2 inches thick. It's messy work that leaves adjacent areas spattered with popcorn-textured gobs.

Direct-applied fire protection must be done before finishes are installed. In a modular factory, spraying a cementitious material requires the work area to be separated or sealed off so that overspray doesn't foul up nearby work or equipment. Drying time slows the assembly process. Portions of the steel frame must still be left bare for bolting modules together in the field. It all translates into time and money.

With the help of Bill Webb, a fire safety engineer who I knew from my Polshek days, we tackled the fire protection problem. We started from basic concepts and came up with a hybrid membrane and direct-applied solution. We then selected three types of fire-resistive materials, each best suited for the part of the VUC that it would protect.

Building codes rest on a chain of certifications from recognized authorities, and each system of fire-resistive construction, comprising both the structural member and its method of fire protection, requires testing and the imprimatur of a recognized laboratory. The VUC was a new type of structure. Without testing, code officials would not be able to approve our fire protection design. Further, while the fire-protective materials that we selected were each laboratory-certified, the use of those materials as a combined system could not be approved without testing them in combination.

We began working on a testing program. In the spring of 2007, Webb and I went to Northbrook, Illinois to visit Underwriters Laboratories, the same UL that stands behind toasters and coffee makers. We were taken on a tour of UL's vast testing facility, as big as several airplane hangars, where all manner of testing is done on everything from appliances to building components. Fire tests on floors, walls, beams, and columns are conducted in chambers heated by giant gas-fueled burners, where full-size mock-ups are torched from one side and instruments record the time and temperature rise on the other side.

After the tour, we retreated to a conference room where Webb and I presented our VUC fire protection system to a group of engineers. Shouldering the responsibility of certifying safety under the UL label confers a certain gravity, and our audience was deadly serious about

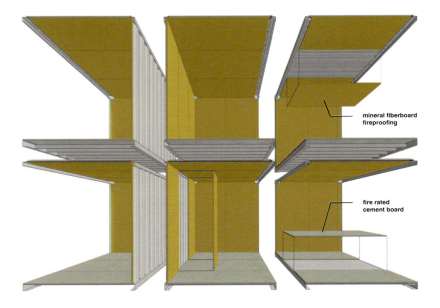

mineral fiberboard
fireproofing

fire rated
cement board

6.51
Panelized membrane fireproofing at interiors of VUCs.

6.52
Intumescent fireproofing,
a thin coating, is used at
the perimeter of VUCs to
facilitate the attachment of
facades.

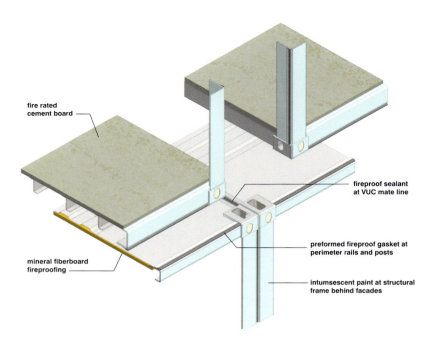

fire rated
cement board

fireproof sealant
at VUC mate line

preformed fireproof gasket at
perimeter rails and posts

mineral fiberboard
fireproofing

intumsescent paint at structural
frame behind facades

their business. At the same time, the group was thoroughly engaged and helpful. While they could not offer a prediction as to whether our approach would test successfully, there were no apparent fatal flaws in our thinking. Our takeaway was that the approach we had developed was feasible. The next step would be to build mock-ups, and have UL conduct a series of tests on VUC floor, wall, column, and beam assemblies.[18]

Integrated Partitions and Cabling

One of the anachronisms of contemporary construction is the way electrical wiring is installed. Other industries use cable harnesses, bundles of electrical wiring that are planned in advance and prefabricated by a specialty manufacturer. In building construction, circuits are laboriously wired one at a time by threading cables through holes in studs, after which gypsum board is applied. To integrate cable harnesses with intermodal modular architecture requires us to think about partitions and electrical wiring as an integrated system.

We designed stressed-skin honeycomb-core panels to eliminate the need for studs every 16 inches. Panels can be prefabricated to standard widths in 4-inch increments up to 48 inches. The panel facing material can be ordinary gypsum board, with joints taped and spackled, or any material that can be glued to a core—wood veneer, ceramics, fabric, composites, thin stone, porcelain-enameled metal, and so on.

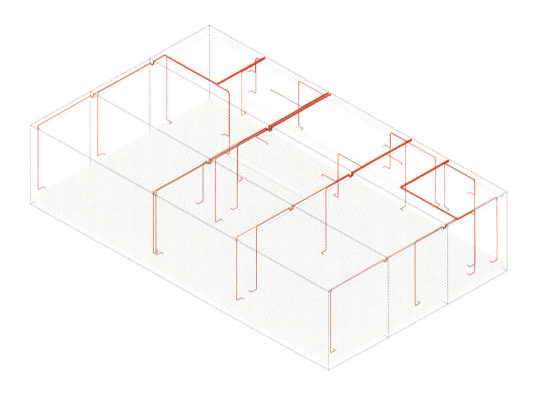

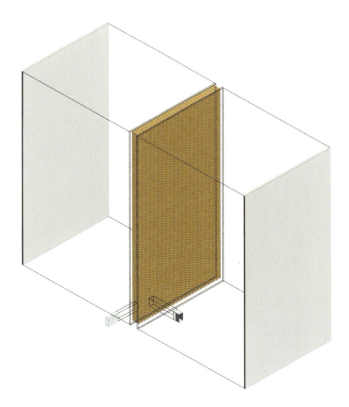

6.53
Apartments are
circuited by cable
harnesses that
run in overhead
raceways. Quick-
connect devices allow
circuits to be rapidly
completed between
VUCs in the field.

6.54
Honeycomb-core
partition panels.

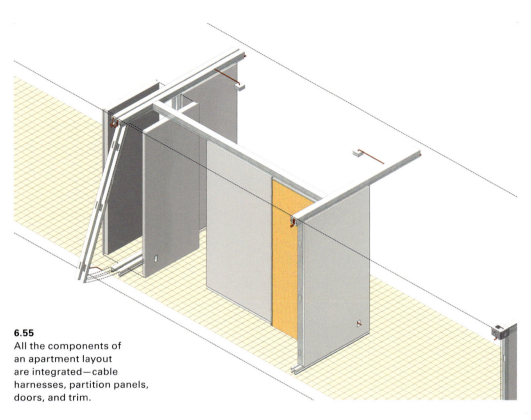

6.55
All the components of
an apartment layout
are integrated—cable
harnesses, partition panels,
doors, and trim.

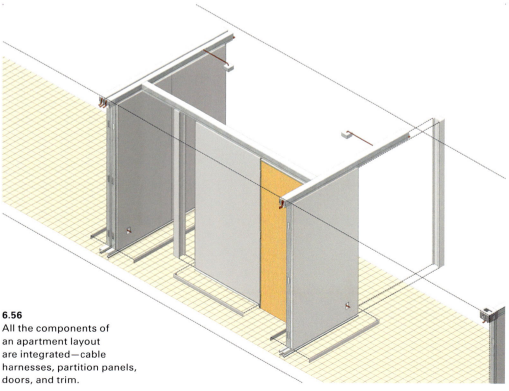

6.56
All the components of
an apartment layout
are integrated—cable
harnesses, partition panels,
doors, and trim.

In the integrated approach that we developed, partition panels are attached to a snap-fit framing system that includes an overhead wireway, a baseboard receptor, and light-gauge posts to support the edges of partitions, spaced up to four feet apart. Standard size partition panels can be pre-ordered and stocked as supply chain components without having to know the dimensions of an apartment layout in advance. Panels can be affixed to the framing system with "industrial trade range" Velcro,[19] eliminating screws that must then be spackled.

Typologies and Cores

Like a living organism, buildings require life support systems, or "services". Water, waste, ventilation, power, natural gas, air-conditioning refrigerant, as well as the movement of people up and down stairs, elevators, and along corridors, all need to be organized in such a way that no system interferes with the functioning of any other system. Building services are expensive, with mechanical, electrical, plumbing, and sprinkler systems accounting for up to a third of a building's cost. Because of the need to organize systems economically, most housing tends toward typical forms, or "typologies". Common typologies are row housing, perimeter blocks, high-rise slabs, and towers. By creating a hybrid of two or more typologies, large projects occasionally achieve both the density of high-rise housing and the human scale of row housing.

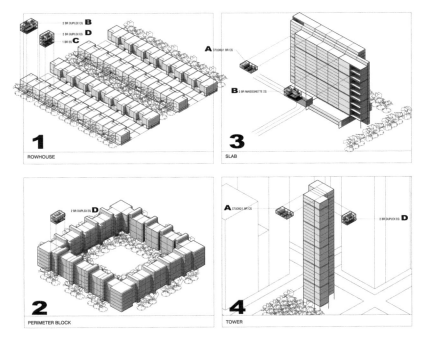

6.57
Housing typologies with VUCs: row housing, perimeter block, slab, and tower.

The Intermodal Modular System

6.58
Housing typology cores with VUCs.

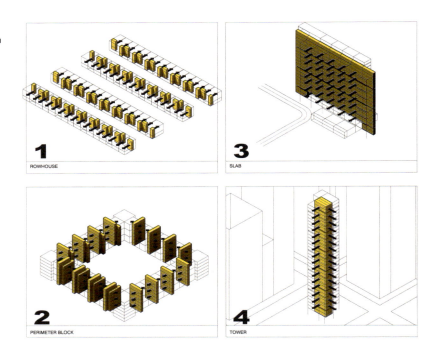

Intermodal modular architecture requires typological solutions for building cores as well as for apartments. We developed specialized core VUCs to incorporate service risers and vertical transportation, as well as strategies to connect those risers to VUCs that comprise apartments.

We take it for granted in high-rise buildings that there will be elevators to take us up and down, and fire stairs to get us out of the building in an emergency. In conventional modular construction, stair and elevator cores are often site built, as they would be in a fully site-constructed building. Why not incorporate stairs and elevators into VUCs? We found ways to adapt VUCs for cores, including a hinged stair to facilitate transportation, and with this last piece of the puzzle in place we had a complete system that would allow us to stack a building from the ground up comprised entirely of VUCs.

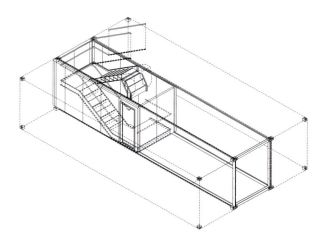

6.59
Stair cores.

6.60
Elevator cores.

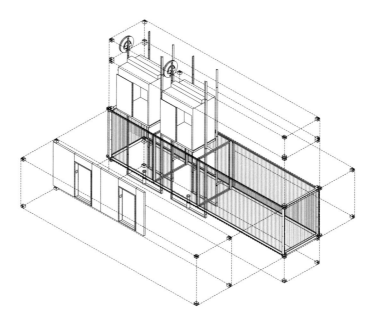

Building Services

Quoting Louis Kahn:

> I do not like ducts, I do not like pipes. I hate them really thoroughly, but because I hate them so thoroughly, I feel that they have to be given their place. If I just hated them and took no care, I think that they would invade the building and completely destroy it.[20]

Pipes and ducts are the veins, arteries, lungs, and bowels of a building, too often considered beneath the dignity of architecture.

Modular architecture will either succeed or fail on the matter of pipes and ducts. The technical problem is how to gain access to and make connections between pipes and ducts from module to module. It is not really that hard once you break the problem down into its constituent parts. Each and every pipe, duct, and conduit, no matter how small, must be assigned its place in advance of manufacturing.

The Building Information Model, or BIM, is a digital design tool that originated in the automotive and aerospace industries and has supplanted ordinary CAD drafting for the preparation of architectural drawings. The BIM embeds intelligence—specifications, performance data, and other attributes—in a three-dimensional computer model. The BIM is a collaborative platform shared by the various design and engineering disciplines. Engineers can now design building services in a virtual three-dimensional environment to ensure that pipes and ducts are coordinated with the surrounding architecture.

The VUC, by virtue of precise manufacturing, facilitates the interconnection of prefabricated building services. With factory fabrication controlled by jigs, a VUC can be within a one-eighth-inch tolerance, many times more precise than field-constructed steel or concrete frames. Pre-manufactured "cassettes" containing a bundle of risers can be reliably positioned so that when VUCs are stacked, each pipe and duct will be aligned with the pipes and ducts above and below. Cassettes can be prefabricated to fit in chase walls, or, say, above kitchen ceilings in apartments. Cassettes containing multiple trades—plumbing, HVAC, sprinklers, and even lighting—can be sourced from specialty manufacturers as supply chain components, scheduled to arrive at the assembly plant ready for rapid installation. At the building site, quick-connect devices are used to join piping and ductwork across mate-lines.

6.61
Student housing, BIM model of mechanical, plumbing, and fire sprinkler systems.

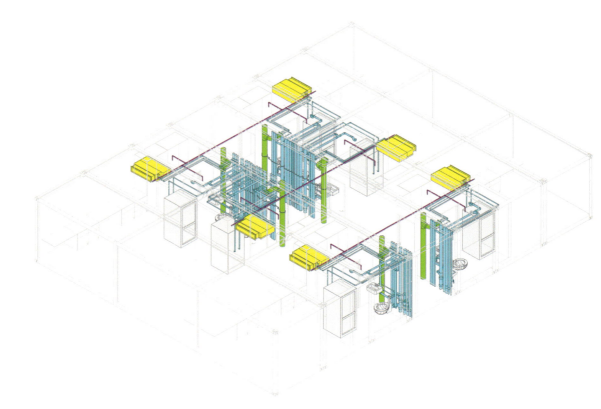

Systems Thinking

The traditional separation of building trades has not kept pace with the integration of technical systems. For decades, materials and products have been organized according to a numerical system officially known as MasterFormat, a kind of Dewey Decimal System for construction, overseen and regularly updated by the Construction Specifications Institute. In MasterFormat, materials and products are organized in isolation. MasterFormat makes no pretense at coordinating or integrating its vast array of materials and products. That is left up to the architect, and year by year, as new materials and products proliferate, the task of integrating them into a building becomes increasingly complex.

In Refabricating Architecture, Stephen Kieran and James Timberlake compare and contrast the traditional MasterFormat classifications with the approach widely used by manufacturers in the aerospace, automotive, and electronics industries.[21] In industry, as Kieran and Timberlake point out, the technical ingredients of complex components are organized systemically and/or spatially. In an automobile, to take one of their examples, the cockpit assembly contains instrumentation, heating and air conditioning, media, and GPS, housed in a self-supporting enclosure. The design and manufacture of the cockpit assembly can be sourced from vendors not under direct control of the automobile manufacturer, and the evolution of cockpit technology advances as competition between cockpit manufacturers drives innovation. (It's worth reflecting on the fact that an integrated systems approach for architecture was pioneered 60 years ago by Ezra Ehrenkrantz in the SCSD project discussed in Chapter 5.)

Similarly, intermodal modular manufacturing will separate the technical development of the VUC and its components from the design of buildings. The implications for architectural practice of this separation will be discussed in Chapter 10.

6.62
System org chart. The components of intermodal modular architecture are grouped under five basic system categories: *EXT*erior, *INT*erior, the *VUC*, *E*nvironmental *C*ontrol *S*ystems, and *COR*es.

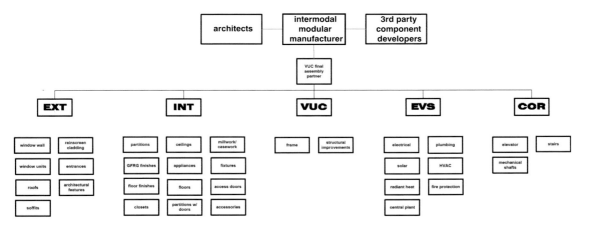

PRINCIPLE #**8** COMPONENT ASSEMBLY

The Addressable Grid

To maximize interchangeability for supply chain procurement, the dimensions of the various components that go into a VUC must be standardized, and every component, sub-component, virtually every screw and bolt must have a spatial address within the three-dimensional grid of the VUC.

I can already hear readers groaning. Standardization equals endless boring repetition. An understandable reaction... but it need not be so. Take, for example, shoe sizes. Feet come in infinitely varied dimensions. When shoes became a manufactured product a "dimension convention" was established with a few dozen lengths and a handful of widths, and billions of people walk around every day in myriad styles of properly fitting shoes.

We need standardization and at the same time we want design flexibility. What is the right mix—how much standardization and how much variety? In modular architecture, there should be a dimensional increment small enough to allow for sufficient design variation, yet large enough to keep the number of variations manageable.[22]

After trying out different grid dimensions, our team settled on a 4-inch increment for controlling the position of partitions and other components in the floor plan, and a 6-inch[23] vertical module as the increment for façade components. Four inches divides evenly into the dimensions of our 8×40-foot (as well as ISO standard 8×20-, 8×48-, and 8×53-foot) VUCs.[24] These increments meet the need for flexibility without over-complicating the supply chain. The apartment layouts previously illustrated were planned on the 4-inch grid, and it was not difficult to make them work.

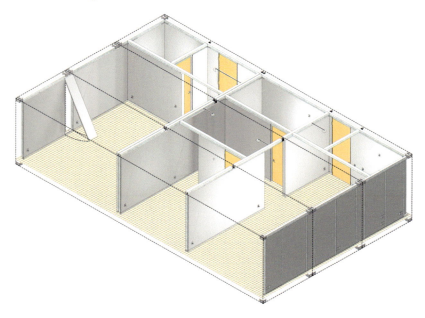

6.63
The 4-inch planning grid.

The addressable grid has ramifications beyond supply chain procurement and manufacturing. With its addressable grid and rules-based design, the VUC is well-suited to the application of artificial intelligence, which is now being adopted by architectural firms as a design tool.[25] Still, while a machine can generate iterations, the architect's *critical* intelligence is needed to evaluate and select from among a range of options.

Digital Design Interface

At the beginning of our research, when we were doing stacking studies, we saw the potential for a front-end digital design interface to facilitate the selection of pre-engineered, plug-and-play components from a BIM library. There should be no need for an architect to laboriously build a BIM model from scratch. Design and technical rules embedded in each component of the VUC will ensure that the arrangement of those components into a building meets structural and other technical constraints. The design process then becomes block play. I often get a reaction when I describe this to people: "it's like LEGO's!" Well, yes... the architect should experience the design process being as pleasurable as playing with that iconic Danish toy, but to make it possible at the scale of a building there has to be thorough behind-the-scenes engineering that ensures the technical resolution of the many possible combinations of elements.

The digital design interface is partitioned into three parts. There is the front-end menu of components with which the architect assembles a building; in the middle is a library of BIM objects that contain not just geometric properties, but information such as specification data, cost

6.64
Front-to-back end digital design interface.

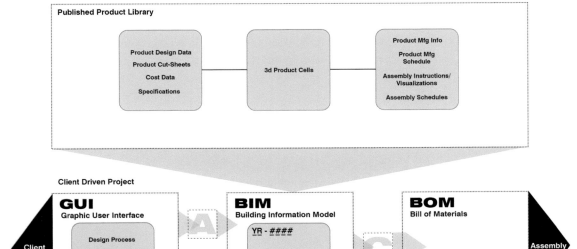

data, embodied greenhouse gas impact, structural properties, etc.; and the back-end is an enterprise software system that tracks inventory, cost, logistics, schedules, and so on.

Other technology comes into play. When the logistics people organize shipment, the order in which the VUCs are stockpiled and shipped will be coordinated with the erection sequence at the jobsite. Radio Frequency Identification (RFID) technology is used to monitor the location of shipping containers in real time anywhere in the world.[26] RFID will follow a VUC from the factory to the jobsite and will ensure that the right module is being craned into the right place in the building.

UrbanMODe: Infrastructure Overbuild

In 2017, I led a competition entry with FXCollaborative in which we proposed an innovative intermodal modular solution that we named UrbanMODe. The competition, sponsored by World Architecture News, called for proposals that would increase housing density and affordability in London's city core. Site selection was left up to the entrants, and our team decided to showcase the advantages of intermodal modular architecture for building above railways and other urban infrastructure. Infrastructure cuts, which often bifurcate neighborhoods, are among the last large, unbuilt sites within developed urban centers, and London is a city crisscrossed by railways. The drawback to overbuild projects is that the structural deck needed to cover the tracks and knit neighborhoods back together is expensive and its cost must be factored into the development financial model. This is where lightweight buildings constructed with VUCs offer significant benefits by reducing the quantity of steel in the overbuild deck that supports those buildings. We'll take a closer look at the weight benefits in Chapter 7.

We chose a site called Camden Cutting, a short walk from Euston Station, and not far from Regents Park. The neighborhood comprised Georgian-style row housing on one side of the tracks, and large free-standing homes on the other—a sensitive context in which to add density. However, a master plan had already been established for Camden Cutting that proposed mid-rise housing blocks over the railway cut, and that gave us a point of departure. Our proposal preserved intimate street-scale urbanity while increasing density by interweaving a contextually sensitive mix of typologies, including town houses, mid-rise bars, and a high-rise tower.

VUCs can economically span long distances using the internal trusses that we developed for our student housing proposal, thus greatly reducing the number of columns that must be painstakingly located so as not to interrupt the tracks or rail operations below. Reduced column touch-downs have the added benefit of freeing up the ground

The Intermodal Modular System

6.65
UrbanMODe: exploded
diagram illustrating mixed
typologies comprising 2,856
standard 8×40-foot VUCs.

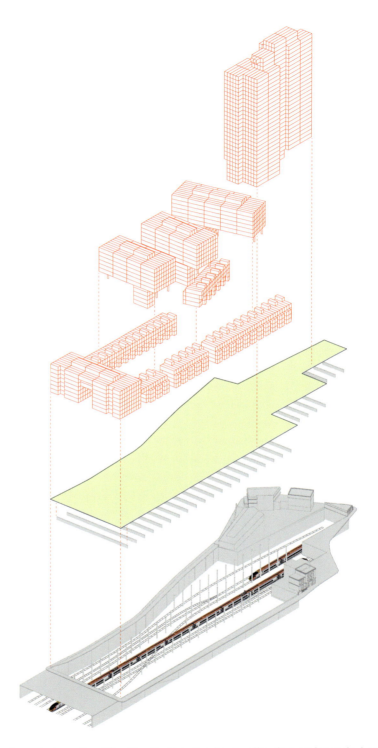

plane below the "floating" mid-rise bars, allowing unimpeded use of a landscaped public garden. We were able to simultaneously achieve overall construction economies and at the same time provide a valuable urban amenity.

6.66
UrbanMODe, site plan and section.

6.67
UrbanMODe, VUC typologies.

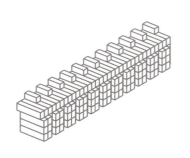

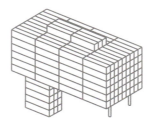

ROW HOUSE   ELEVATED BAR   TOWER

6.68
UrbanMODe, street view illustrating VUC row housing with mid-rise bars.

6.69
UrbanMODe, street view illustrating VUC high-rise housing at the commercial town center.

6.70
UrbanMODe: aerial view.

• • •

In Part 3, we'll situate intermodal modular architecture in a broader environmental, social, and cultural context. In Chapter 7, we'll look at the environmental impact of buildings constructed with VUCs, including embodied greenhouse gas emissions as well as the associated impacts of density and land use efficiency. In Chapter 8, we'll discuss the ramifications of disruptive innovation. Entrenched resistance in the construction industry will have to be overcome before there can be widespread adoption of intermodal modular architecture, but the disruption that it will cause must be managed fairly and equitably. In Chapter 9, we'll speculate on intermodal modular architecture as a new global vernacular—a shared, open-source language of construction. Continuing that discussion into Chapter 10, we will show how the new global vernacular has the potential to re-shape architectural practice as well as the relationships among all the participants in the housing process—architects, developers, policy makers, the intermodal modular enterprise, VUC component manufacturers, and urban "consumers" of housing. We'll then conclude the book with a chapter that delineates the proper place of a globalized housing industry in our locally constructed urban and personal environments.

The world-wide project of intermodal modular architecture is a new way of thinking about, talking about, and making buildings that will draw on the power of "distributed intelligence". The vision we've outlined here is only the beginning of an ongoing, evolving project. It calls on us to pool our collective imagination to bring intermodal modular architecture to fruition.

Notes

1 GBM is no longer in operation, and Alex Abrams and Eldon Scott are no longer involved with the company. Abrams went on to a career as a New York State affordable housing executive, and Scott runs Urbanspace in New York City, an affiliate of Urbanspace in London, formerly Urban Space Management.

2 The following statement by Joel Turkel elaborates nicely on the idea of a "delivery system" that we pursued at GBM:

> The future of pre-fab is an increasingly non-architectural problem. Traditionally, architects have tried to design things to be pre-fabricated using either existing or new means, as opposed to designing functional and integrated delivery methods... Real development for the industry will come from [those] who are able to think in terms of complete front-to-back business models. They are aware of the needs and limits of manufacturing processes but also are versed in new technologies, entrepreneurial methods, how capital works, strategic partnerships, and the importance of marketing and branding. This group will not design buildings but rather solutions for distributed delivery methods...
>
> As quoted in Ryan Smith, *Prefab Architecture: A Guide to Modular Design and Construction* (Hoboken, NJ: Wiley, 2010), 46.

3 Rain screens make it possible to wrap buildings in a thermal blanket, outside of the structural frame, so there are no "cold bridges" that allow heat to escape.

4 Transcript of the April 18, 2006 New York City Landmarks Preservation Commission Hearing.

5 See the Glossary.

6 "Containers," CIMC, accessed July 27, 2020, http://www.cimc.com/en/index.php?m=content&c=index&a=show&catid=36&id=1.

7 "Steel Sheet in Coils," CargoHandbook, accessed July 27, 2020, https://cargohandbook.com/Steel_sheet_in_coils.

8 CIMC subsequently established their own modular division after acquiring Verbus, a U.K. modular start-up.

9 In their book Refabricating Architecture, Stephen Kieran and James Timberlake offer a well-researched theory of manufacturing applied to building, which has greatly influenced this book.

10 Le Corbusier's Maison Domino, for example, was the distillation of reinforced concrete construction into a prototype that led to his "Five Points of Architecture".

11 372 Lafayette Street structural drawings, sheet S-4.9, May 1, 2006.

12 By this time, GBM had closed down and I had established an architectural practice. I continued to pursue opportunities to advance intermodal modular architecture such as this feasibility study, which was done in collaboration with FXCollaborative.

13 The alternative would have been a conventionally fabricated steel truss sandwiched between VUCs, which was not a true modular solution. At the Atlantic Yards modular tower in Brooklyn (discussed briefly in Chapter 3), a conventional truss created erection problems due to mis-matched tolerances between modules and trusses.

14 My client was the New York developer RAL Partners & Affiliates. I subsequently brought the project to FXFowle (now FXCollaborative) and took a position with the firm, where I led the design.

15 The 2012 International Energy Conservation Code and technical standards such as ASHRAE 90.1.

16 Damage to façade seals during craning was a significant problem during construction of the modular tower at the Atlantic Yards in Brooklyn discussed in Chapter 3.

17 The Prefabricator's Toolbox was created by Professors James Garrison and Deborah Gans. Funding for research was provided by the Institute of Design and Construction.

18 We designed test specimens, and UL gave us a proposal for testing services, but when GBM ceased operations at the end of 2007, we didn't have an opportunity to follow up.

19 "Velcro Companies Introduces 'Industrial Trade Range' of Solutions for Construction Applications," Velcro, accessed July 27, 2020, https://www.velcro.com/press-and-news/velcro-companies-introduces-industrial-trade-range-solutions-construction-

applications/. Professor James Garrison is credited here for the idea of using Velcro in prefabricated partitions for modular construction.

20 Louis I. Kahn quoted in *World Architecture One* (London: Studio Vista, 1964), quoted in Dean Hawkes, *The Environmental Tradition: Studies in Architecture of Environment* (London: Taylor & Francis, 1996), 73.

21 Stephen Kieran and James Timberlake, *Refabricating Architecture* (New York: McGraw-Hill, 2004), 39–41.

22 There was a robust discussion of planning modules in the U.K. during the post-war years. See Christene Wall, *An Architecture of Parts: Architects, Building Workers and Industrialization in Britain, 1940–1970* (London and New York: Routledge, 2013).

23 A 4-inch vertical increment would have been preferable, but a standard hi-cube shipping container is 9 feet 6 inches high, and does not divide into 4-inch increments.

24 The use of imperial dimensions was established when shipping container dimensions were standardized during the early 1960s, a legacy of post-war American economic dominance.

25 Mimi Kirk, "Will the Advent of Artificial Intelligence Affect Small Firms?" AIA, *Architect Magazine*, February 1, 2019, https://www.architectmagazine.com/aia-architect/aiafeature/will-the-advent-of-artificial-intelligence-affect-small-firms_o.

26 ISO 17363:2013 Supply chain applications of RFID – Freight containers.

Part 3

7   Is Intermodal Modular Architecture Sustainable?

As this book argues, we need economies of scale for modular architecture to bring about substantial cost reductions in urban housing, which means that like other industries, the intermodal modular enterprise must operate globally. Globalization as a trading system, however, is in a state of flux, if not crisis. The current pandemic has exacerbated forces that have been at work for several years, and we are in a "period of radical uncertainty, an order of magnitude greater than we're used to".[1] Saying that globalization is in crisis, however, is not the same as saying that it is over.[2] Even if the future of our relationship with China is unclear,[3] it seems likely that the exchange of goods with overseas trading partners will continue. Some analysts predict that the global trading system will reorganize along regional lines.[4]

In Chapter 2, we discussed the rate of global urban population growth and the need to produce mid- and high-rise housing at a commensurate speed and scale. In Chapter 3, we demonstrated that economical long-distance transportation—which means intermodal transportation—is necessary to achieve economies of scale. While we can expect the nature of globalization to change, it seems reasonable to assume that the global movement of goods unleashed by the advent of the shipping container, as discussed in Chapter 4, will continue. This naturally raises questions about long-distance transportation of building modules and sustainability.

In this chapter, we will address the greenhouse gas (GHG) and energy impacts of intermodal modular architecture. We'll look at those impacts from a range of perspectives, starting with the scale of the building, moving on to the scale of the city, and beyond to regional scale. At the scale of the building, we'll examine the embodied GHG emissions and embodied energy of buildings constructed using the Volumetric Unit of Construction (VUC) as compared to conventional on-site construction. Next, we'll look at the operating energy of a highly efficient building to see how embodied impacts appear in comparison. We'll then isolate the impact of transporting VUCs on the intermodal system over varying distances to assess transportation's contribution as a proportion of the total embodied and operating energy.

Expanding our perspective to the next scale, we'll look at "location efficiency", or the energy impact associated with various patterns of development. Location efficiency leads us to a comparison of low-density low-cost suburban development to high-density high-cost urban development. We'll analyze the dollar cost of VUCs in comparison to the conventional stick-built home to show how scale, transportation, density, cost, and energy use are all connected.

Long-Distance Transportation

As a proponent of a system of modular construction based on intermodal transportation, I am often asked if shipping building modules halfway around the world makes sense from an environmental standpoint. Fair question. There are really two answers, one of which is simple, and one more complex. The simple, but narrow, answer is that maritime transportation is about ten times more fuel efficient per ton of cargo moved per mile (ton-mile) than trucking, so shipping modules across oceans translates into one-tenth of the GHG emissions if that distance were traveled by a semi-trailer over the highway. Rail freight is about three times as efficient.[5]

7.1
CO2e comparison among shipping modes.
Source: Natural Resources Defense Council.

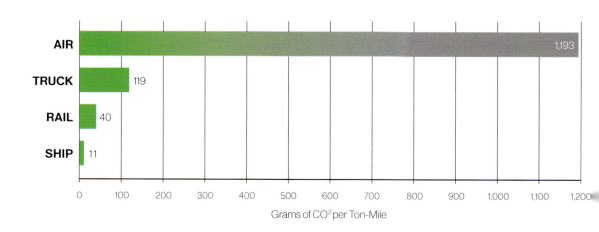

Grams of CO^2 per Ton-Mile

The 9,000 miles from Shanghai to Los Angeles, for example, is roughly equivalent to 900 miles on the highway. Via the Panama Canal, the trip from Shanghai to New York is about 12,000 miles, or the equivalent of 1,200 highway miles. Given the light weight of the all-steel VUC, which is about one-third the weight of a conventional steel frame building with precast concrete floors,[6] we would expect to be able to transport VUCs an even longer distance with the same GHG emissions output. Shipping lightweight VUCs from Shanghai to New York works out to the equivalent of about 400 miles on the highway. While there are variables that bear on each specific building location and design, the order of magnitude comparison is what matters.

Table 7.1 System Comparison: Weight

Baseline: Steel Frame + Hollow-Core Precast Plank	
Structure	116.67 lb/sf
Superimposed Dead Load (Enclosures, Partitions, etc.)	17.00 lb/sf
Total Baseline	133.67 lb/sf
Volumetric Unit of Construction (VUC)	
Structure	26.08 lb/sf
Superimposed Dead Load (Enclosures, Partitions, etc.)	17.00 lb/sf
Total VUC	43.08 lb/sf
Comparison: VUC to baseline	32.23%

Over the next few decades, freight transport—all modes—will become more efficient as energy policies and new technologies are implemented. Truck fuel economy standards in the U.S. are expected to yield CO2 reductions of 30–45 percent over the period from 2010 to 2027.[7] Increased fuel efficiency in maritime transport is also anticipated, with CO2 reductions of 40–60 percent over the period from 2012 to 2050.[8] Moreover, fuel economy standards in maritime transport are under the aegis of the International Maritime Organization (IMO) and are independent of the U.S. government's inconsistent environmental policies. Clearly, other nations are taking the lead here. A Norwegian initiative is well underway to build a net-zero, battery-powered container ship (with autonomous navigation), which will undergo sea trials in 2020. Named the Yara Birkeland, it is a small vessel, designed solely for inland waterways. With a capacity of only 120 TEU—smaller even than Malcom McLean's first container ship—it will replace 40,000 truck trips a year.[9] But if the Yara Birkeland proves out, we can expect container ship design to advance along similar lines with increasing size and range.

In the context of conventional container ship fuel efficiency, it's reasonable to ask if transporting materials 400 "equivalent highway miles" is a sustainable distance. Shouldn't we be obtaining our building materials more locally? To put that question in context, we'll need to dig a little deeper. The more complex answer requires "Life Cycle Assessment", or LCA, an accounting for all of the energy inputs and GHGs emitted over the course of the extraction of raw materials, manufacture, construction, operation, demolition, and beyond to include recycling and/or disposal. At present, "whole building" Life Cycle Assessment is a nascent discipline, just beginning to emerge as a formal course of study.[10]

Embodied GHG and Energy

When I was a young parent living in Brooklyn, the environmental issue of the moment was: cloth diapers or disposables? Which is less damaging to the environment—the energy and water resources consumed in washing and drying a reusable cotton diaper, or the energy consumed in the manufacture and the impact on landfills plumped up by the disposal of a synthetic diaper? Like other received notions among our set of young, urban, progressive friends about things "natural" as opposed to artificial, it was a given that cotton cloth diapers were more environmentally friendly. Imagine our conflicted feelings when we learned about an LCA study reported in *The New York Times*[11] which showed that the energy consumed in washing and drying cloth diapers, and the damaging algae blooms caused by detergents, made cloth diapers on balance more environmentally harmful. As Allen Hershkowitz of the NRDC stated at the time (this was the early 1990s): "The Earth does not benefit from symbolic gestures. People are wrong to think that simply using cloth diapers puts them on a higher moral plateau".[12] Now, three decades later, the balance has shifted slightly the other way[13] with the development of a new compostable cloth diaper. Life Cycle Assessment can be applied to any aspect of material and energy consumption, and it leads us to a better understanding of the "circular economy", or the cradle-to-cradle life cycle. Buildings are far more complex than diapers, of course, but there are now software tools available that allow architects who don't have specialized expertise to create LCA models that help us choose materials and systems more wisely.

Athena Impact Estimator[14] is an LCA modeling tool frequently used to support LEED[15] certification. By international agreement,[16] whole building LCA models allocate impacts for the building structure and enclosure within four "system boundaries", which are: the product stage, the construction process, the use stage, and the end-of-life stage (Figure 7.2). As a four-stage sequence, these are often referred to as the "cradle-to-grave" life cycle. When we refer to the "cradle-to-cradle" life cycle, we are including reuse, recycling, and recovery potential. Such system impacts beyond the end-of-life stage might include, for example, the "benefits and loads" from making recycled steel with material harvested from demolition.

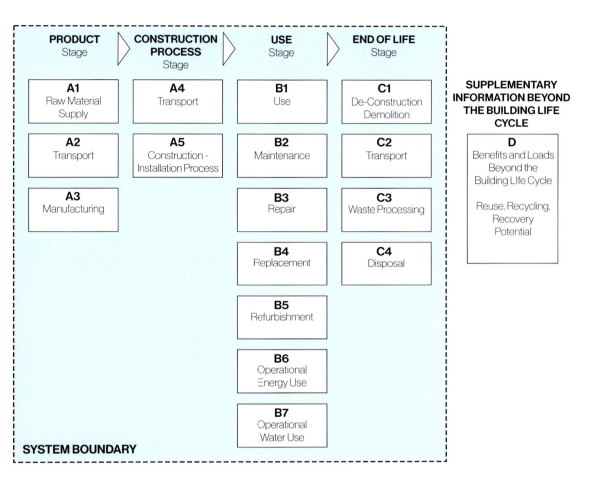

PRODUCT Stage	CONSTRUCTION PROCESS Stage	USE Stage	END OF LIFE Stage	SUPPLEMENTARY INFORMATION BEYOND THE BUILDING LIFE CYCLE
A1 Raw Material Supply	**A4** Transport	**B1** Use	**C1** De-Construction Demolition	
A2 Transport	**A5** Construction - Installation Process	**B2** Maintenance	**C2** Transport	**D** Benefits and Loads Beyond the Building LIfe Cycle Reuse, Recycling, Recovery Potential
A3 Manufacturing		**B3** Repair	**C3** Waste Processing	
		B4 Replacement	**C4** Disposal	
		B5 Refurbishment		
		B6 Operational Energy Use		
		B7 Operational Water Use		

SYSTEM BOUNDARY

7.2
European LCA reporting standards.
Source: Athena Sustainable Materials Institute.

Let's return to the study that we discussed in Chapter 6, in which we looked at the feasibility of using the VUC system to build a high-rise student housing facility. Located in a downtown residential neighborhood, the design featured six connected tower blocks of slightly varying heights that were to be constructed using a steel frame with hollow-core precast concrete plank floors. To compare the GHG footprint for the steel-and-plank building to a building of identical design constructed with VUCs, we modeled one representative block to simplify accounting for material quantities. Our model is based on a 12-story building with an 8,960 SF floor plate, totaling 107,520 SF.

Working with Athena's software, we compared the baseline building to a building constructed with VUCs. Because structure accounts for most of a building's mass, we initially modeled only the structural systems of our two buildings. This allows us to isolate and compare the most significant material differences and their impacts. We will assume that the GHG impact of other building components (enclosures, partitions, etc.) remains constant. Note that our first model does not include superimposed dead loads, again to isolate the differences in structural systems. When we get to a deeper look at transportation impacts, we'll add back superimposed dead loads. For now, we are not including the use stage. Later, we will also address the most significant aspect of the use phase, operational energy.

Athena produces results in nine categories of environmental impact.[17] For the sake of brevity, we are initially focusing only on Global Warming Potential (GWP), as measured in kg/CO2e. Carbon dioxide equivalent, or CO2e, encompasses all GHGs with their impact benchmarked to the impact of carbon dioxide, which is assigned a value of 1. Methane, which has a far greater GHG impact than carbon dioxide,[18] is accounted for within in CO2e with a weighted value of 25.[19] We selected the project location "USA" from the Athena menu, which is based on nationwide averages for energy sources and transportation distances.[20] Our objective here is a broad overview; specific geographic locations would of course produce different results due, for example, to regional variations in the fuel mix and percentage of renewable energy used to generate electricity. Other aspects of our modeling method can be found in the endnotes.[21]

Looking first at the embodied GHG impact, we found that over the cradle-to-grave life cycle the VUC system outperformed the baseline system by about 9 percent, a decent, albeit modest improvement. When we turn to the cradle-to-cradle impact (phases A to D), however, the results are more impressive. The VUC system has about 26 percent less GHG impact, mainly because VUCs are manufactured entirely of steel, 100 percent of which can be recycled. (Some virgin steel must still be produced to

Table 7.2 System Comparison: Global Warming Potential

LCA measures	Unit	Product (A1 to A3)	Constr'n Process (A4 to A5)	Use (B1 to B7)	End of Life (C1 to C4)	Beyond Building Life (D)	Total Effects	
		Total	Total	n/a	Total	Total	A to C	A to D
Baseline Steel/Precast Concrete	Kg CO2e	1,750,000	208,000	n/a	83,800	79,300	2,040,000	2,120,000
VUC	Kg CO2e	1,650,000	162,000	n/a	47,700	-298,000	1,860,000	1,560,000
Comparison: VUC to Baseline		−5.71%	−22.12%	n/a	−43.08%	−126.61%	**−8.82%**	**−26.42%**

Table 7.3 System Comparison: Energy

LCA Measures	Unit	Product (A1 to A3)	Constr'n Process (A4 to A5)	Use (B1 to B7)	End of Life (C1 to C4)	Beyond Building Life (D)	Total Effects	
		Total	Total	n/a	Total	Total	A to C	A to D
Baseline Steel/ Precast Concrete	MJ	22,700,000	3,010,000	n/a	1,230,000	364,000	27,000,000	27,300,000
VUC	MJ	27,100,000	2,380,000	n/a	693,000	(1,370,000)	30,200,000	28,800,000
Comparison: VUC to Baseline	MJ	19.38%	−20.93%	n/a	−43.66%	−376.37%	**11.85%**	**5.49%**

keep up with demand, so average recycled content in steel products today is about 86 percent.)[22] The concrete used in the baseline can only be "downcycled"—which means crushing it for use, say, as road base. Otherwise, it ends up in landfills.

Concrete is an excellent structural material and has many essential uses, but it is one of the most significant contributors to GHG emissions, accounting for up to 8 percent annually of all emissions worldwide.[23] More than half of those emissions are the byproduct of the chemical reaction inherent in the manufacture of Portland cement,[24] which occurs regardless of the energy source used in the manufacturing process.[25]

Even though the GHG impact for the all-steel VUC system is lower, it consumes about 12 percent more energy during the cradle-to-grave cycle. We can infer that the Portland cement chemical reaction is the reason why there can be a higher GHG impact yet lower energy impact for the baseline system, which uses precast concrete. It's worth mentioning that the student housing baseline construction system, with steel frame and hollow-core precast plank floors, uses far less concrete than typical high-rise residential structures which are commonly built with an entirely cast-in-place concrete structure.

Researchers are working to de-carbonize the chemical reaction in cement manufacture, and other GHG impacts can be addressed with renewable energy sources. But even advocates of low-carbon concrete acknowledge that a significant reduction of demand for concrete is necessary.[26] The VUC offers a pathway toward that goal in multi-story housing, a major segment of the construction industry. There is also a remarkable feature of the VUC end-of-life stage, not accounted for in the model, which is its inherent ability to be disassembled and reused rather than recycled. We'll come back to this toward the end of the chapter.

Transportation as a Component of Embodied Energy

Now let's assess transportation's contribution to the cradle-to-grave environmental impact, including operating energy. Sustainable design practice tends to favor locally sourced materials as being environmentally preferable to materials sourced across long distances.[27] While that may be the case for strawberries, when it comes to buildings, we should be wary of oversimplification. For our discussion going forward, we no longer need a baseline comparison—what we want to understand is whether long-distance VUC transportation is a significant factor when seen in the context of the total embodied and operating energy attributable to an intermodal modular building.

Because buildings in different regions operate using energy from varied types of fuel, as already noted, we'll make this next comparison in terms of energy rather than the GHG emissions attributable to specific fuel sources. While GHG impact is the critical measure, accounting for those varied impacts is beyond the scope of this study. We can, however, look at operating energy[28] independently, without analyzing the complex factors that go into determining GHG impact, simply to understand the relative importance of transportation energy to other embodied energy and to the operating energy consumed over the life of the building. The correlation to GHG impact is approximate but still useful.

Using the data for embodied energy from the Athena model, we'll plug in an Energy Use Intensity (EUI) to simulate the operational energy component of the use stage. EUI is a unit of measure representing the amount of energy consumed by a building per square foot per year.[29] We'll use a stringent EUI of 38.1 kBTU, or 40.2 MJ per square foot per year (source energy).[30] This was the EUI benchmark for a recently constructed Passive House[31] certified high-rise student housing facility at Cornell Tech in New York City.[32] We want to look at VUC transportation from a worst-case perspective by using a stringent EUI to magnify the significance of transportation energy by comparison.

Table 7.4 shows the comparison, in units of energy (MJ) and by percentages, of components of the life cycle energy consumed by the VUC building over a relatively short 20-year life cycle.[33] We are using a 20-year life cycle, rather than a typical 50-year life cycle,[34] to magnify, again, the impact of transportation. It's striking to find that the transport component of embodied energy, which within the U.S. relies on trucking, is a mere 1.77 percent of the total cradle-to-grave life cycle.

What if we did a similar analysis of long-distance overseas transport for various global cities? Athena doesn't have an international transportation database, so we used another source, the EcoTransIT Online Calculator.[35] EcoTransIT calculates freight transportation impacts[36] for every imaginable city-to-city combination. It accounts for all three types of intermodal transport[37]—container ship, truck, rail—and provides separate data, including mileage, for each. We selected global cities that represent a broad

Table 7.4 VUC System Student Housing – USA Cradle-To-Grave Life Cycle Energy Consumption

	VUC Transport (A5 Only)[a]	**All Other Embodied Energy[a]**	**Operating Energy (20 Years)**	**Total**
MJ	2,330,000	42,823,920	86,440,979	165,521,864
%'age of Total	1.77%	32.54%	65.69%	100.00%

[a] From Athena Impact Estimator.

spectrum of manufacturing locations and destinations. We included two possible U.S. manufacturing locations that are in proximity to container terminals and which might offer cost competitive labor rates, San Diego and Cleveland. (Cleveland, a rust-belt city in need of a new industrial base, can access global shipping via the St. Lawrence Seaway;[38] an operation based in San Diego would have access to Mexican manufacturing and supply chains in Tijuana, and would ship from the Port of San Diego.) Figure 7.3 isolates the VUC transport impact.

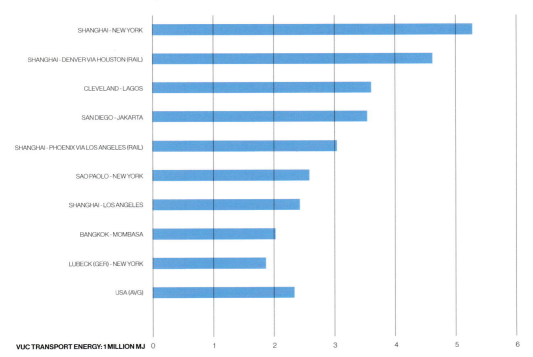

VUC TRANSPORT ENERGY: 1 MILLION MJ

7.3
City-to-city VUC transport energy comparison.
Source: EcoTransIT.

Viewed in isolation, the VUC transport impact from Shanghai to New York is more than double the U.S. average. But to understand that impact in context, we then added the balance of the embodied and operating energy consumed in the overall cradle-to-grave life cycle (Figure 7.4). Viewed within that frame of reference, it's clear that the energy consumed in long-distance overseas transport is, in fact, a minor proportion of the total. As a percentage of overall energy, the least energy-consuming transit between Lubeck, Germany, and New York represented about 1.4 percent of the total energy budget, and the most energy-consuming transit, between Shanghai and New York, represented about 3.9 percent.

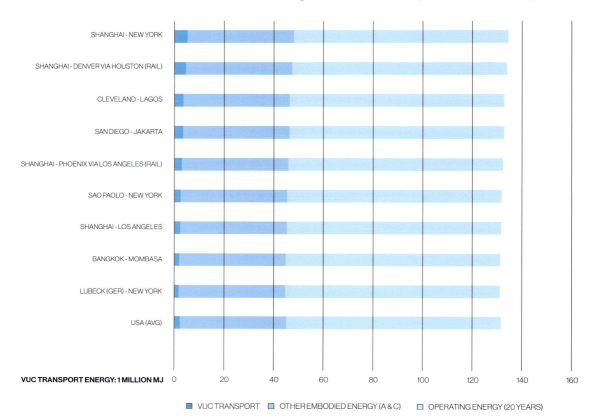

VUC TRANSPORT ENERGY: 1 MILLION MJ

■ VUC TRANSPORT   ■ OTHER EMBODIED ENERGY (A & C)   □ OPERATING ENERGY (20 YEARS)

7.4
City-to-city total energy comparison.
Sources: EcoTransIT, Athena Sustainable Materials Institute, Buro Happold.

Should even these small percentages be ignored? Of course not. Transportation, as much as any other sector, must phase out fossil fuels and convert to renewables, but transport impacts do need to be contextualized. We'll be looking at a still broader context shortly. Before we do that, however, let's return to our student housing study and touch on other aspects of intermodal modular architecture and sustainability.

Indirect Benefits

The VUC system creates indirect benefits that ripple outward. For example, the light weight of the VUC can reduce the materials used in supporting structures and foundations. The 1,400-bed high-rise dormitory was situated on top of a three-story classroom podium that, in turn, sat above a three-level below-grade athletic facility with a basketball court and an Olympic-size pool. To keep the athletic facility column-free, long-span steel trusses were required to transfer the weight of the dorm towers and classroom podium to the outer foundation walls. The lightweight VUC system would have reduced the amount of steel in those transfer trusses by about 25 percent,[39] with a corresponding reduction of GHG impact as well as cost savings. The direct and indirect weight reductions would have also reduced the number of expensive foundation caissons required to carry the building.

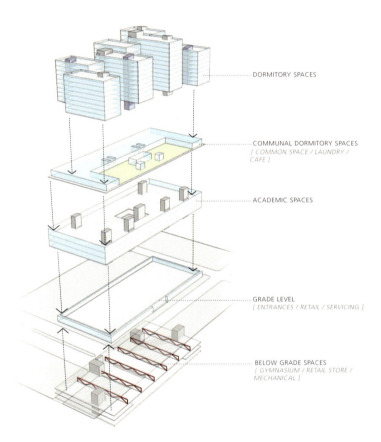

DORMITORY SPACES

COMMUNAL DORMITORY SPACES
[COMMON SPACE / LAUNDRY / CAFE]

ACADEMIC SPACES

GRADE LEVEL
[ENTRANCES / RETAIL / SERVICING]

BELOW GRADE SPACES
[GYMNASIUM / RETAIL STORE / MECHANICAL]

7.5
Student housing project, exploded view.

Our study also revealed that there were environmental benefits for the neighborhood. Surrounding streets are narrow, with room for one lane of traffic and parking on either side. The myriad daily truck trips to and from a job site to deliver materials to construct a conventional building in a congested city already burdened with heavy traffic have a significant emissions impact. You've probably noticed around construction sites that trucks are queued up waiting for their turn to make a delivery, with engines idling, spewing tailpipe fumes. Our intermodal modular dormitory would require about 1,400 VUCs. On a large site with two cranes, the VUCs could be stacked up in less than four months, averaging eight VUC deliveries and crane placements per day per crane (a conservative assumption). The project construction manager, a large international firm, determined that there would be at least 50 percent fewer truck trips required in the process of delivering VUCs as compared to the delivery of construction materials in individual truckloads of steel, concrete, sheet rock, copper pipe, and so on.[40]

The overall duration of on-site construction would be significantly reduced. The construction manager estimated that conventional construction for the baseline dormitory (starting at the top of the podium) would take 16 months, as compared to about 10 months for our intermodal modular approach.[41] To neighbors and passers-by, the modular building would appear complete after four months; during the next six months,[42] the work would be happening inside—hook-ups, mate-line patching, and commissioning.

With intermodal modular, there is practically no waste[43] at the job site—far fewer dumpsters and roll-on roll-off truck pick-ups. Again, fewer emissions and a fraction of the noise and dust. The area needed for staging materials is greatly reduced, which in a dense urban context means that less sidewalk and street space needs to be cordoned off. Less traffic congestion means further reductions of tailpipe emissions and less pedestrian inconvenience.

The number of construction hoists can be reduced, since all materials are either already part of the VUC, or in the case of materials for mate-line patching are preloaded into the VUCs before craning. The baseline building needed three hoists for 16 months. The intermodal modular approach required two hoists during craning and only one hoist to carry the workforce during the interior completion period.[44]

Developable sites in densely built cities like New York are increasingly scarce. Building over railroad tracks and other infrastructure, as at New York's Hudson Yards, is a solution that both repairs the urban fabric and creates new development opportunities in dense city cores. Hudson Yards required the construction of an expensive structural deck above 28 acres of active rail tracks to create a new urban ground plane—not only for office towers but also for public spaces and cultural buildings. A major challenge for this type of project is to find suitable locations between closely spaced tracks to insert building foundations. As in the student housing project, massive steel trusses were needed to transfer the enormous weight of high-rise buildings in order to stay clear of critical railroad operations.

New York City's Economic Development Corporation commissioned FXCollaborative to do a feasibility study for a rail overbuild at Amtrak's 180-acre Sunnyside Yards facility in Queens,[45] where a costly transfer structure will be required to support mid- and high-rise buildings that must span across the tracks. We asked our structural engineer, LERA, to evaluate the potential savings in the transfer trusses that could be realized by using the VUC system to construct housing. They found that a 50–65 percent reduction in steel tonnage could be achieved,[46] resulting in cost

7.6 (opposite above) Section Perspective, Amtrak Maintenance Yard Overbuild. Courtesy of FXCollaborative.

7.7 (opposite below) New York City Sunnyside Yards overbuild, weight savings in transfer deck using VUCs.
Source: LERA Consulting Engineers.

reductions of 11–15 percent in the transfer structure.[47] (Savings varied depending on the transfer span, which ranged from 20 to 115 feet, and building height, which ranged from 15 to 69 stories. Cost in this case is not linearly related to tonnage.) Of course, reduced steel tonnage means reduced GHG impact.

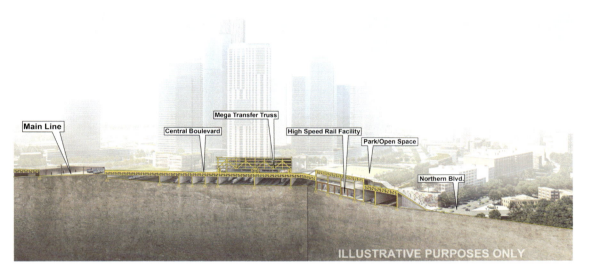

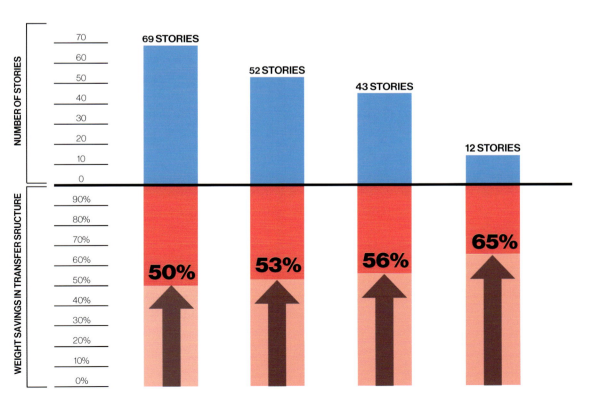

LERA also believes that there are further advantages of the lightweight VUC system that would require wind tunnel testing to prove out. In a recent wind tunnel study for a supertall building in Seoul, they found that a stiff, lightweight structure can dramatically reduce wind loads as compared to a heavier concrete or steel-concrete hybrid structure. Improved behavior under wind loads will become increasingly important as the intensity of severe weather events increases with climate change.

Location, Location, Location

Yet as meticulously as we might account for the complex cradle-to-grave or cradle-to-cradle environmental impacts of an intermodal modular building and the associated indirect benefits such as lightened transfer structures, we would still have neglected to consider broader external impacts—for example, how patterns of real estate development might shift in favor of more energy-efficient land use through the adoption of low-cost intermodal modular housing.

When we turn to a consideration of development patterns, the cost of urban housing turns out to be a powerful sustainability driver. This includes not only the cost of affordable housing for the poor and working poor, but also, importantly, the cost of housing for middle-class families. The VUC system can reduce the cost of multi-story urban housing across all income categories in comparison with conventional site-built housing. When we expand our frame of reference beyond the individual building to the larger development context, it will become clear that we've so far only scratched the surface. If we can make mid- and high-rise urban housing an affordable and attractive choice for the middle class—not only for young people but for all family units and age groups—we could see a remarkable reduction in energy use and GHG emissions.

Think of a pyramid representing energy savings and their economic cost, in which the biggest environmental bang for the buck is at the broad base where simple and low-tech solutions are found. As you climb the pyramid, costs increase as returns diminish. Energy-efficient building design often follows a three-tiered approach[48] that starts with basic considerations such as building shape, orientation, and the design of well-insulated and air-tight envelopes. Then at the second tier, passive techniques are added—for example, the use of thermal mass to absorb solar heat during the day and release it during the evening, or the use of solar light shelves to reflect daylight deeper into a building. Only after the first two tiers have been optimized should active energy-consuming mechanical and electrical systems for environmental conditioning and lighting be designed.

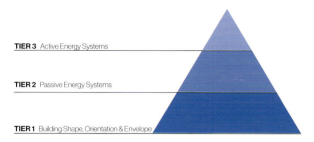

TIER 3 Active Energy Systems

TIER 2 Passive Energy Systems

TIER 1 Building Shape, Orientation & Envelope

7.8
Three-tiered energy pyramid.

The current standard of energy-efficient building is "Net Zero Energy", or NZE. Net-Zero Energy is defined by the U.S. Department of Energy as "an energy-efficient building where, on a source energy basis, the actual annual delivered energy is less than or equal to the on-site renewable exported energy".[49] This means that you need to install enough solar panels on site to fully offset the energy you consume. (Another path to NZE is to obtain off-site renewable energy through district energy systems, or, while not universally agreed, through Renewable Energy Credits (RECs).) In NZE design, a fourth tier is added at the top of the pyramid, which is the technology (e.g. photovoltaic (PV) panels) required to generate the "on-site renewable exported energy".

TIER 4 On-site Renewable Energy

TIER 3 Active Energy Systems

TIER 2 Passive Energy Systems

TIER 1 Building Shape, Orientation & Envelope

7.9
Four-tiered energy pyramid.

But there is still another tier that must be added at the base of the pyramid: land use. Simply by building cities, as opposed to suburbs—regardless of how energy efficiently you build those suburbs—you reduce energy consumption and GHG emissions. Let me clarify—the dramatic gains in energy efficiency are found in multi-story cities like New York, not low-density cities like Phoenix, which are essentially sprawling suburbs.

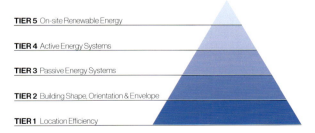

TIER 5 On-site Renewable Energy

TIER 4 Active Energy Systems

TIER 3 Passive Energy Systems

TIER 2 Building Shape, Orientation & Envelope

TIER 1 Location Efficiency

7.10
Five-tiered energy pyramid.

The Jonathan Rose Company, a real estate firm that specializes in environmentally responsible development, did a landmark study in 2011[50] that compared household energy consumption in Transit Oriented Development, or TOD,[51] to conventional suburban patterns of land use (Conventional Suburban Development, or CSD). The Rose Company's findings challenge accepted notions about energy-efficient building. They discovered that when you step back and consider housing density, housing type (single family versus multi-family), and proximity to energy-efficient public transportation, the gains that are achieved simply by adopting sustainable planning strategies like TOD outshine the gains from constructing energy-efficient single-family homes in suburban subdivisions. For example, according to the Rose study, a family living in an ordinary multi-story apartment building—constructed without energy-efficient features—in a neighborhood with access to transit consumes 39 percent less energy per year than an energy-efficient free-standing suburban house.

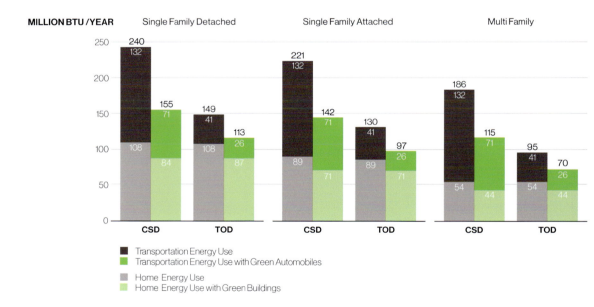

7.11
Energy consumption and location efficiency.
Source: Jonathan Rose Companies.

The Rose study revealed that land use planning that reduces the energy consumed during daily transportation—commuting, shopping, picking the kids up from school, getting to and from activities—is far more impactful than simply building green. Yes, energy-efficient construction does matter, and by bringing that urban multi-story apartment building up to reasonably stringent energy standards, the Rose study shows an overall 55 percent reduction compared to an equally efficient house in the suburbs, for an additional 16 percent improvement. Still, at the building scale, that additional 16 percent reduction in energy consumption is not enough. Today, we know that we can and must go further.

Drawing the Net-Zero Energy Boundary

The Rose study used a 20 percent improvement in energy efficiency as the benchmark for green building.[52] In so doing, they left a lot of potential gains on the table. Why not build Net-Zero Energy suburban houses? Wouldn't that be the silver bullet? Well, no. There is an unintended consequence—one that is generally overlooked, and which further underscores the need for a holistic approach that accounts for location efficiency. Using the Rose study as a point of departure, David B. Goldstein and Jamy Bacchus,[53] in a paper for the Natural Resources Defense Council, showed how environmentally virtuous land use strategies that encourage density and vertical development in proximity to mass transit can be perversely undermined by policies that promote rooftop PV solar panels.[54] Using data from Rose, the average single-family home consumes about 108 MBtu or 31.6 KWh of source energy annually.[55] Goldstein and Bacchus estimate that the capacity of a PV array must equal 30 percent of that household's total annual energy needs,[56] or about 9.5 KWh, to achieve NZE. A PV system with that output requires a substantial roof area to be covered with panels. With, say, an average output of 325 watts per panel,[57] a total panel area of 528 SF will meet that requirement (assuming optimal orientation and no shade). When roof edge setbacks and the inevitable inefficiency in panel layouts are factored in, a total south-facing roof area of about 700 square feet is required. Since half of a gabled roof faces the wrong way, the overall total roof area comes to about 1,400 square feet, or roughly equivalent to the roof of an average new American two-story single-family home. Multi-family/multi-story construction cannot yield adequate roof area, since the ratio of roof to floor area decreases with each additional story. Neighboring multi-story buildings can interfere with sun angles, reducing efficiency. The land use patterns that are ideal for rooftop PVs, Goldstein and Bacchus found, resemble nothing other than Sunbelt sprawl!

Where you draw a boundary to define the limits of a Net-Zero Energy system can be misleading. You can succeed, with technology, in achieving a Net-Zero suburban house, but the land use patterns that go along with that, as Rose showed, are energy- and resource-intensive. Does that mean that solar panels are bad? Absolutely not. Please, put solar panels on your house. The point is that as a model for future land use, even a Net-Zero Energy suburban development must account for personal transportation energy, and once you do that the unsustainable paradox of Net-Zero Energy sprawl becomes apparent. Even with the introduction of electric vehicles, it will be decades before we make the transition to a fully electric and net-zero automobile fleet.[58]

The Impact of Bad Rules

The economist Edward L. Glaeser has also studied the comparative energy use of U.S. cities and suburbs, tallying the impacts of heating fuel, electrical consumption, driving, and public transportation, and finds evidence that some, although not all, American cities are far more energy-efficient than their suburban counterparts. Glaeser takes into account that much of the existing housing stock in cities is old, with poor insulation, drafty windows, and inefficient heating systems, whereas suburban housing stock tends to be newer and more efficient. (As anyone who has lived in an old apartment building knows, steam radiators produce far more heat than needed or wanted, and windows are often thrown wide open in the dead of winter.) Glaeser shows that even with those inefficient buildings in the mix, for example, "an average New York City resident emits 4,462 pounds less CO_2 annually than an average New York suburbanite".[59] Since the region surrounding New York has a well-used commuter rail system, the comparison in this case is with a relatively energy-efficient suburban ring.

The reasons are not hard to discern. Aside from the energy consumed by personal transportation, the isolated suburban house, with one family living in it, presents four walls and a roof to the elements, and no matter how well that house is insulated, there is energy transfer across a greater surface area than in multi-story apartment buildings, where most dwelling units present only one or two surfaces to the outdoors.

Glaeser goes on to analyze the differences among cities, and not surprisingly, New York is among the top-ranked, while Sunbelt cities like Atlanta, Houston, and Phoenix are at the bottom. Glaeser collected data for 48 U.S. cities, including cities with disparate climates—temperate San Francisco, chilly Chicago, sweltering Houston—and including cities ranging from sprawling Phoenix to towering New York, and found that across the board "households in dense urban areas have significantly lower carbon emissions than households in the suburbs".[60]

Glaeser's research suggests that we can add a sixth, and even broader base to the pyramid—the inherent energy saving advantage of building in temperate climates.[61]

TIER 6 On-site Renewable Energy
TIER 5 Active Energy Systems
TIER 4 Passive Energy Systems
TIER 3 Building Shape, Orientation & Envelope
TIER 2 Location Efficiency
TIER 1 Climate Efficiency

7.12
Six-tiered energy pyramid.

The San Francisco Bay area has just the right combination of cool summers and mild winters to minimize energy consumption for heating and air conditioning. Glaeser notes that land use regulations in California are the most restrictive in the nation, and suggests that restrictive regulations in California raise the cost of construction and drive development to unregulated Sunbelt states like Texas—places with lots of flat land and highways that encourage inexpensive but energy-intensive sprawl. In other words, environmentally virtuous California has simply shunted development to far less energy-efficient states and has inadvertently increased overall emissions. Glaeser attributes the relative lack of dense urban development in the U.S. to bad rules, in particular to restrictive land use regulations that drive development further away from city cores. Much has been written in the last few years about the California housing crisis that corroborates Glaeser's 2011 findings.[62]

Urban Multi-story Construction— Sustainability and Cost

This chapter began with an LCA model, which compared the VUC system to a conventional site-constructed building. We showed that with the all-steel VUC, there were significant cradle-to-cradle reductions in GHG emissions. We then showed that long-distance intermodal transportation of VUCs is not significantly impactful, accounting for between roughly 2–4 percent of the building's embodied and operating energy consumption, using an extremely low EUI over a comparatively short 20-year period. We discussed the indirect benefits of building with lightweight VUCs and the associated reductions in material used for overbuild structures and associated GHG emissions. We've reviewed a series of studies that demonstrate the overwhelming impact of land use patterns on energy efficiency. It's time to state our next intermodal modular principle.

PRINCIPLE #9 **LOCATION EFFICIENCY MATTERS. LOCAL SOURCING DOES NOT**

In distilling this complex issue down to a concise statement, we do not advocate for heedless transportation of VUCs across excessive distances, especially by diesel-powered truck. However, if environmentally virtuous land use is the goal, then the cost of mid- and high-rise urban housing is the driver. That cost must be reduced to a point where urban living becomes an attractive and economically viable alternative to "drive till you qualify".[63]

Why don't more middle-class families want to live in cities? The attractions of quiet suburban life may exert a strong pull, but a significant factor that discourages urban living is simply the high cost of multi-story construction, compounded by the high cost of land in desirable cities. Young couples in cities like New York face a difficult lifestyle choice once they start rearing children. Stay, and accept the high price for a cramped apartment, most likely in a neighborhood with a 30- to 45-minute commute by mass transit; or pay the same price for a much larger house with a yard and make a longer commute by car. Small surprise that most will sooner or later give up city living and move to the suburbs.[64]

For a presentation at Greenbuild 2015,[65] my colleague Jamy Bacchus developed a model that charts multi-story urban construction costs against suburban tract development costs, tracing the effect of density on the combined costs of construction and land. Our hypothesis is that the lower construction cost achievable with intermodal modular can overcome the high cost of urban land to make middle-income urban housing viable. The model uses a range of urban land values, from $20/SF to $1,000/SF. (At the extreme end of the scale, land in Brooklyn Heights, among the most expensive in the U.S., is valued on average at about $41,160,300 per acre,[66] or $945/SF.)

Average multi-story construction costs (2019) in U.S. cities range from about $300/SF in Denver to nearly $500/SF in San Francisco. Average in New York City is about $400/SF. Globally, the average in cities like London and Hong Kong exceeds $500/SF. Sydney is comparable to New York.[67]

For comparison, we used a benchmark construction cost of an average U.S. suburban house at $100/SF. Place that house on a half-acre lot, account for the cost of subdivision development, including the construction of roads and infrastructure, and all-in cost comes to about $235/SF.[68] The model included the cost of land for public rights-of-way, roads, and infrastructure construction, all pro-rated by yard frontage for each building lot. (These are costs not typically carried by urban residential construction.)

In Figures 7.13 and 7.14, density is represented on the vertical axis as Floor Area Ratio (FAR), which is a typical zoning regulation that multiplies the lot area to get allowable floor area. "All-in" (land plus building) dollar-per-square foot multi-story construction cost is represented on the horizontal axis. Each curve represents all-in dollar-per-square foot development cost for each land value. (Note that because zoning regulations typically limit the amount of lot area that a building can cover, FAR does not correspond to the number of stories. In New York City, under "standard tower rules" that limit lot coverage to 40 percent, FAR 12 can generate a 30-story building. Advocates for affordable housing in New York are lobbying to increase the residential cap beyond the current FAR 12.[69] The upper limit shown here is FAR 15.) At $400/SF, multi-story construction cannot come even close to the suburban benchmark. However, at about $200/SF, multi-story construction becomes a viable alternative up to about $400/SF land cost. Average land prices (2018) in Kings County, NY (Brooklyn) are in the range of $275/SF, in Alameda County, CA (Berkeley, Oakland) about $77/SF, and in Santa Clara County, CA (Palo Alto) about $109/SF.[70]

Is Intermodal Modular Sustainable?

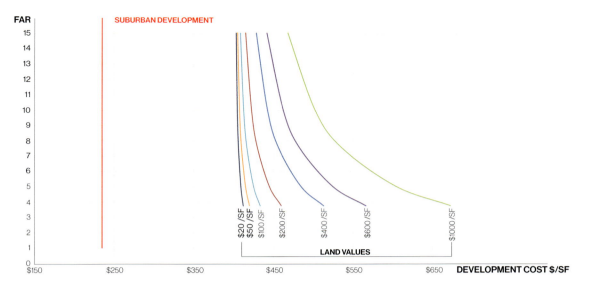

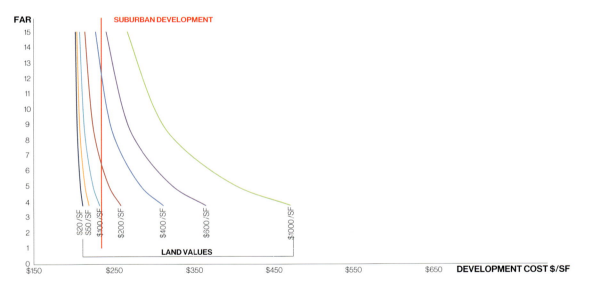

7.13 (above)
Development cost, $400/SF
construction cost applied to
a range of land values.
Source: Jamy Bacchus PE, LEED
AP BD+C, BEMP.

7.14 (below)
Development cost: $200/SF
construction cost applied to
a range of land values.
Source: Jamy Bacchus PE, LEED
AP BD+C, BEMP.

Let's revisit the student housing project discussed earlier, located in one of the highest cost union labor markets in the U.S. The construction manager compared our intermodal modular solution to the conventional scheme in side-by-side cost estimates. Because we were uncomfortable at that stage with the risk of overseas manufacturing, we partnered with one of the U.S. legacy modular manufacturers to develop a cost analysis of VUCs. The cost estimate bottom line showed that our intermodal modular approach achieved a 4 percent cost saving (not including indirect savings to transfer trusses and foundations). The cost of VUCs was $217/SF[71] (including transportation), and the cost of the on-site craning, hook-ups, and mate-line patching was $175/SF[72] for a total of $392/SF.[73] The 4 percent savings over conventional construction were not enough to convince our client to pursue the VUC system and the project moved ahead on a conventional track.

The following year, a major international facade manufacturer expressed interest in partnering with Global Building Modules. As part of their due diligence, they did a cost estimate based on the same student housing design to see what effect manufacturing in Asia would have and to evaluate the feasibility of long-distance VUC transport. As expected, we found that the cost of VUCs manufactured in Asia dropped dramatically, to $78/SF[74] (including transportation). Holding $175/SF for on-site work, we were now at $253/SF, for a 38 percent saving. Table 7.5 shows these numbers as well as projections of further cost reductions. It's not unreasonable to assume that with increased economies of scale, manufacturing costs will come down, and as installation experience is gained, those on-site costs will come down as well. While hypothetical, $200/SF for high-rise intermodal modular construction as illustrated in Figure 7.14 seems within reach. At that price point, the choice to stay and raise a family in the city would no longer be driven by cost.

We might also ask how big does an urban apartment really need to be? A pure dollar-per-square foot comparison is misleading. Urban living doesn't require the same square footage as living in the suburbs. The average suburban house has grown from 1,525 square feet from 1973 to 2,435 square feet in 2018.[75] If a suburban family can live comfortably in 1,525 square feet, an affordable 1,200–1,500 square-foot three- or four-bedroom city apartment should be ample. Apartments of that size, currently only affordable by the very wealthy, must be made affordable for the middle class.

The ballooning of the suburban house is driven by consumer demand for private amenities—spa-size bathrooms, status kitchens, recreation rooms, and so on. Newly developed apartment buildings now have common amenities such as gyms, indoor pools, roof gardens, even

Table 7.5 Cost Comparison (Costs are adjusted to 2015 dollars to align with Figures 7.13 and 7.14)

		VUC Cost		On-site Cost	Total	Savings
Conventional construction					$409/SF	
Intermodal modular manufactured U.S.		$217/SF		$175/SF	$392/SF	4%
Intermodal modular manufactured overseas		$78/SF		$175/SF	$253/SF	38%
Projected economies of scale: overseas intermodal modular	−20%	$63/SF	−20%	$140/SF	$203/SF	48%

screening rooms as standard features. Luxuries can be shared. New buildings frequently offer basement storage space. You don't need the three-car garage. In exchange for a smaller but still comfortable living space, you get less commuting and easy access to the entertainment, cultural resources, and educational enrichment that cities offer.

Keep in mind that our cost projections are not real estate development models. Soft costs (fees, financing, taxes, marketing, etc.) and profit are not included. We are not accounting for housing subsidies or tax incentives. We can't predict the degree to which markets in desirable locations would skew price, allowing developers to simply pocket the cost savings. These are questions that policymakers will need to address. Our purpose here is simply to present the case for bringing multi-story construction costs down to a level that could make city living a viable alternative to suburban living.

If dense urban land use is the base of the energy pyramid, and if the cost of construction is the barrier to making high-rise urban living an affordable alternative for middle-class families, then a construction cost solution— which means industrializing the construction process—goes hand in hand with an environmental solution. As this book argues, a robust, scalable modular building industry depends on access to global markets, and access to global markets depends on low-cost long-distance transportation across blue water. The VUC, as a building block for equitable urbanism, is an energy saving technology that on a per household basis is far more effective than, for example, a suburban subdivision covered in solar panels.

• • •

Before we conclude this chapter, there are a few additional topics worthy of discussion.

Design for Disassembly

569 million tons of construction and demolition (C&D) waste were generated in 2017, more than double the amount of municipal waste that year. About 90 percent of C&D waste is generated during demolition, at the end of the cradle-to-grave life cycle.[76]

Sustainable design practice means specifying materials with recycled content wherever possible. The results of our LCA model showed that over the cradle-to-cradle life cycle the all-steel VUC is 26 percent less impactful than the baseline steel frame and concrete plank building. We attributed this to the fact that steel, unlike concrete, is a recyclable material. Even with the inherent recyclability of steel, energy must still be expended to recover steel after demolition and to return it back to a usable form. Is there a way to reduce that end-stage impact?

Theoretically, it is possible, and an emergent branch of the green design movement, called Design for Disassembly, or DfD, aims to codify the principles for doing so.[77] DfD promotes modularity and prefabrication, as well as simplified and standardized methods for constructing buildings that allow for easy deconstruction The constituent pieces and parts should be salvageable and reusable, or able to be "upcycled".

So far, DfD remains a set of well-intentioned principles that have yet to be widely adopted in conventional design practice. Within the building industry, advocates for DfD face an uphill battle. It requires the design team to expend significant time thinking through the end phase of a building's life cycle, decades in advance. It can seem very much like an abstraction as budgets are strained, deadline pressures mount, and time-critical tasks take precedence.

One of the virtues of the intermodal modular approach is that buildings made of VUCs are inherently deconstructible, but more importantly, they are inherently *re*constructable. Not only is the VUC a standard modular dimension, with standardized bolted connections, but all the components and subcomponents are also modular. A building comprised of VUCs, like LEGO blocks, can be taken apart and reassembled into the same or, for that matter, into a new configuration. There is no reason for a VUC to enter the waste stream. Design for deconstruction and reconstruction is embedded in the system's DNA, with no extra design effort and at no extra cost.

Embodied Intelligence

A criticism often leveled against volumetric modular construction is that you are shipping empty boxes full of air. Flat pack is presumed to be the efficient way to ship prefabricated buildings. That criticism is based, however, on a flawed understanding of buildings, which unlike furniture are interlaced throughout with complex systems—very different from a knock-down bed from IKEA. With volumetric modular construction in general, and intermodal modular specifically, what is being shipped is a highly organized microcosm of constructed value, or better stated, embodied intelligence.

In order to create any habitable space—using conventional or modular methods—technical systems that provide structural support, weathertight and thermally efficient enclosure, environmental conditioning, electrical power, lighting, internet connectivity, plumbing, fire protection, partitions, storage, fixtures, appliances, and finishes must be arranged in an intelligent configuration. The space that is created within that carefully coordinated arrangement accommodates the varied functions and pleasures of living. Much like the eastern concept of "ma", space within a VUC properly understood has a positive value, even if it has no substance or weight.

Flat pack prefabrication, limited to the primary building structure, accounts for about 15 percent of a building's economic value. In certain instances, prefabricated unitized facades are delivered to the job site, accounting for another 15–20 percent for a total of about 30–35 percent. In contrast, volumetric modular accounts for about 80–90 percent (some interior work must be completed in the field). It is meaningless to talk about shipping air as if that air surrounded by embodied intelligence has no value. In terms of dollars per square foot, this so-called empty space has a precise value. Stacked VUCs represent far more value of completed construction than a prefabricated flat pack structural system. In maximizing dollar value in the factory, intermodal modular architecture inherently maximizes environmental value.

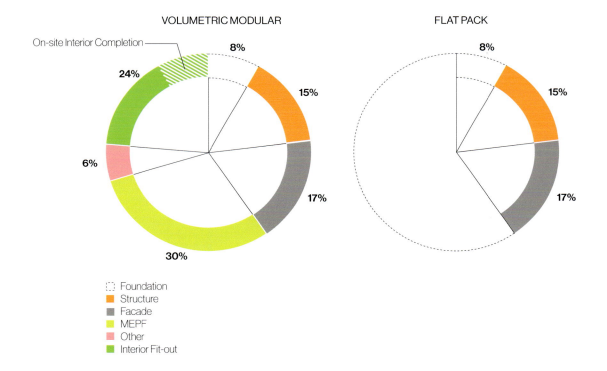

7.15
Value of construction, volumetric to flat pack comparison.[78]

Real-Time Design Dashboard

An intermodal modular manufacturer will source from regular suppliers, making the provenance of materials and components easily traceable and their embodied energy and GHG impact predictable, project after project. VUCs and their various components and subcomponents will be pre-engineered and represented by BIM objects in a central database. Each object in the BIM library will be tagged with accurate embodied energy and GHG values. Transportation energy from alternative manufacturing locations will be drawn from a master data set like EcoTransIT. A Life

Cycle Assessment dashboard will appear on the computer screen, making it possible for a designer to view data for embodied energy in real time as the building form is assembled from modules and components. Think TurboTax for carbon accounting.

With the real-time dashboard, design at the conceptual stage will be fully informed by energy metrics as the building is assembled in the model from pre-engineered BIM components. At the same time, item by item costs will appear side by side with energy readouts, enabling the designer to make informed choices at each critical decision point. It will be possible to see payback cycles that correlate with energy-efficient building features that might have a higher first cost. As every architect knows, the process that is euphemistically referred to in the building industry as "value engineering" is in reality simply cost cutting that often takes place late in the design process, sacrificing long-term value in exchange for short-term savings. The dashboard will render value engineering obsolete and will replace it with "value design".

• • •

The worldwide increase in urban population over the next several decades is poised to go in one of two directions. It can follow the American Sunbelt pattern, of low-density automobile dependent sprawl, or it can be modeled on high-density vertical cities like New York. In one direction lie increased GHG emissions. The other path, requiring a concerted effort to foster dense urban development, would achieve significant GHG reductions. If intermodal modular architecture is adopted as a solution to making cities livable and affordable for the middle class, it will be because increased living space, better quality, more design options, lower energy footprint, and all of the above for less money make it a logical choice.

No matter what choice you make, whether you are an urbanite, or you commute to the city, energy has a major impact on your life and will have an ever-increasing impact in the future. The type of energy you consume, the price you pay for it, and the external costs that are imposed by it that must be paid for somewhere down the line all affect your standard of living and that of your children and grandchildren.

Severe weather events and wildfires over the last decade have erased any lingering doubt that climate change and its disastrous impact may pose an existential threat. We are headed down a path of mutually assured environmental destruction if we do not get our house in order, or more accurately, our housing—beginning at the base of the energy pyramid by first and foremost considering the location and density of our development patterns.

LESS GREEN

MORE GREEN

7.16

The explosive rate at which global populations are urbanizing, and at which development is sprawling, calls for a housing solution of equal scale and power. This book argues that a sustainable, scalable, industrialized approach to construction based on the ocean-spanning intermodal transportation system will change the economics of multi-story construction, and will make city living an affordable and desirable alternative.

Notes

1 Adam Tooze, Columbia University, quoted in Neil Irwin, "It's the End of the World Economy as We Know It," *New York Times*, April 16, 2020.

2 Elizabeth Economy, Council on Foreign Relations, quoted in Neil Irwin, "It's the End of the World Economy as We Know It," *New York Times*, April 16, 2020. "There will be a re-think of how much any country wants to be reliant on any other country [but] I don't think fundamentally that this is the end of globalization".

3 Thomas Friedman, "China and America are Heading toward Divorce," *New York Times*, June 23, 2020.

4 Bruce Mehlman, "De-Global: 10 Trends Defining the New World," *Mehlman Castagnetti Rosen & Thomas*, last modified November 13, 2019, https://mehlmancastagnetti.com/wp-content/uploads/De-Global-2019.pdf.

5 "Clean by Design: Transportation," Natural Resources Defense Council, April 2013, Table 1.

6 The steel and precast concrete plank building data used here was developed for a student housing feasibility study discussed in more detail later in the chapter.

7 Alan McKinnon, "Freight Transport in a Low-Carbon World: Assessing Opportunities for Cutting Emissions," *TR News*, November/December 2016, no. 306 (2016): 14.

8 McKinnon, 14.

9 "Autonomous Ship Project, Key Facts About Yara Birkeland," *Kongsberg*, accessed June 22, 2020, https://www.kongsberg.com/maritime/support/themes/autonomous-ship-project-key-facts-about-yara-birkeland/.

10 "History," GHG Management Institute, accessed June 22, 2020, https://ghginstitute.org/history/. In 2012 the GHG Management Institute began offering "the world's first and only professional certification for GHG practitioners—the EP(GHG)—accredited to ISO standards".

11 John Holusha, "Consumer's World; Diaper Debate: Cloth or Disposable?" *New York Times*, July 14, 1990.

12 Holusha, 1990.

13 Mary Widdicks, "Are Cloth Diapers Really Any Better for the Environment, Your Wallet, or Your Baby?" The Goods, *Vox*, October 15, 2019, https://www.vox.com/the-goods/2019/10/15/20892011/cloth-diapers-debate-parenting-advice.

14 "Home," *Athena Sustainable Materials Institute*, accessed June 22, 2020, http://www.athenasmi.org/.

15 "LEED v4 for Building Design and Construction," *U.S. Green Building Council*, 2019, https://www.usgbc.org/sites/default/files/LEED%20v4%20BDC_07.25.19_current.pdf. LEED, or Leadership in Energy and Environmental Design, is a rating system that awards points for sustainable building design in various credit categories. LEED v.4 offers points for Whole Building Life Cycle Assessment.

16 Athena Sustainable Materials Institute, *Athena Impact Estimator for Buildings: User Manual and Transparency Document* (Ottawa: Athena Sustainable Materials Institute, 2019), https://calculatelca.com/wp-content/uploads/2019/05/IE4B_v5.4_User_Guide_May_2019.pdf. Athena Impact Estimator "conforms to the EN 15804/15978 system boundary and reporting format".

17 These are: Global Warming Potential, Acidification Potential, HH (Human Health) Particulate, Eutrophication Potential, Ozone Depletion Potential, Smog Potential, Total Primary Energy, Non-renewable Energy, Fossil Fuel Consumption.

18 Matthew Brander, "Greenhouse Gases, CO2, CO2e, and Carbon: What Do All These Terms Mean?" White Pages, *Ecometrica*, September 4, 2012, https://ecometrica.com/white-papers/greenhouse-gases-co2-co2e-and-carbon-what-do-all-these-terms-mean.

19 Jessica McDonald, "How Potent is Methane?" *FactCheck.org*, last modified September 24, 2018, https://www.factcheck.org/2018/09/how-potent-is-methane/. Methane is also said to be 84 times more powerful over the first 20 years of its release, which is when we need to draw down climate. The ~25 times factor used by Athena is over a 100-year cycle.

20 Because Athena does not include data for locations outside of the U.S., an LCA of intermodal modular architecture manufactured overseas is unfortunately beyond the scope of this book. Further research is needed to account for different fuel mixes used in generation of electricity in various overseas locations.

21 The "Project Extra Materials" feature of Athena Impact Estimator was used to input actual structural material quantities based on known concept-level designs for each structural system. In other words, Athena's built-in structural calculator was overridden in order to incorporate more accurate data that reflects high-rise

structural design. Factors such as lateral load design and progressive column loading for a 12-story building have thus been accounted for.

22 "Steel is the World's Most Recycled Material," Steel Recycling Institute, accessed June 22, 2020, https://www.steelsustainability.org/recycling. According to the Steel Recycling Institute, "Steel is the most recycled material on the planet, more than all other materials combined. Steel retains an extremely high overall recycling rate, which in 2014, stood at 86 percent".

23 Johanna Lehne and Felix Preston, "Making Concrete Change: Innovation in Low-carbon Cement and Concrete," *Chatham House Report* (London: The Royal Institute of International Affairs, 2018), 1, https://www.chathamhouse.org/sites/default/files/publications/2018-06-13-making-concrete-change-cement-lehne-preston-final.pdf.

24 Lehne and Preston, 3.

25 United Nations Environmental Programme, *Sand and Sustainability: Finding new solutions for environmental governance of global sand resources* (Geneva: GRID-Geneva, 2019), https://wedocs.unep.org/bitstream/handle/20.500.11822/28163/SandSust.pdf?sequence=1&isAllowed=y. Further, it turns out that good quality sand, which constitutes about 30 percent of a typical concrete mix, is becoming a scarce global commodity.

26 Lehne and Preston, vii.

27 "LEED v4 for Building Design and Construction," *U.S. Green Building Council*, (2019), https://www.usgbc.org/sites/default/files/LEED%20v4%20BDC_07.25.19_current.pdf. In LEED V.4, Building Product Disclosure and Optimization includes a multiplier bonus for locally sourced materials. The credit states "For credit achievement calculation, products sourced (extracted, manufactured, and purchased) within 100 miles (160 km) [emphasis added] of the project site are valued at 200% of their base contributing cost. For credit achievement calculation, the base contributing cost of individual products compliant with multiple responsible extraction criteria is not permitted to exceed 100% its total actual cost (before regional multipliers) and double counting of single product components compliant with multiple responsible extraction criteria is not permitted and in no case is a product permitted to contribute more than 200% of its total actual cost".

28 Operating energy is broadly divided into primary energy, which is the energy drawn from sources outside of the building such as the electric utility, and site energy which comes from energy sources such as building fuel tanks or photovoltaic panels. Operating energy comprises space and water heating, space cooling, lighting, and plug loads (computers, appliances, and other such items that aren't part of the building but use power).

29 Athena Impact Estimator does not have a function that accepts EUI inputs, so we created a separate Excel model to apply EUI to the student housing project.

30 "The difference between source and site energy," Energy Star, accessed June 22, 2020, https://www.energystar.gov/buildings/facility-owners-and-managers/existing-buildings/use-portfolio-manager/understand-metrics/difference. Site energy is "the amount of heat and electricity consumed by a building as reflected in your utility bills". Site energy can come from on-site fuel or PV panels (primary energy) or from utilities (secondary energy). Source energy "represents the total amount of raw fuel that is required to operate the building. It incorporates all transmission, delivery, and production losses".

31 Passive House is an international organization that promulgates ultra-low energy building performance standards to minimize energy use while maintaining healthy and comfortable indoor environments.

32 "The World's Tallest and Largest Residential Passive House," *Burohappold Engineering*, 2016, https://www.burohappold.com/wp-content/uploads/2016/05/bhe-cornell-tech-casestudy-web2.pdf.

33 Within the parameters of a 20-year building life, we are ignoring other use impacts such as embodied energy due to replacement of secondary construction elements – finishes, cabinetry, etc.

34 Aneurin Grant and Robert Ries, "Impact of Building Service Life Models on Life Cycle Assessment," *Building Research & Information* 41, no. 2 (2013): 168–186. doi:10.1080/09613218.2012.730735. "Life cycle assessments (LCAs) of buildings often use an operational lifetime of approximately 50 years…"

35 "Calculation," EcoTransIT World, accessed June 22, 2020, https://www.ecotransit.org/calculation.en.html.

36 For our calculations, we used EcoTransIT's Well-to-Wheels (WTW) function to account for direct as well as indirect energy sources – i.e. source energy.

37 EcoTransIT's energy consumption for container shipping is about 19% higher per ton-mile than the NRDC data cited earlier.

38 Harry Valentine, "Improved Prospects for Container Ships on the St. Lawrence Seaway," Editorials, *Maritime Executive*, October 6, 2018, https://www.maritime-executive.com/editorials/improved-prospects-for-container-ships-on-the-st-lawrence-seaway.

39 [Project name withheld], Modular Study Final Presentation, Transfer System Savings, May 20, 2009, 50.

40 [Project name withheld], Modular Study Summary Report, July 2009, 12–14.

41 [Project name withheld], Modular Study Summary Report, July 2009, Appendix II, Schedule.

42 Six months of interior work was very conservatively projected by the construction manager's schedule, reflecting uncertainty about the nature of the VUC system.

43 Athena Impact Estimator accounts for waste in manufacturing.

44 [Project name withheld], Modular Study Summary Report, July 2009, Appendix I, Comparative Logistics Plan. This is a conservative estimate. Up to 90 percent reductions have been cited by others (see James Wilson, "The Potential of Prefab: How Modular Construction Can Be Green," Building Green, September 9, 2019, https://www.buildinggreen.com/feature/potential-prefab-how-modular-construction-can-be-green).

45 New York City Economic Development Corporation, Sunnyside Yard Feasibility Study, February 6, 2017. The author was with FXCollaborative from 2014-2019, and worked on the modular aspect of the study.

46 LERA Consulting Structural Engineers, in an email to author, July 2, 2020.

47 Sunnyside Yard Feasibility Study (cost data provided by HR&A Consultants based on structural analysis by LERA Consulting Engineers with input from WSP USA/ Structural Engineering).

48 Norbert Lechner, *Heating, Cooling, Lighting: Sustainable Design Methods for Architects* (Hoboken, NJ: John Wiley & Sons, 2014), 9.

49 "DOE Releases Common Definition for Zero Energy Building, Campuses, and Community," Office of Energy Efficiency & Renewable Energy, Energy.gov, published September 16, 2015, https://www.energy.gov/eere/buildings/articles/doe-releases-common-definition-zero-energy-buildings-campuses-and.

50 Hernandez, Lister and Suarez, March 2011.

51 Transit Oriented Development is a planning strategy for creating neighborhoods within walking distance of mass transit, in order to reduce the use of automobiles.

52 Hernandez, Lister and Suarez, March 2011. The Rose paper uses Energy Star standards to define "energy efficiency" as a 20 percent improvement over "standard homes".

53 Disclosure: Jamy Bacchus consulted to GBM in 2006–7, helping to analyze the energy footprint of the intermodal modular system.

54 David Goldstein and Jamy Bacchus, "A New Net Zero Definition: Thinking outside the Box" (presentation, ACEE Summer Study on Energy Efficiency in Buildings, Pacific Grove, CA, August 2012).

55 Hernandez, Lister and Suarez, March 2011. The Rose paper cites the Energy Information Administration's 2005 Household Residential Energy Consumption Survey (RECS).

56 Goldstein and Bacchus, 11–86.

57 Ana Almerini, "How many solar panels do I need?" *SolarReviews* (blog), last modified June 25, 2020, https://www.solarreviews.com/blog/how-many-solar-panels-do-i-need-to-run-my-house. Ben Zientara, "How Much Electricity Does a Solar Panel Produce?" Solar Basics, *Solar Power Rocks*, last modified April 2, 2020, https://www.solarpowerrocks.com/solar-basics/how-much-electricity-does-a-solar-panel-produce/.

58 Thompson Reuters, "Will electric vehicles really create a cleaner planet?" https://www.thomsonreuters.com/en/reports/electric-vehicles.html, accessed December 11, 2020. According to Thomspon Reuters analysts Jon Berntsen and Frank Melum, "By 2040, roughly half of the vehicles on the road will still be powered by fossil fuels, but all new vehicles sold will be EVs. As a result, carbon dioxide production from passenger cars will fall to 1.7 billion metric tons, but total energy required to power the increasingly electric global fleet of cars will have grown to around 1,350 terawatt hours".

59 Edward L. Glaeser, "Green Cities, Brown Suburbs," *City Journal*, Winter 2009, https://www.city-journal.org/html/green-cities-brown-suburbs-13143.html.

60 Glaeser, 2009.

61 Edward L. Glaeser, *The Triumph of the City* (New York: Penguin, 2011): 210–212.

62 Thomas Fuller, "Why Does it Cost $750,000 to Build Affordable Housing in San Francisco," *New York Times*, February 20, 2020, https://www.nytimes.com/2020/02/20/us/California-housing-costs.html. Noah Buhayar and Christopher Cannon, "How California Became America's Housing Market Nightmare," *Bloomberg*,

November 6, 2019, https://www.bloomberg.com/graphics/2019-california-housing-crisis/. James Broughel and Emily Hamilton, "Op-Ed: One reason for the high cost of housing in California may surprise you—overregulation," Opinion, *Los Angeles Times*, July 3, 2019, https://www.latimes.com/opinion/op-ed/la-oe-broughel-hamilton-overregulation-housing-california-20190703-story.html.

63 Scott Wiener and Daniel Kammen, "Why Housing Policy is Climate Policy," Opinion, *New York Times*, March 25, 2019, https://www.nytimes.com/2019/03/25/opinion/california-home-prices-climate.html.

64 Local district school funding and tax deductions on mortgage interest and property taxes also factor into the decision by young families to move to the suburbs.

65 David Wallance, Jamy Bacchus and Jeffrey Ravn, "Moving Parts: Modular Architecture in a Flat World," (presentation at Greenbuild International Conference and Expo, Washington, DC, 2015).

66 Andrew Van Damm, "Detailed data show the value of land under homes across the country," Economic Policy, *Washington Post*, January 23, 2019, https://www.washingtonpost.com/us-policy/2019/01/23/why-its-problem-that-dirt-brooklyn-is-so-much-more-expensive-than-dirt-arkansas/. Article excerpts data from the Federal Housing Finance Agency for the period 2012–2017.

67 "Construction Costs," New York Building Congress, February 2019, https://www.buildingcongress.com/advocacy-and-reports/reports-and-analysis/construction-outlook-update/Construction-Costs.html.

68 Construction costs and land values were based on data from the Lincoln Institute.

69 Moses Gates, Sarah Serpas, Kellan Cantrell and Ben Oldenburg, "Creating more affordable housing in New York City's high-rise areas," Regional Plan Association, February 2018, https://rpa.org/uploads/pdfs/RPA-12-FAR.pdf.

70 William Larson, Jessica Shui, Morris Davis and Stephen Oliner, "Working Paper 19-01: The Price of Residential Land for Countries, ZIP codes, Census Tracts in the United States," Federal Housing Finance Agency, last modified February, 2020, https://www.fhfa.gov/PolicyProgramsResearch/Research/PaperDocuments/wp1901.pdf. Note that this data is for land zoned for single-family development. Due to lack of similar data for land zoned for multi-story development we are using this as a proxy.

71 [Project name withheld] Modular Study Summary Report, July 2009, Appendix II, Modular Cost Estimate. In 2009 the modular cost was $193/SF and the on-site cost was $156 for a total of $349/SF.

72 [Project name withheld], Appendix II, Modular Cost Estimate.

73 The "Cost Estimate for Student Housing Project New York City" prepared in 2009/Q3, and the façade manufacturer's cost study for Asian manufacturing prepared in 2010/Q1 are escalated to 2015 dollars to align with costs in Figures 7.13 and 7.14. For U.S. construction cost escalation, see https://www.rsmeansonline.com/references/unit/refpdf/hci.pdf For Asian inflation, see https://www.macrotrends.net/countries/EAS/east-asia-pacific/inflation-rate-cpi

74 [Project name withheld], "Cost Estimate for Student Housing Project New York City," March 2010. In 2010, the cost was $80/SF. East Asian inflation was negative during the period 2010–2015, so adjusted for inflation the 2015 cost was $78/SF.

75 Peter Andrew, "Is Your House the 'Typical American Home'?" HSH, last modified January 26, 2020, https://www.hsh.com/homeowner/average-american-home.html.

76 "Sustainable Management of Construction and Demolition Materials," EPA, accessed June 24, 2020, https://www.epa.gov/smm/sustainable-management-construction-and-demolition-materials.

77 Fernanda Cruz Rios and David Grau, "Circular Economy in the Built Environment: Designing, Deconstructing, and Leasing Reusable Products," *Reference Module in Materials Science and Engineering* (2019): 7. doi:10.1016/B978-0-12-803581-8.11494-8.

78 Based on high-rise student housing project. Percentages will vary from project to project.

8 Innovators, Entrenched Interests, and Early Adopters

Just after the New Year in 2008, a few weeks after GBM switched off the lights, I began work on a house for the CEO of a global industrial corporation headquartered in mid-town Manhattan. In our first meeting, seated at one end of a polished boardroom table, I presented a rough dollar per square foot budget based on the level of quality one would expect for high-end residential construction in suburban New York. My numbers, squarely within the range of similar houses recently built nearby, were met with a noticeable lack of enthusiasm. My client, a sophisticated European, aspired to a well-designed modern house built with good materials and excellent craftsmanship, comfortable for his family and appropriately scaled for entertaining. He had previously been through the experience of designing and building a house in northern Europe, where residential construction costs are comparatively low, and he was shocked to hear that the cost of his new home would be roughly double the cost of his previous one. I then recommended that he hold a contingency fund in reserve for changes would inevitably occur during construction—some of that contingency to cover unanticipated conditions that would inevitably arise, and some to allow for upgrades and enhancements that he and his family would surely want once the emotional investment in building a home took hold. Enthusiasm dropped another notch at the news that I could not guarantee cost at this early stage in the process.

Our discussion turned to schedule. My client stated, with insistence, that the house must be completed by September of the following year, 21 months away. Impossible, I thought. Eighteen months for construction of this large and complex house, minimum. I took a piece of paper and drew a timeline. Design: six months. Permits: simultaneous with design. I added the 18-month segment of the timeline for construction and said that completion would be in January, 24 months out under the best of circumstances. A perfectly reasonable, if blunt, statement—who could argue? The numbers were simple, and my client did not refute my arithmetic. He simply picked up the pencil, crossed out January, and made an X on the timeline to mark September, three months earlier, as the completion date.

I knew right away that I needed to get us back on course, so I followed my instinct and did the only thing possible under the circumstances. I doubled down. I pulled out another piece of paper and drew a triangle. I wrote SCOPE in the center, and I labeled each corner: COST/TIME/QUALITY. I pushed the paper over to my now clearly annoyed client and said, "I call this the iron triangle of construction. If we keep the size of your house constant, you can choose to control any two of the other three".[1]

8.1
The iron triangle of construction.

My client simply took the pencil from my hand and drew a big X through my iron triangle. He was having none of it. "Your industry can't possibly be that backwards", he said. "Haven't you heard of Six Sigma? In my industry we control cost, time *and* quality".

Six Sigma. That was shorthand for the maximum acceptable number of product or process defects, 3.4 per million opportunities, a metric developed by Motorola in the 1980s to set a benchmark for their production quality standard. Six Sigma has since evolved into a kind of cult of quality, a veritable martial art of quality. There are, in fact, certifications like Six Sigma Black Belt and Six Sigma Master, high achievements that a mere Six Sigma grasshopper aspires to attain. Six Sigma Ninjas are the commandos of corporate quality control.

There are five phases to a Six Sigma quality control process:

> Define: define the problem, improvement activity, opportunity for improvement, the project goals, and customer (internal and external) requirements.
> Measure process performance.
> Analyze the process to determine root causes of variation and poor performance (defects).
> Improve process performance by addressing and eliminating the root causes.
> Control the improved process and future process performance.[2]

Six Sigma is one of several data-driven and analytical systems for industrial quality control. Around the same time as Six Sigma, Toyota introduced an approach they call kaizen, literally translated as "improvement", but understood in context to mean "continuous improvement". In kaizen, the worker is empowered to make small improvements on the factory floor, and when kaizen culture takes root, incremental improvements aggregate and compound geometrically into large-scale improvements.

In kaizen, the question "why" is repeated five times until the root cause of a problem is identified. For example:

> Why did the machine stop?
> There was an overload, and the fuse blew.
> Why was there an overload?
> The bearing was not sufficiently lubricated.
> Why was it not lubricated sufficiently?
> The lubrication pump was not pumping sufficiently.
> Why was it not pumping sufficiently?
> The shaft of the pump was worn and rattling.
> Why was the shaft worn out?
> There was no strainer attached, and metal scrap got in.[3]

While Six Sigma and kaizen are very different and, notably, are culturally distinctive—one is hierarchical, based on a top-down management approach, while the other is horizontal, collaborative, and locally implemented—what they both have in common is this: they are only possible only where processes have been standardized so that improvement in quality, speed, and cost can be achieved iteratively under controlled conditions. They have little resemblance, in other words, to the architect's studio or to the construction site, where each building "re-invents the wheel" and you only get one chance to master each step in the process.

• • •

In the following pages, we'll look back to the origins of interchangeable parts manufacturing and the emergence of industrial quality control 250 years ago. We'll see the resistance of vested interests pitted against disruptive innovation as artisans struggle to retain economic privilege in the face of technological change. We'll note striking parallels between the 18th-century artisanal workshop production and the 21st-century construction industry (and the mid-20th-century shipping industry). Returning to the present, we'll then look at aspects of contemporary construction—declining productivity, archaic trade jurisdictions, and the challenges of job-site safety, all of which contribute to the excessive cost of urban housing. Innovation seems to have been perpetually waiting in the wings. Why has construction been so resistant to change? What is the current state of research and development in construction? To what degree is investment capital flowing into innovative construction technology?

Interchangeable Parts

Honoré Blanc, a French gunsmith, was central to the eventual shift from artisanal workshop production to manufacturing. As an official working for the French army from 1763 until his death in 1801, he perfected a novel method of musket assembly from interchangeable parts. In today's jargon, Blanc's method was truly disruptive. It so threatened the artisanal class that it was suppressed for a generation by the guilds in a clash over political influence. While rational systems and standardization were inherent to hierarchical command-and-control military culture, for the artisans, standardization and technical oversight were an unacceptable infringement on deeply rooted customs and prerogatives. The struggle over control of the workshop turned out to be far more intractable than the comparatively straightforward technical challenge of interchangeable parts manufacturing.

Ken Alder, a historian of technology, has shown through a close examination of late 18th- and early 19th-century French arms manufacture how societal and cultural factors can influence the arc of technological change.[4] He coined the phrase "technological amnesia" to explain the repression of

Blanc's invention of interchangeable parts manufacturing, which was entirely forgotten by the French for a generation. Interchangeable parts manufacturing is popularly associated with Eli Whitney, but Whitney merely capitalized on Blanc's technical achievements, which he learned of through a French pamphlet passed along to him by Thomas Jefferson. Decades later, when "the American system of manufacture" found its way to France, the French had no recollection that it was their invention in the first place.[5]

The military "is the ideal form towards which a purely mechanical system of industry must tend",[6] Lewis Mumford once wrote. Military engineers under Louis XVI were steeped in principles of rational organization, uniformity, and administrative efficiency. Advances in the design and manufacture of artillery, the introduction of mathematics and physics into military education, and the effort to standardize musket production[7] were largely driven by French officers. The military, under the authority of the king, wished to impose its doctrine of mechanical efficiency on artisanal gunsmiths. The new model for musket manufacturing, based on artillery engineering, required transparency and rational standards of measurement for technical knowledge to be shared. The new technique of mechanical drawing, or in Denis Diderot's words, the "geometry of the workshop",[8] was the means by which musket manufacturing standards were to be disseminated.

The officer-engineers who oversaw arms procurement established a corps of inspectors, or "controllers", who were charged with enforcing military standards on artisanal muskets. The controllers inspected gunlocks[9] and other components of muskets, and they could withhold payment for substandard work. However, the controllers were corruptible, and officials sought better oversight. In 1763, Blanc—at 27 already a highly regarded gunsmith—was named chief controller of the French armories. He was to be the instrument through whom the engineers would root out corruption and achieve their goal of standardized musket production.

One of the technical problems Blanc faced, which is hard to imagine from our perspective 250 years later, was how to disseminate a standard set of dimensions and profiles among a group of disparate workshops where fiercely independent artisans resented any imposition on their autonomy. Drawings turned out to be insufficient. The abstraction of mechanical drawing could not convey the three-dimensional and operational complexity of a musket gunlock. To supplement drawings, Blanc created a master set of exquisitely crafted jigs, templates, and gauges, copies of which were distributed to the workshops. The precision jigs and templates greatly reduced the element of variation introduced by hand-held tools guided by the artisan. With jigs, the worker's hand might supply the necessary pressure (later supplanted by mechanical power) but the jig ensured that the tool could only move along a predetermined path. The gauges were then used to determine if the result was within acceptable tolerances.[10] The "workmanship of certainty"[11] was to supplant artisanal autonomy.

The independent armorers under Blanc's authority were obliged to accept his patterns, and much of Blanc's work as the chief controller entailed visits to the workshops to ensure that the patterns were being faithfully and properly used. With jigs, a much less skilled and lower paid worker could perform the same task that previously only a highly skilled craftsman could accomplish, and with their skill devalued, the leading artisans could no longer command premium prices.

By 1790, Blanc had advanced beyond jigs, having perfected a method of manufacturing muskets using interchangeable parts. He hoped to win a contract to supply vast quantities of muskets to the army of the new French Republic. Blanc convened a group of distinguished military and government elites at the Hotel des Invalides in Paris to witness a demonstration. Gunlocks comprised 26 separate parts, all which had to work together with the precision of a watch. To dramatize his breakthrough, Blanc filled a row of 26 buckets, one for each type of part, and randomly selected one part from each bucket. Like a magician performing a difficult trick before a skeptical audience, he assembled several working gunlocks. The French brass, who regarded the manufacture of muskets as a hand-crafted, one-off process—even if controlled by jigs—immediately grasped the implications of Blanc's method. Not only would quality standards be predictable, but replacement parts could be stocked to quickly repair damaged or malfunctioning muskets. Costs would come down. The workshops could be re-organized and divided for more efficient manufacture of identical parts. A skilled and therefore highly paid artisan would no longer be needed to carry out a final fitting process, a heretofore critical task. Production would accelerate. Perhaps most important was that pricing could also be standardized, based on a time/task analysis for each part. Transactions would be transparent.

The state-employed French technical-managerial class advocated for interchangeable part manufacturing. The artisans, of course, did not share management's enthusiasm and jealously guarded their right as private entrepreneurs to set prices and production schedules. Their autonomy was being undermined by the application of rational management principles.

The traditions of artisanal production were deeply intertwined with economic transactions, social relations, and kinship. As Alder shows, in a town like St. Etienne, the center of French arms manufacturing, armorers and the merchants who sold their products, as well as the negociants who sold the armorers raw materials, were neighbors and may often have been relatives, bound by blood or by marriage. At times, roles may have overlapped. Among artisans, there was a respected hierarchy of master, journeyman, and apprentice, and among merchants and negociants, status accrued with success and wealth.[12] Blanc's method was a revolution and posed a clear and present danger to the established order.

Bureaucratic infighting between two high-ranking officers determined the fate of interchangeable parts. François Marie d'Aboville stood with the engineer-managers and rational manufacturing; Jacques-Bassilien Gassendi aligned himself with the guilds. Gassendi prevailed, and by 1806 had silenced the last hold-outs who supported Blanc's method. Napoleon threw his support behind the guilds as he moved to consolidate power. Interchangeable parts manufacturing was discredited and forgotten by the French arms industry for a generation, later to be taken up and re-introduced by Eli Whitney.[13]

The erasure of Blanc's innovation resonates with the history of modular and prefab housing in the 20th century. Take, for example, the epic dismantling of the Lustron Corporation by an enraged Congress in 1950, a debacle that undoubtedly contributed to a half-century or more of technological amnesia about industrialized housing. The stigma of the Lustron affair left a long-lasting mark, and nothing comparable to Lustron's million-square-foot factory able to produce 100 houses a day has since been proposed. A confluence of hostile interests, crusading politicians, and a cynical press shut down the Lustron plant despite the fact that production was ramping up and prospects were promising. Yet, the resurgence of interest in modular architecture over the last decade is evidence that technological amnesia may be in remission.

Construction Productivity in Decline

It might come as a surprise, but productivity in the U.S. construction industry has declined since the 1960s, according to Paul Teicholz, a professor of engineering at Stanford University. Meanwhile, during the period from 1964 to 2012, non-farm industrial productivity rose 150 percent. Construction productivity since 1964 has declined about 20 percent, for a comparative decline of about 170 percent. There is no reason to think that these trends have changed since 2012. The major underlying causes identified by Teicholz remain firmly entrenched, including "fragmented process for procuring a project" and "inefficient use of labor at site".[14] The divergence between industrial and construction productivity means that each year a dollar of construction purchases less and less building in terms of quality or quantity relative to manufactured goods. It is true that new materials, labor saving equipment, and information technology are being brought to bear at the construction site—but these innovations do not seem to be making a significant dent in the trend, and are at best a holding action.

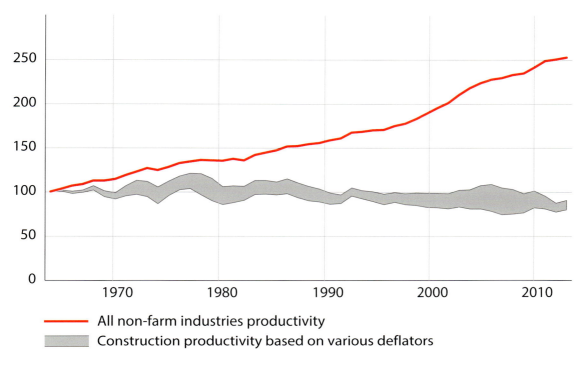

──── All non-farm industries productivity

░░░░ Construction productivity based on various deflators

8.2
Construction labor
productivity, 1964–2012 the
bottom curve represents
a range of C30 (Bureau
of Labor Statistics/Value
of Construction in Place)
figures based on various
deflators[15] 1964 = 100.
Source: Project Production
Institute.

Did you ever pass by a building site and hear the racket of jackhammers pounding away at concrete? It almost always means that something had been done wrong and now must be chipped away, broken up, or cut through. It might have been due to a measurement error or maybe a coordination oversight. Sometimes, a jackhammer is a little too crude, and a diamond-bit drill cores out a hole for piping to pass through—a sound more like a low-pitched dentist's drill. Whenever you hear concrete being pulverized, it is a sign that productivity is in trouble.

On a large-scale construction project, the work must be divided into dozens of specialties. Each is the province of a subcontractor, who on a union project is to a great extent at the mercy of the trade union that "owns" the work in question. In New York City, there are unions for ironworkers (who erect structural steel), lathers (who fabricate steel reinforcement for concrete), steam fitters (plumbers who work on heating and cooling systems)... and the list goes on to include some 60 or more trade locals.[16] When new technology is introduced into the construction process, a power struggle to "claim" the work ensues, with a history of claims dating back to the late 19th century when entirely new structural materials and technologies were first introduced and did not fit traditional trade categories.

New York City is generally considered the most recalcitrant of union towns, and perhaps it is not entirely fair to use New York to represent construction practices throughout the country, but to varying degrees the division of labor and disputes over trade jurisdiction are endemic to construction everywhere. New York is a useful example if only because the tendencies are so exaggerated that the irrationality of contemporary construction based on the fragmentation of trades is that much easier to see.

With the advent of steel and reinforced concrete, along with the introduction of elevators, new building techniques led to a scramble by the various trades to control the work and reap the economic reward. In 1903, a collective bargaining agreement was drawn up, meant to end years of bitter factional fighting, called The New York Plan for Settlement of Jurisdictional Disputes. The New York Plan became an institution, consulted and amended year after year, and is still the touchstone for New York construction trade labor arbitration. The precedents embodied in more than a century of decisions are cited to resolve contemporary disputes over which trade should perform which task, disputes that frequently erupt in the middle of construction. The time it takes to find a resolution can slow down or even stop progress at the job site.

The logic of The New York Plan decisions is often convoluted. The trades who are competing for jurisdiction will each argue that they are the ones with the skills and the tools to best handle a task—for example, electricians, with good reason, claim the installation of light fixtures. Carpenters will argue, with justification, that they are best suited to handle finish work such as the installation of the suspended ceiling systems that are ubiquitous in contemporary commercial construction. It has been enshrined in The New York Plan for some time that carpenters install the ceiling suspension grid and panels, and electricians install the light fixtures. But who installs the lens that completes the light fixture and integrates it with the finished appearance of the ceiling? The ensuing arguments are almost Talmudic. The electricians win lens installation. The system works well enough, until the next new situation arises that doesn't so neatly fit categories of ceiling, fixture, and lens.

For the new offices of a Wall Street law firm, an architect specified a technically innovative translucent plastic membrane ceiling that diffuses the light cast by the light fixtures mounted 12 inches above the membrane. Should the membrane be considered a light fixture lens? What defines a lens? Does a lens need to be directly supported by the light fixture? The carpenters claimed that the membrane ceiling is not a lens. They said it is simply a ceiling. The electricians made their counterclaim, perhaps believing that because the photons emitted by their light fixtures would pass through the translucent membrane 12 inches away, they, like toll collectors on a bridge, should collect the wages for its installation. The work stops. The arbitrators gathered the disputants before them. Arguments were presented in solemn tones. The New York Plan was scoured for precedents. Although the carpenters have been highly trained by the manufacturer in the technique of heating the membrane to cause it to shrink and stretch tight while leaving it clean and fingerprint-free, the arbitrator decided that this innovative product is by precedent a lens, and therefore the work belonged to the electricians.[17] A month later, on appeal, that decision was reversed, and the work was awarded to the carpenters.[18]

In a trendy and expensive downtown condominium, an architect specified electrically heated towel bars. Lacking a New York Plan precedent for heated towel bars, the precedent for unheated towel bars was consulted. Who installs? Plumbers, of course. (Here is the logic: towel bars are in bathrooms; toilets are in bathrooms; plumbers install toilets, ergo, plumbers install towel bars. Somewhere along the way the carpenters and tile setters lost out, each of whom could have, based on their skills, made an equally cogent case for towel bars.) Electricians, naturally, install electrical devices, and since the heated towel bars were wired, the electricians made their claim. With kingly wisdom, the arbitrator decreed that the installation of the towel supporting element—the bar—would be done by the plumbers, whereas the installation of the towel heating element concealed within the bar would be done by the electricians.[19] The electricians, perhaps sensing that the absurdity of two-trade towel bar installation would not hold up under closer scrutiny, filed for appeal and six weeks later won the exclusive right to install.[20]

The two foregoing cases were selected almost at random from decisions and appeals over an 18-month period on matters solely concerning electricians, plumbers, and carpenters. Trade union arbitration in New York City is itself a minor industry. While it's easy to poke fun at the perpetual scrum of union jurisdictional disputes, the arbitration process does provide a forum for people with clashing interests to resolve their differences. The absurdity of the arrangement is accepted with a New York shrug simply to get on with the high-stakes business of construction.

But at the heart of the productivity problem is the proliferation and increasing technical sophistication of manufactured building components that blur the boundaries between what were formerly discreet building trades. A modern building is no longer crafted at the job site from raw materials—it is an amalgam of low-tolerance site construction and high-tolerance industrial products, awkwardly joined.

In product manufacturing, the design of the process is inextricable from the design of the product. The industrial designer works with the process engineer to develop an integrated solution that meets the requirements of performance, aesthetics, and production economy. The process/product is taken through iterative stages of development, first as a prototype, and eventually as a production run. Lessons learned in production are then fed back into the process/product cycle. Cumulative cycles lead to advances that increasingly add value to the product, by improving performance, reducing costs, and increasing efficiency. Every new product is perfected through iteration after iteration. When high value-added products arrive at the construction site, with multiple trade jurisdictions, who determines the process? At the construction site, the role of process engineer is up for grabs, and at last resort, it is assumed by the trade labor arbitrator.

Will the tradition-bound world of the construction trades come to terms with an entirely new way of assembling buildings with VUCs? In 19th-century France, the guilds resisted technical progress with political power, but the productivity and transparency that interchangeable parts brought to musket manufacturing ensured that the new method would eventually prevail. Unions, as did the guilds before them, always fight a rear-guard action against change. Construction, like work along the waterfront, has ancient roots and traditions. Yet as much as we may cherish tradition and honor precedent, stagnant productivity in construction, decade after decade, is unsustainable. The longshoremen's unions were eventually undone by the unsentimental economics of Malcom McLean's corrugated steel box. Is construction finally ready for technological change?

The New Housing Assembly Process

Can assembly line methods be used to "manufacture" a high-rise building from VUCs at the job site? The Levitts were able to achieve something approaching assembly line efficiency with their 27-step process for building wood-frame houses. Levittown was built on a horizontal site. Is there anything fundamentally different about going vertical?

The intermodal modular building site will be different from a conventional construction site. Constructing an intermodal high-rise will be more akin to assembly than to construction. Stacking, bolting, and stitching VUCs will require a new set of technical skills. The intermodal modular construction force will be craning modules into place and making structural connections, as is traditionally done by operating engineers and ironworkers, but with the finesse and care required in the handling of a finished product. There will be no reason for the standard division of trades. Beam stitching (the interior bolting of VUCs along mate-lines) has more in common with the installation of plumbing fixtures in a finished bathroom than with traditional ironwork. A highly trained modular technician should be able to make structural connections and plumbing connections equally as well. The job site should be understood an extension of the factory, and a modular assembly crew with a sense of ownership of the entire on-site process would foster quality control practices like kaizen.

The unions, like the guilds before them, will face a choice: embrace the changes that intermodal modular will bring to the construction site, re-tool and re-organize, or obstruct innovation. For a while, they may cede conventional construction to lower paid non-union workers who are a steadily increasing share of the workforce,[21] but that will only forestall the inevitable. By committing to a new union job site that embraces industrial quality control principles instead of archaic practices, that values systems integration over trade disputes, and that has a stakeholder's investment in the success of the enterprise, the unions could secure preferred status on projects using intermodal modular construction.

Unions need not—should not—be weakened. With real gains in productivity, which means shifting 70–80 percent of the work to factories, wages can remain high. As today's high-tech longshoremen would attest, a strong union can co-exist with technical progress and productivity. There may be fewer on-site construction jobs in intermodal modular housing, but more projects will be economically viable—smaller slices, but more pies. With robotics and advanced manufacturing technology, the factory workforce will be small, but highly skilled. This is no different from the changes that have been re-shaping American manufacturing for decades.

One thing must be insisted upon—there can be no division of trades and no jurisdictional disputes. Modular technicians will have to agree to belong to one union, and that is the same union whether in the factory or at the site. As part of the bargain, intermodal modular enterprises will have to offer the union board representation, as is common in Germany and as was recently proposed for U.S. corporate governance by Elizabeth Warren.[22] Labor's interests must be aligned with management's.

The legacy modular manufacturers are no model for labor organization. In the legacy modular plants, the workforce is drawn from the same pool of ironworkers, carpenters, plumbers, and electricians as those who carry out the work at a building site. Those trades can be just as resistant to systematic procedures in a factory as at the building site. During a visit to one such plant, I learned that the plumbers insisted on varying the way that they installed the piping in a series of identical bathrooms that were set up in a row on the factory floor. Bored by repetition, the plumbers made the day go by faster by arranging the pipes a little bit differently each time. While we can acknowledge that there is a place for individual autonomy and agency in the industrial workplace—a topic that is beyond the scope of this book—there are larger issues to address. We have an urgent and unmet need for housing, which means that we need more productivity and better quality for less money. In that context, the plumber's insistence on variation is gratuitous.

We need to go further, in fact. The benefits of modularity should be implemented at every stage of the process. The cutting and fitting of piping, the unspooling and connecting of electrical cable, and other methods inherited from construction have no place in the VUC assembly plant. Plumbing, wiring, HVAC, and other components should be manufactured as plug-and-play components by supply chain partners.

For example, prefabricated "wet wall" units, integrating multiple trades—plumbing, tile, fixtures, even electrically heated towel bars—should arrive at the assembly plant ready to insert into the VUC. Ceiling "cassettes" integrating fan coil units, fire sprinklers, and light fixtures should be similarly componentized. Scale and standardization are required, but that doesn't mean that every apartment design from now on needs to be identical. We don't want vertical Levittowns. It does mean that the design of the parts must be governed by a set of dimensional rules, along the same lines as European kitchen systems. Bathroom wet walls, ceiling cassettes, and similar integrated components can be produced in varied series and still be manufactured with common subcomponents. The VUC, with its dimensional standards and addressable grid, is set up for variation in design while achieving economies of scale.

Before concluding this section, a few remarks on job-site safety are in order. The inefficiency of construction is starkly illustrated by statistics on construction injuries and fatalities and is reflected in the high cost of workers' compensation insurance claims.[23] Most construction management firms, acutely aware of the human and financial costs of accidents, make job-site safety a paramount concern. But no matter how diligent a safety program is implemented and enforced, building sites are inherently dangerous places to work—far more dangerous than factories. In a factory, the work is performed indoors at floor level, obviously reducing the likelihood of injury from a fall. Safe materials management methods along with good lighting, safety striping, and other measures reduce the likelihood of accidental contact with equipment and objects. Ergonomically designed equipment and workstations reduce the likelihood of overexertion. By shifting most of the work to a factory, resources diverted to excessive workers' compensation premiums can be put to better use, and the human cost of injury and death at the construction site can be minimized.

Innovation

Innovation requires the commitment of resources to imagine, design, engineer, prototype, test, and evaluate new ideas. An enterprise that funds its own research and development must generate enough surplus revenue to spend it without expectation of an immediate return on investment. Profit margins in the construction sector are thin, and research and development funding in construction is scarce. Among architecture firms, it is all but non-existent.

How does the construction sector compare with other industries in R&D spending? R&D intensity, which is the ratio of research and development spending to revenue, is one of the metrics used for assessing innovation. Among the world's largest publicly listed corporate R&D spenders, average R&D intensity was 4.5 percent in 2018. Of 24 industrial sectors worldwide, the top three sectors in R&D intensity were Technology at 31.3 percent, Pharmaceuticals & Biotechnology at 18.7 percent, and Automobiles and Components at 16.8 percent, together representing two-thirds of the total. Construction, Real Estate & Engineering has an R&D intensity of 1.7 percent.[24]

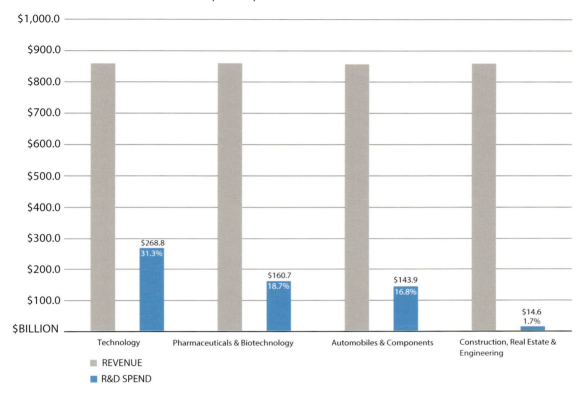

8.3
R&D intensity comparison research & development in construction compared to top three industrial sectors. Note that while all four sectors have comparable revenue, R&D spending in construction is a fraction of the other three.
Source: Idea to value.[25]

In 2018, $14.6 billion in total was spent on construction R&D among the companies on the Global Innovation 1000[26] list. Of that, Chinese enterprises account for $11.12 billion. China is outspending the U.S. in construction R&D by more than 18 times.[27]

R&D intensity doesn't tell the whole story, however. Innovation is not simply a matter of how much is spent on R&D—it matters how strategically that spending is used. An annual survey by the consulting firm Strategy& (formerly Booz & Company) looks at "high-leverage" innovators and finds that the companies that are the most successful innovators, as measured by growth and profitability, had lower R&D intensities than their industry as a whole. Strategy& identifies six key characteristics shared by high-leverage innovators:

1. They closely align innovation strategy with business strategy.
2. They create company-wide cultural support for innovation.
3. Their top leadership is highly involved with the innovation program.

4. They base innovation on direct insights from end users.
5. They rigorously control project selection early in the innovation process.
6. They excel at each of these first five characteristics and have been able to integrate them to create unique customer experiences that can transform their market.[28]

High-leverage innovators make innovation central to every aspect of business. It is not a luxury option. It drives everything that the company does, at every level.

Investment in innovative construction enterprises, including a few modular start-ups, has sharply accelerated in recent years. As reported by the Wall Street Journal, "venture investment in private construction-technology companies leaped to $6.1 billion in 2018, from $352.1 million in 2016".[29] Based on the first six months, the WSJ projected even greater investment in 2019. While this tells us that innovative companies are suddenly being funded, the WSJ does not indicate how much of this funding is allocated to R&D. We will have to assume that R&D funding associated with this surge is reflected in the Global Innovation 1000 data for 2018 cited above. From that, might we conclude that R&D intensity in construction has not been significantly affected, and that much of this investment has been put to other uses?

One example is Katerra, a construction start-up founded by former tech executives, which had raised $2 billion by the end of 2018 and used it to acquire manufacturers, contractors, and A/E (architecture/engineering) firms, creating a large vertically integrated construction enterprise focused on a new method of heavy timber prefabrication. The theory behind Katerra's massive acquisition is that by consolidating the entire design, manufacturing, and construction process under one roof, they will have the ability to squeeze out inefficiencies that afflict each operation, as well as inefficiencies in the fragmented project delivery chain. So far, the results have not been convincing. There were stumbles mastering the prefabrication of cross-laminated timber structural panels, unrealistically low-cost estimates that proved illusory and resulted in projects losing money, failure to deliver projects on schedule, and dubious interlocking owner/customer relationships of the kind that led to the collapse of WeWork.[30] (Both Katerra and WeWork were financed by SoftBank, which itself has imploded.) It's too early to know if these missteps are the result of growing pains or if there is a more fundamental flaw in the company's strategy. Katerra is operating at scale, has significant financial resources, and with a proven executive team may be able to right the ship.

Still, even if Katerra rights the ship, they may be headed in the wrong direction. Simply spending massive sums on acquisition of technology does not mean that Katerra is innovating. Katerra's top-down, command-and-control culture is oddly out of touch with our contemporary open-source, collaborative, and horizontal world.[31] The future of modular architecture will hinge on whether the cultural, political, and social forces that stymied innovation in the past can be overcome. It will require the participation of diverse stakeholders committed to innovation at all levels. The emergent discipline of "design thinking" is far better suited for that kind of challenge than the top-down approach.

Design Thinking

Design thinking is a branch of knowledge that grew out of a critique of systems analysis. It had become clear by the late 1960s that certain challenges—poverty, crime, the environment, urban planning, to name several—could not be acted upon effectively through conventional methods of analytical problem solving. The premise of the analytical approach is that it's possible to identify all relevant factors, prescribe measures that address those factors, execute those measures, and thereby achieve a satisfactory and stable solution. In a seminal paper, Dilemmas in a General Theory of Planning, a professor of design, Horst W. Rittel and an urban planner, Melvin M. Webber, dismantled the linear analytical model. They coined the phrase "wicked problems", not because a problem happens to be bad or evil but to describe a class of problems that are too open-ended to allow for a definitive or comprehensive understanding.

The solving of a wicked problem might never stop. In Rittel and Weber's words, wicked problem solving "should be based on a model of planning as an argumentative process in the course of which an image of the problem and of the solution emerges gradually among the participants, as a product of incessant judgment, subjected to critical argument".[32] Wicked problems are not solved; they are endlessly "re-solved". Purely technical problems, by contrast, are "tame problems" in which there is a finite, or determinate, solution that is objectively verifiable. Wicked problems have indeterminate solutions because there is no yes/no answer, only a spectrum of possibilities, all involving trade-offs. Most design problems are indeterminate and are therefore wicked problems.

The nature of wicked problems is such that any solution produces unanticipated effects that ripple beyond the problem's boundary, or defined frame of reference. Dealing with wicked problems starts with an understanding of that boundary. For example, in the name of economic development, Syracuse, NY (like many cities during the 1950s and early 1960s) built interstate highways to alleviate traffic congestion and improve traffic flow. The analytical model went something like this: (A) the goal was economic improvement; (B) the analysis concluded that time spent in traffic was holding back business development; therefore, (C) the solution was to build elevated highways to move people to, from, and within the city more rapidly. Planners failed to recognize the consequences that would occur outside of the problem's boundary, or that there was even a boundary at all. As a result of highway construction, neighborhoods were decimated, and those who were able to afford it used the new interstate to leave the city and commuted from the suburbs. The city's population shrank, its economy declined, and tax revenue dropped. A cycle of urban poverty was set in motion.[33] It's fair to say that the planners who designed the highway had none of this in mind at the time,[34] and within a systems analysis framework, they would not have understood the problem any differently.[35] The planners mistook a wicked problem for a tame problem.

Design thinking is a practice for dealing with wicked problems. Out of the universe of possibilities, no two designers will arrive at the same solution, and it is impossible to say that one designer's solution is right and another's is wrong. It can only be said that one is better or worse than the other in particular aspects. Design thinking has evolved into a methodology, which has been codified as:

1. Empathize. Design is a form of social action. Engaging (or imagining) the end user and understanding the nature of the problem come before technical or aesthetic decisions are made.
2. Define. Using the insights gained in step one, form a conceptual framework. Because each designer brings their "world-view", acquired from schooling and experience, each designer's conceptual framework will be different. (For this reason, design thinking, as a mode of knowledge, is entirely unlike scientific knowledge.)
3. Ideate. Synthesize multiple solutions while knowledge continues to be gathered and processed. The first attempts are generally messy. Iterate until one or more solutions are ready to pursue to the next stage.
4. Prototype. Create a working model of the proposed solution or solutions. This doesn't have to be sophisticated, at least at first. It can start as a crude mock-up.
5. Test. Subject the prototype(s) to real-world users. If necessary, go back to previous steps and reiterate. Or, go on to...
6. Implement.[36]

Each stage is conceptually clear and at the same time open-ended. Together, these stages form a general armature that can support an infinity of particulars. There is no rule that requires linear progression, and designers might find themselves skipping forward or stepping backward. The boundaries between stages may at times blur. What this rubric provides is a language that helps the designer reflect on the design process.

Innovation itself is a wicked problem because it is indeterminate. Innovation requires an imagining of possibilities that do not yet exist, of needs that users may not yet be aware of, and of ramifications and ripple effects that cannot reliably be predicted. Intermodal modular architecture will be an ongoing innovation project that over time will evolve, grow, and respond to the needs of users and stakeholders. It must be a collaborative endeavor.

In the next two chapters, we'll explore aspects of intermodal modular architecture and open-source collaboration that will thrive on design thinking as a continual process of *re*solution and ideation. The organic growth of intermodal modular architecture will happen on a horizontal, non-hierarchical field where multiple contributors will "write the code", as it were, of a new global vernacular. Intermodal modular architecture, like the internet itself, will be "an architecture that possesses a center of gravity, but which allow[s] loose networks of soloists to collaborate".[37]

PRINCIPLE # 10   DESIGN THINKING

Breaking the Iron Triangle

We have trapped ourselves in an iron triangle on a global scale, of which the three rigidly fixed sides are the growing economies of the developing world, climate change, and the aspirations of a worldwide middle class. We are trapped, not because the iron triangle is in any sense real, but because our assumptions about boundaries are false. As Paul Romer has written:

> Every generation has perceived the limits to growth that finite resources and undesirable side effects would pose if no new recipes or ideas were discovered. And every generation has underestimated the potential for finding new recipes and ideas. We consistently fail to grasp how many ideas remain to be discovered. Possibilities do not add up. They multiply.[38]

We often hear, for example, that the recent and rapid growth of emergent economies, especially China, is the cause of American wage decline. Economist Joseph Stiglitz, who has been an outspoken critic of policies that exacerbate economic inequality, rejects the view that globalization, liberal trade policies, and technology are to blame. Steiglitz has dismissed these ideas as "self-serving ignorant falsehoods".[39] The solution to American wage inequality, as Stiglitz has pointed out, lies in policies that address the root problems in areas such as taxation and investment in education and infrastructure.

In the previous chapter, we showed that a globalized intermodal modular industry and a solution to climate change go hand in hand. Location efficiency, i.e. dense vertical urbanism, is key to that solution. The challenge is to bring the cost of generously scaled apartments in high-rise buildings down to a point where middle-class families can be attracted back to cities. The manufacture of VUCs is a means to an equitable and affordable urbanism and at the same time to a significant reduction in GHG emissions.

Will VUCs be manufactured in the U.S., or will they be manufactured in low-labor-cost countries like China? It depends. To drive down the cost of manufacturing in the U.S., there will need to be significant investment in advanced manufacturing technology. With adequate investment, we could become exporters of urban housing to cities in Asia, South America, and eventually Africa. Or, an offshore intermodal modular manufacturer could leverage low manufacturing costs to sell into high-construction-cost U.S. markets, primarily in our densely developed and prosperous coastal cities. Under that scenario, investment in technology may take longer but eventually a technically advanced plant in the U.S. would be viable. The long game, in which intermodal modular manufacturing becomes a U.S. export industry, is where time and global trends may be favorable.

The zero-sum worldview—the iron triangle—holds that we cannot have a solution to climate change without damaging the American economy, that overseas manufacturing is the cause of American wage inequality, and that the aspirations of a growing global middle class require us to erect trade barriers to protect our standard of living. If dense urban development is central to sustainability and if intermodal modular architecture for multi-story urban buildings is both scalable and cost-effective, then a global intermodal modular industry can change the zero-sum equation. We must simply apply to buildings what industries that have broken the iron triangle have long known how to do, and harness an interchangeable parts architecture to designing, manufacturing, and assembling livable cities.

Notes

1 Stephen Kieran and James Timberlake, *Refabricating Architecture* (New York and London: McGraw-Hill, 2004), 8–9. In *Refabricating Architecture*, Kieran and Timberlake state this proposition as an equation: Quality × Scope = Cost × Time.
2 "The Define, Measure, Analyze, Improve, Control (DMAIC) Process," ASQ, accessed June 23, 2020, https://asq.org/quality-resources/dmaic.
3 "Lean Thinking and Methods – Kaizen," EPA, last modified September 12, 2019, https://www.epa.gov/sustainability/lean-thinking-and-methods-kaizen.
4 Ken Alder, "Innovation and Amnesia: Engineering Rationality and the Fate of Interchangeable Parts Manufacturing in France," *Technology and Culture* 38, no. 2 (April 1997): 273–274.
5 Alder, 273–274.
6 Lewis Mumford, *Technics and Civilization* (New York: Harcourt Brace & Company, 1934), 89.
7 Charles Coulston Gillispie and Ken Alder, "Engineering the Revolution," *Technology and Culture* 39, no. 4 (1998): 734–736, doi: 10.2307/1215848.
8 Denis Diderot, quoted in Alder, "Innovation and Amnesia," 282.
9 The gunlock is the critical mechanism in an 18th-century musket that controls the action of the flint. When the gunlock is actuated, the flint ignites a small spoon of gunpowder. The explosion of gunpowder then propels a lead ball toward the intended victim.
10 Alder, "Innovation and Amnesia," 283. Tolerance was a concept introduced by artillery engineers in the ancient regime.

11 David Pye, *The Nature and Art of Workmanship* (New York: Bloomsbury Academic, 1995), 24–26. Pye, a design theorist writing in the 1960s, coined the phrase "workmanship of certainty", to characterize how jigs or other methods of controlling a tool could be relied upon to alter the material as predicted, as distinguished from "the workmanship of risk" that accompanies the inevitable variation of work done with hand-held tools.

12 Alder, "Innovation and Amnesia," 284–289.

13 Robert S. Woodbury, "The Legend of Eli Whitney and Interchangeable Parts," *Technology and Culture* 1, no. 3 (Summer, 1960): 235–253.

14 Paul Teicholz, "Trends in Labor Productivity in the Construction Industry" (presentation, Project Production Institute Symposium, San Francisco, CA, December 9, 2015).

15 Julia Vitullo-Martin and Hope Cohen, *Construction Labor Costs in New York City: A Moment of Opportunity*, report (New York: Regional Plan Association, June 2011), appendix.

16 *New York Plan for the Resolution of Jurisdictional Disputes, In the Matter of the Arbitration between Local Union No. 3, IBEW and New York City District Council of Carpenters*, § 100-S, 1–4 (2011) (statement of Richard Adelman, Chairman).

17 *Plan for the Settlement of Jurisdictional Disputes in the Construction Industry: In Arbitration between IBEW Local Union No. 3, and New York City District Council of Carpenters*, Case No. H10-047, 1-6 (2011) (Robert M. Hirsch, Arbitrator).

18 *New York Plan for the Resolution of Jurisdictional Disputes: In the Matter of Arbitration between IBEW Local #3 and Plumbers Local #1*, § 100-O, 1–4 (2009) (statement of Eric J. Schmertz, Chairman).

19 *Plan for the Settlement of Jurisdictional Disputes in the Construction Industry: In the Matter of Arbitration between IBEW Local #3 and United Association of Journeymen and Apprentices and Pipe Fitting Industry of the United States and Canada, and Tishman Construction Corp.*, § 100-P (Appeal to 100-O), 1–7 (2010) (statement of Tony A. Kelly, Arbitrator).

20 Vitullo-Martin and Cohen, 20.

21 "Empowering Workers through Accountable Capitalism," Warren Democrats, accessed June 23, 2020, https://elizabethwarren.com/plans/accountable-capitalism.

22 "Employments by major industry sector," U.S. Bureau of Labor Statistics, last modified September 4, 2019, https://www.bls.gov/emp/tables/employment-by-major-industry-sector.htm. "Workers Compensation and the Most Dangerous Industries in the U.S.," *Eastern Kentucky University Online* (blog), accessed June 23, 2020, https://safetymanagement.eku.edu/blog/workers-compensation-and-the-most-dangerous-industries-in-the-u-s/. "Chart Book (6th edition): OSHA Enforcement and Injury Costs – Workers' Compensation in Construction and Other Industries," The Center for Construction Research and Training, accessed June 23, 2020, https://www.cpwr.com/chart-book-6th-edition-osha-enforcement-and-injury-costs-workers%E2%80%99-compensation-construction-and.

23 Nick Skillikorn, "Top 1000 Companies that Spend the Most on Research & Development (Charts and Analysis)," *Idea to Value* (blog), last modified August 8, 2019, https://www.ideatovalue.com/inno/nickskillikorn/2019/08/top-1000-companies-that-spend-the-most-on-research-development-charts-and-analysis/#industries. Data was aggregated by Skillikorn from Strategy& (PWC Network) 2018 Global Innovation 1000 Study, 2018 EU Industrial R&D Investment Scoreboard (World 2500 companies), and Fortune 500 2018.

24 Brad Goehle and Robert Chwalik, "The Global Innovation 1000 Study," last modified December 17, 2019, https://www.strategyand.pwc.com/gx/en/insights/innovation1000.html.

25 Skillikorn, 2019.

26 Barry Jaruzelski, Robert Chwalik and Brad Goehle, "What the Top Innovators Get Right," Tech & Innovation, *Strategy + Business*, October 30, 2018, https://www.strategy-business.com/feature/What-the-Top-Innovators-Get-Right?gko=e7cf9.

27 Konrad Putzier, "Momentum Builds for Automation in Construction," Real Estate, *Wall Street Journal* (New York, NY), July 2, 2019. Putzier used data from research done by CREtech.

28 Kathryn Brenzel and David Jeans, "Warped Lumber, Failed Projects: TRD Investigates Katerra, SoftBank's $4B Construction Startup," *The Real Deal*, December 16, 2019, https://therealdeal.com/2019/12/16/softbank-funded-construction-startup-katerra-promised-a-tech-revolution-its-struggling-to-deliver/.

29 Steve Denning, "How Not to Fix US Health Care: Copy the Cheesecake Factory," Leadership, *Forbes*, August 13, 2012, https://www.forbes.com/sites/stevedenning/2012/08/13/how-not-to-fix-us-health-care-copy-the-cheesecake-factory/#79d5a9ec2bd2. Atul Gawande, "Big Med," Annals of Health Care, *New Yorker*, August 6, 2012, https://www.newyorker.com/magazine/2012/08/13/big-med. In a review of Atul Gawande's *New Yorker* article *Big Med*, Steve Denning points out that

the command-and-control approach implemented successfully by the Cheesecake Factory restaurant chain, which Gawande extolls as a model for the American health care system, is the wrong model for health care. Denning suggests that top-down management works poorly in "knowledge work" such as software development and health care, where the workers know more than management about what needs to be done. In creating a scalable solution for modular housing, we need to unleash the creativity and resourcefulness of autonomous knowledge workers in architecture and product development.

30 Horst W. Rittel and Melvin M. Webber, *Dilemmas in a General Theory of Planning* (Berkeley: Institute of Urban and Regional Development, University of California, 1973), 162.

31 Joseph F.C. DiMento, "Stent (or Dagger?) in the Heart of Town: Urban Freeways in Syracuse, 1944–1967," *Journal of Planning History* 8, no. 2 (2009): 133–161, https://journals.sagepub.com/doi/10.1177/1538513208330768.

32 Alana Semuels, "The Role of Highways in American Poverty," Business, *Atlantic*, March 18, 2016, https://www.theatlantic.com/business/archive/2016/03/role-of-highways-in-american-poverty/474282/.

33 This is not to overlook other factors at play in the economic decline of cities like Syracuse, including policies of red-lining, slum clearance, exclusionary zoning in the suburbs, and the availability of Federal money for interstate highway construction.

34 Rikke Friis Dam and Teo Yu Siang, "5 Stages in the Design Thinking Process," Interaction Design Foundation, last modified May 2020, https://www.interaction-design.org/literature/article/5-stages-in-the-design-thinking-process. The five-stage rubric was originated by the Stanford d. school and has been widely promulgated. The descriptions of each stage are by this author.

35 David Brooks, "What Machines Can't Do," Opinion, *New York Times*, February 3, 2014, https://www.nytimes.com/2014/02/04/opinion/brooks-what-machines-cant-do.html.

36 Paul M. Romer, "Economic Growth," Econlib, *Concise Encyclopedia of Economic Growth*, 2nd ed. (Carmel, IN: The Liberty Fund, 2007), https://www.econlib.org/library/Enc/EconomicGrowth.html.

37 Joseph Stiglitz, "Inequality is Holding Back the Recovery," *New York Times*, January 20, 2013.

38 C30 deflated by annual construction labor cost index, annual consumer price index, annual construction value in place index, house price index, index of new one-family house under construction, annual building value in place index.

39 Skillikorn, 2019.

9   Toward a Global Vernacular

In this chapter, the first of two that speculate on changes in architectural practice that might occur with the widespread adoption of intermodal modular architecture, we'll explore the notion of a new global vernacular.

Briefly:

The loss of vernacular traditions during the industrial revolution left Western architecture without an authentic wellspring of indigenous culture. Adolf Loos, acutely attuned to this "crisis of culture",[1] strove to reestablish authenticity in the design of "utilitarian" architecture by rejecting inauthentically appropriated ornament. Loos posited a distinction between "utilitarian" architecture and "the monument and the tomb", or architecture of symbolic significance. The Modern Movement, in adopting Loos' rejection of ornament, overlooked his nuanced distinction and wholly rejected symbolism. The evolution of post-war curtain wall facades demonstrates that the repression of the symbolic impulse was unsustainable, and today the building as a representational object is central to design practice. Meanwhile, an entire category, "everyday architecture" (what Loos referred to as "utilitarian"), languishes in a state of aesthetic impoverishment. Intermodal modular architecture is a vehicle for the creation of a vibrant modern vernacular, a revitalized everyday architecture.

The word vernacular, with a Latin origin in vernaculus, "native, from verna, slave born in the master's house"[2] appears to be inextricably bound to the idea of the local. Vernacular architecture as commonly understood is made from materials harvested or extracted at the building site. Because the availability of wood or the species of stone varied from location to location, vernacular architecture has always had, like wine, a character that is inseparable from its place. The techniques of vernacular architecture, handed down through generations, were similarly local, with building cultures differentiated according to the methods devised by local builders to work with local materials, and in response to local climactic conditions. Owing, perhaps, to the winnowing of form and construction by continual trial and error, vernacular architecture seems always to have a "rightness" about it.

In the 18th century, pattern books were published and widely disseminated that blurred the distinction between vernacular and learned architecture. With pattern books in circulation, the vernacular was no longer chained, like a slave, to the local. The forms and details of Georgian domestic architecture were available to builders in the far-flung British colonies. American colonial houses derived from Georgian models constituted "a remarkably pervasive voluntary adoption of an exceedingly comprehensive, centralized design standard".[3] Was this "the point at which true vernacular began to disappear",[4] or were pattern books the beginning of a new kind of vernacular in a more globally connected era? Even with pattern books, there was local adaptation. The development of the verandah as an additive shading system and outdoor living space in southern states, or the saltbox roof that shielded the New England house from northerly winter winds were climactically responsive local adaptations of the Georgian model. Pattern books disseminated a shared language of architecture that could be regionally differentiated within a common set of standards.

The absence of a modern vernacular appears to have left us in a situation where every architect strives, to a greater or lesser degree, to make a "statement", and every statement is made in isolation. Vernacular architecture, in contrast, was always a communal project. The digital revolution that began during the late 20th century has created new conditions that make a modern vernacular possible through internet connectivity and social media platforms. Intermodal modular architecture is an open-source collaborative endeavor, and the VUC, as a system with inherently digital properties, is a physical medium on which a digitally connected global vernacular can be built.

Ornament and Crime

Adolf Loos' frequently misunderstood essay, "Ornament and Crime", was a meditation on indigenous culture and modernity. He did not say that ornament *is* crime, as is so often misunderstood. He took pains throughout his life, in fact, to repudiate the notion. Loos was urbane Viennese in the era of Sigmund Freud, and his ideas were intertwined with a keen awareness of the relationship between eros and creativity.

Admittedly, upon reading Ornament and Crime today, it is hard to take some of it seriously. Loos linked modern-day tattooing to criminality, but he made a point to distinguish between tattoos in contemporary Vienna and tattoos of indigenous tribes. Among the Viennese demi-monde tattooing was a sign of decadence, whereas tattooing among indigenous peoples signified a legitimate cultural expression, an aesthetic urge. Loos couldn't have foreseen that the 21st-century population of Williamsburg, Brooklyn would be as inked as a tribe of Papuans. Tastes do change. But what he was really grappling with in Ornament and Crime was the problem of creativity and self-consciousness in the new industrial era, in which architects had lost an organic connection with the roots of architecture as indigenous construction. Loos' formulation that "cultural evolution is equivalent to the removal of ornament from articles in daily use"[5] was a statement on the problem of authenticity. Because early 20th-century city-dwellers had lost the connection with an indigenous heritage, it was, for Loos, an affectation to decorate objects for no reason other than to evoke an ersatz past.

Loos was careful to confine his disapprobation of ornament to utilitarian buildings and articles of daily use. For architecture of symbolic significance, ornament was acceptable. He believed that the classical tradition was permitted under certain circumstances. His interiors were veneered with marble so exotically variegated that it amounted to a decorative motif. Loos used ornament, and he justified it within his stated principles. One of his dicta was that interior design should be expressive of the life of a building's inhabitants, whereas the design of façades called for a circumspect public decorum.

Despite this nuanced and easily misunderstood argument, Le Corbusier and others co-opted Loos' seemingly anti-ornament rhetoric. By temperament an outsider, Loos distanced himself from modern architects with whom he might have found an alliance. He dismissed the white geometric abstractions of the post-World War I era as a self-conscious avant-garde aesthetic, which he regarded as equally disconnected from the present as the over-ornamented facades that he denounced. Loos sought cultural continuity, not revolution. As Hilde Heynen has written:

> [Loos] does not treat modernity as a new beginning, as a completely unique period that deliberately breaks with tradition. On the contrary, he sees modernity as a very specific continuation of the tradition. His ideas are not avant-garde in character: one does not find any rejection of the existing order in his work, any call for a tabula rasa or repudiation of our cultural inheritance.[6]

Loos insisted that architects eschew artistic expression in utilitarian buildings. He wrote: "We have the style of our time. We have it in those fields in which the artist... has not yet poked his nose".[7] By establishing a hierarchy of building types, and the degree of ornament and richness of material that would be appropriate for each, he drew a categorical distinction between buildings that were to any degree utilitarian, and the "very small part of architecture [that] belongs to art: the tomb and the monument. Everything that fulfills a function is to be excluded from the domain of art".[8] Loos placed housing squarely in the utilitarian camp, arguing for

> for a strict separation between architecture and dwelling: architecture was not meant to be a reflection of the personality of its occupant; on the contrary it should be kept separate from dwelling. Its task was to make dwelling possible, not to define it.[9]

The shock of successive waves of industrialization and urbanization during the 19th century shattered the link between culture and tradition. The revival of historic styles that flourished until the early 20th century was a rear-guard action aimed at clinging to a rapidly receding past. The avant-garde polemicists of the Modern Movement turned toward engineering, technology, and function as the basis for a new architecture that had no need for history. We are in the habit of equating the modern with an avant-garde program, with the shock of the new, but Loos' categorical distinctions lead to an unfamiliar idea: utilitarian architecture, being rooted in the present, can be the most modern.

The idea of a modern vernacular is an unfinished modernist project. The codification of the International Style could perhaps be viewed as an attempt to create a modern vernacular grounded in functionalism, but few architects were able to transcend the conventions of International Style modernism to achieve the kind of local adaptation and evolution that is the essence of a living vernacular.[10]

• • •

Before returning to the idea of a modern vernacular, let's pause here to consider two fundamental and surprisingly different "construction mentalities": (1) stacking and (2) framing/cladding, which suggest parallel distinctions between everyday and atelier architectures. Stacking, which has ancient roots in Neolithic structures, seems to arise from a primal instinct. Cladding, by contrast, begins with an image. As Loos wrote: "the artist, *the architect*, first senses the effect that he intends to realize and sees the rooms he wishes to create in his mind's eye"[11] (emphasis in the original). While the passage refers to the design of interiors, it refers equally to the design of facades. Modern curtain wall architecture, construction technology at its most advanced, is pure framing/cladding. In this schema, Mies van der Rohe is an unusual figure who straddles both modes. He was an artist/technologist who single-handedly invented curtain wall architecture; yet, he was also a vernacular architect for whom the rules for stacking bricks underpinned form.

Stacking

The stacking instinct is universal among children and ancient builders alike. To construct by stacking seems to almost be hardwired into the eye/hand/mind connection. Children as young as 18 months will pick up blocks and stack them into towers... then knock them down and stack them back up again, over and over. Block play seems so ingrained in early childhood development[12] that it is hard not to believe that it reaches back in time and across cultures.

9.1
Block play.

Pre-historic monumental structures, dating as early as 7,000 BCE, known variously as dolmens, cromlech, quoits, and goindol, at sites ranging from Western Europe to the Mediterranean and eastward to Asia, were little more than rock piles, sometimes covered with earth to form a mound. While they were associated with rites of burial, these Neolithic structures were not necessarily built for actual entombment of the dead; they may in some instances have served a purely symbolic function. The structural principle was the lintel, with a monumental capstone spanning two or more pillars. Dolmen (and their variants) constituted a universal architecture.

9.2
Poulnabrone Dolmen.

Stacking served builders well for thousands of years. Brick making is believed to have begun at least 6,000 years ago with mud-formed bricks baked in the sun. Fired brick is known to have been used around 2,500 BCE to replace the mud brick of the Ur ziggurat in ancient Mesopotamia.[13] The hand-held brick, a modular masonry unit, allows a single laborer to erect a wall. If for no other reason than that, the brick remains our most common unit of construction.

Stacked structures are balancing acts, a mass here counterbalancing a mass there. The joints between stone blocks are a narrative of the act of stacking, blocks arranged in courses, courses completing stories, stories becoming structures. The completed building makes its appearance as it rises from the ground up. What you stack is what you get.

9.3
Habitat 67 Montreal, Safdie Architects.

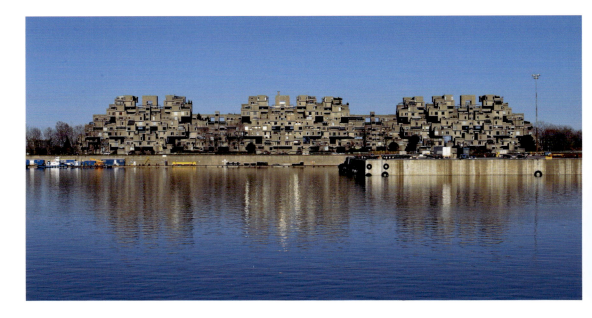

Stacked structures can be improvisational when constructed over extended periods. The cathedral builders had the opportunity, given the slow pace of the work, to alter the upward branching of ribs and vaults. Since the construction of cathedrals often took generations, each successive master mason could apply new knowledge and new sensibilities to the undertaking. This could only be possible with walls that rose progressively and complete at each stone course.

Indigenous building evolved organically. It went unrecorded[14] until it was endangered by industrialization. In "The Rock is My Home", Werner Blaser, a student of Mies, analyzes vernacular stone dwellings in Alpine villages, which he documented in photographs and measured drawings. Blaser wrote that these houses "are remarkable for one constant feature: the form of the building is varied by a method of addition determined by objective requirements. This is reflected in the structural arrangement of surfaces within the geometrical organization of the whole".[15] By "objective requirements", Blaser is not referring to conscious design criteria, and certainly not to dictates of style. He means that the method of building with stone never attempts to impose on itself a form that doesn't follow from the logic of stacking, the shape of the units being stacked, and the implacable discipline of gravity.

In his unbuilt projects and pedagogy based on load-bearing brick masonry, Mies gave the impression that he had established an unassailable approach that connects the act of building—stacking—to the creation of a building image. Mies trained his students at the Illinois Institute of Technology to draw detailed cross sections of load-bearing brick structures with every brick placed according to the rules of "bonding", or the cross-lapping that both holds the masonry mass together and gives a wall its characteristic pattern (e.g. running bond, Flemish bond, English bond, and so on). Mies' well-known project for an unbuilt Brick Country House was "re-constructed" by Blaser in 1964, 41 years after Mies designed it. In plans and details, Blaser meticulously placed each brick through the full thickness of the wall, organizing headers and stretchers, turning corners, presenting the precise form of the brick country house as having emerged from a close study of bonding and coursing. Blaser's drawings have often been mistaken for originals, which has led some historians to conclude that there was an attempt to create a misleading narrative.[16] However, even if there is no evidence from the surviving 1923 drawings that bonding and coursing was part of the original design procedure, it remains entirely possible that such studies were done but have been since been lost. Regardless of whether the reconstructed version was a recovery of the original idea or post-rationalized, Mies' intention was clear: to ground architecture firmly in the act of construction.

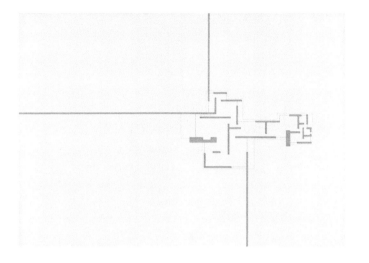

9.4
Mies van der Rohe, Brick
Country House Project,
1923, drawing by Werner
Blaser, 1964. © The Museum
of Modern Art/Licensed by
SCALA/Art Resource, NY. ©
2020 Artists Rights Society
(ARS), New York / VG Bild-
Kunst, Bonn.

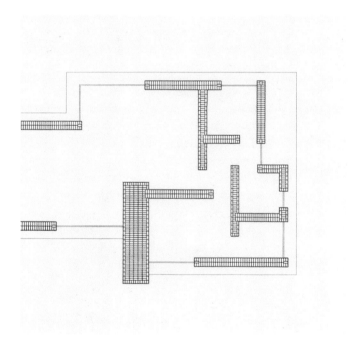

9.5
Brick country house project,
enlarged detail. © The
Museum of Modern Art/
Licensed by SCALA / Art
Resource, NY.

Form and structure in stacked construction are one and the same. When
you really think about it, this idea is so far from contemporary architecture
as to seem startling. The contemporary notion of first conceiving an
autonomous form independent of structural principles and then inserting
an engineered armature to support it did not, and could not, occur to the
educated architect, and certainly not to the vernacular builder prior to
the industrial revolution. The pre-industrial architect conceived of form
and structure as a unity. The plan of the building was largely determined

by the problem of directing the weight of large masses of masonry (or timber) down to the ground. The architect had to be in control of the load paths to create form.

Framing/Cladding

In contrast to stacking, structures that are built first as a frame and are then covered in weatherproof cladding present the architect with the problem of reconciling the tension between what Kenneth Framption has referred to as the "representational" and the "ontological".[17] Framed architecture, whether it is a Japanese teahouse or a modern office building, requires the architect to decide how the cladding is to express an architectural idea. Is the expression of cladding an image that is entirely independent of the structure? Is the structure itself exposed to the weather and expressive of the building's image? Or is the cladding a proxy that expresses a concealed structure but isn't structural? Whichever it is determines the relationship between the framed structure and its weatherproof enclosure. It is nearly impossible for a contemporary architect to avoid the problem of representation.

With the founding of the Ecole Polytechnique during the French Revolution, the disciplines of engineering and architecture split. With the advent of structural steel and reinforced concrete toward the end of the 19th century, framing-cladding became the primary construction system for most institutional and commercial buildings, as well as for multi-story housing. Advances in the mathematical validation of structural design forced the architect to hand over responsibility for organizing load paths to a technically educated engineer. The architect, having reserved for himself the role of aesthetician, withdrew from the role of constructor.

A progression toward our contemporary non-load-bearing curtain wall mounted on a structural frame began with the Chicago-school office buildings designed by Louis Sullivan and others in the late 19th century. There was an apparent retrenchment during the Beaux-Arts period at the end of the 19th and early 20th centuries, in which modern steel structures were buried within massive masonry envelopes, but the very fact that engineered steel frames carried the loads down to the ground meant that a strict aesthetic discipline was required to create the illusion of a stacked architecture. The Beaux Arts simulated but did not replicate the architecture of compressive loads that underpinned the history of architecture going back thousands of years. That approach can work if there are enough resources to build convincing simulacra, but by World War II depleted resources along with the demise of classical architectural education marked the end of the Beaux Arts. European emigres educated a new generation of modern architects, and the development of curtain wall enclosures began in full during the late 1940s.

Curtain wall architecture in its early days adhered to the aesthetic principles of Cartesian geometry and repetition. To maintain a philosophical stance that modern architecture should be non-representational required the repression of expressive impulses. At first—under the hands of Mies, Gordon Bunshaft, and Eero Saarinen, among others—a preoccupation with geometric purity and austere composition appeared to reflect objectivity and an honest attitude toward structure, but this was really more an ideological position than a technical inevitability. Mies' application of I-beams to facades was for optical effect.

By the mid-sixties however, the heroic style of curtain wall design had run out of steam and other forms of façade expression began to emerge. The advent of reflective glass coatings ushered in a new monolithic sculptural architecture, exemplified during the early seventies by I.M. Pei's John Hancock building and Kevin Roche's U.N Plaza towers. In 1978, the professional establishment was outraged when the first renderings of Philip Johnson's AT&T headquarters, with its Chippendale top and coursed granite pilasters (all hung from the steel frame), were published. Johnson, more than anyone, understood that the aesthetics of modern facades had nothing to do with construction logic. Post-modernism in the 1980s released architects entirely from the dictates of modernist aesthetics. With theoretical justification provided by Robert Venturi's and Denise Scott Brown's writings, Michael Graves and others showed how facades could perform an illustrative and ironic role in alluding to classical traditions. Recently, Frank Gehry's Beekman Place tower in Manhattan has achieved the transmogrification of curtain wall into thick sculptural form, stainless steel as tin-knocker's poché, hung from the structure with the same underlying curtain wall technology that Mies used. Whether one prefers one style to another has become a relative question, a matter of personal preference. It is certainly not a matter of agreement on conventions or of the inherent nature of construction, nor is it a matter of codification of what is appropriate on what occasion.

With the sudden break with tradition during the 19th century, epigrammatic dictates like "form follows function" reflected an underlying anxiety about where form does actually come from. If form no longer derives from traditional sources, constrained by traditional materials and methods for spanning space and articulated by the ancient ornamental orders, then something had to be found to replace those received traditions. The Modern Movement, in aspiring for objectivity, required an objective-appearing style. Even so, mid-century architects who strove for "structural honesty" found themselves transferring the image of an idealized but concealed structure to the outer skin.

Mies expounded rhetorically upon the importance of structural expression and objectivity; yet in his constructed work, he treated the building skin as the image rather than the substance of structure. Another example, prior to Seagrams, is the façade of the IIT Alumni Memorial Hall, which appears at first to be a straightforwardly expressed steel frame with brick infill. The visible steel framework on the facade is in reality a non-load-bearing grid of steel-plate pilasters and spandrels set flush to the brick cladding, an ornamental system that denotes the structural steel frame buried behind the cladding. (There were sound technical reasons for this, having to do with the necessity of fireproofing the structural steel frame, which meant that it could not be left exposed.)[18] Far from being a structural purist, Mies accepted, even embraced, the image-making nature of his framed and clad architecture. The framing/cladding construction mentality, at its root, is the same as the steel-framed Beaux Arts.

Mies was a complex figure. He navigated the tension between the representational and the ontological as an artist and allowed himself a certain inconsistency. As a teacher, however, his instruction in the logic of brick construction and his efforts to promulgate an after-the-fact Brick Country House narrative show that he meant his students and colleagues to understand and adopt his thinking that architectural form is rooted in the act of construction.

• • •

At the end of the 19th century, with the shift to framing as the predominant structural system for buildings, the structural engineer relieved the architect from responsibility for gravity. With the advent of air conditioning, responsibility for comfort was handed over to the mechanical engineer. These and further technical specializations have changed the nature of architectural practice. The architect today is dependent on various specialists to execute the design of a building, and practice is highly collaborative. We will not be returning to the era of the architect as a master builder, any more than we will be going back to the age of massive masonry buildings. We can, however, look forward to a new stacked vernacular of lightweight steel-framed VUCs. The structural design of the VUC itself, and the interconnections between VUCs, will be the province of an engineer, but the most basic level of structural design, the stacking and aggregation of modules, will be the domain of the architect. In determining the arrangement, the architect will be intuitively guided by the constraints of balance, overturning and building stance, seeking an equilibrium that will allow the stack to stand up. The engineer, now working on the manufacturing side rather than as a consultant to the architect, will ensure that the stacking arrangement is safe and that the internal construction of VUCs and their interconnections are valid for each specific building design. This activity will remain largely behind the scenes.

Vernacular Today

Vernacular architecture as a living tradition no longer exists in most of the developed world, and vernacular traditions in the developing world are rapidly vanishing, overtaken by ever-accelerating modern development. Pockets of indigenous culture with a living vernacular remain, but for how long?[19]

Vernacular architecture shows us how builders with limited resources and rudimentary technology and local materials can take advantage of the sun, wind, and local climactic patterns to shape environments. In his book *Architecture Without Architects*, Bernard Rudofsky educated a generation of architects with case studies of environmentally responsive indigenous buildings, but as a source of design inspiration, indigenous models have limitations. The architect is rarely able to re-interpret archaic forms or apply analogs at the scale of modern buildings. The most successful efforts have come from an understanding of first principles rather than a literal emulation of vernacular form.

Is the notion of a global vernacular an oxymoron? Nassan Al-Sayed, a scholar of vernacular architecture, has written that "for anything to be considered vernacular, it has always been assumed that it must be native or unique to a specific place, produced without the need for imported components or processes, and possibly built by the individuals who occupy it. In the twenty-first century, as culture and tradition are becoming less place-rooted and more information-based, these particular attributes of vernacular have to be recalibrated to reflect these changes".[20] He continues: "the idea of modern knowledge as different from and possibly opposite to, vernacular knowledge, must be abandoned... the vernacular may in fact be in some instances the most modern of the modern".[21] Taking Al-Sayed's insights as a starting point, perhaps we can come up with a serviceable theory of a modern global vernacular. Here are three propositions:

1. *The vernacular evolves continuously*. It exists in the present and looks neither backward nor forward. This is why we can think of a global vernacular, in Al-Sayed's words, as the "most modern of the modern". The new global vernacular evolves in synch with the present, not ahead or behind. To be modern in this sense requires us to achieve "unself-conscious virtues in an age peculiar for its self-consciousness".[22]

   We no longer inhabit a world in which vernacular builders pass along their skills and know-how from generation to generation absent historical consciousness, independent of the flow of time. Contemporary practitioners have no choice but to be fully conscious of temporality. But while the individual architect may not be able to subsume in the present moment, perhaps a network of architects could join in a continuum of thought. Imagine an architectural hive mind collaborating on a vernacular language, in which a multiplicity of static points of view would, like cinema, approximate temporal flow.

2. *The vernacular is a shared language.* Well, perhaps this is obvious... but what language, with what rules, what grammar? Where is this shared language going to come from? In the vernacular of indigenous cultures, the shared language of construction was unselfconsciously transmitted from generation to generation. A father taught a son where to site a house, how to mix mortar, lay bricks, thatch a roof. The models were all the other houses built in the same manner, going back generations. No need to consciously "design". If there is going to be a new vernacular form of building, we have no choice but to consciously set about creating one. The common language of intermodal modular, based on the VUC as the basic element of grammar, is where a new global vernacular architecture can begin.

3. *The vernacular is a language with embedded rules.* The Brick, as quoted by Louis Kahn, said "I like an Arch".[23] Kahn had divined the embedded constructional rules in bricks spanning space. If a common language of construction is going to launch a living modern vernacular, a critical requirement is that the language has embedded rules. Dennis De Lucca, in an essay about a still living tradition of vernacular building on the island of Malta, wrote, "it is perhaps significant in this respect to point out that in Malta, the limestone block itself is of cubic shape and typically measuring 58cm (23in) in length, 15–23cm (6–9in) in widtch, and 28cm (11in) in height, is very much a reflection of the completed building, and vice-versa".[24]

In traditional Japanese architecture, the 3×6-foot tatami mat is a modular panel that formed the basis of floor plans from tea houses to palaces. The arrangement of tatami in a range of scales and in varying degrees of complexity is governed by the nature of "stacking" those modules on a horizontal plane. A traditional Japanese builder would never cut a tatami mat to a custom dimension, or cut it on the diagonal, or into a curved shape, just to attain a new building form. Why not? It would have been easy enough to do. The answer seems straightforward: the ability to transmit the language of Japanese building from generation to generation depended on preserving the inherent modular properties of tatami. To undermine that modular discipline would remove the embedded rules that govern the language, tantamount to abandoning it.

To repeat: the vernacular
...evolves continuously.
...is a shared language.
...is a language with embedded rules.

While many architects are inspired by the vernacular architecture of the past, most have no intention of building in a true vernacular. No one talks about the idea of a modern vernacular. The architecture schools don't teach it (we barely even know what it is) and there are no professional rewards for pursuing it.

• • •

We can now state our next principle, the basis for a new global vernacular in our digitally connected and networked world.

PRINCIPLE # 11   OPEN SOURCE

The open-source approach to intermodal modular architecture, which would not have been possible before the digital revolution, undergirds the three essential features of a modern vernacular. First, it enables the global vernacular to *evolve continuously* as an iterative and collaborative process independent of the design and construction of any single building. Second, the ordering principles (standardization, addressable grid) of the VUC are physical properties with digital values, enabling intermodal modular architecture to become a *shared language*. Third, the digital design interface, with behind-the-scenes engineering and with technical attributes attached to each object, creates a language with *embedded rules*, an open-source architectural "operating system".

Architects, by nature inclined to customize, may still want to participate in the technical evolution of the modular system and develop their own design variations. In fact, this is desirable and is the very essence of the new vernacular, and we will return to that idea in the next chapter. With the participation of architects networked across the globe, the catalog of systems-based components will evolve and grow like smartphone apps.

Lest anyone think that I am advocating a modern vernacular as an answer for all forms and occasions, let me be clear: I am not. Our public buildings and our cultural buildings will always require the hand of an artist. There are also occasions for historicism just as there are for virtuoso flights of architectural invention. But lacking a connection among architects and across generations, historicism too often lapses into kitsch, and virtuoso overreach, well, overreaches.

• • •

As the linchpin of a modern vernacular, the stacking of VUCs returns architects to the primal origins of building, in which form and structure are a unity, and in which the design process at the conceptual stage is a true analog to the process of construction. By recovering a vital new vernacular, in which stacking puts architects once again in touch with the instinct to construct, we can address a critical need to revitalize everyday architecture. We would also engage atelier architecture in a fruitful dialog. As so incisively written by Nicholas Habraken 60 years ago:

> The architect-poet finds himself in a terrible situation. In his perambulation through the town, he finds that daily chatter has ceased. He hears only his own verses and those of his colleagues being recited. They are spoken by uniform choirs. Every sound he utters is answered only by the lines of his confreres.
>
> Is it any wonder that sterility threatens and that, cut off form the source which feeds him, he is in danger of losing himself in empty jargon? Looking around for a foothold, the architect grabs at the only thing he can work with – material – and inclines to exaggerated expression. Is it any wonder that, in looking for inspiration and lacking normal criteria, he will search for ever-new forms? He is not motivated by a society of which he is a part and he is in need of ideas. These ideas will gradually make him repeat himself. The poet who no longer hears everyday conversation will exhaust himself in increasingly artificial syntax. He will call forth any sound he can utter, for he hears no echo.[25]

The Collaborative Project

My architectural education at Cooper Union in the 1970s began with the nine-square grid, a legendary pedagogical tool devised by John Hejduk, Robert Slutzky, and their colleagues, a group known collectively as the Texas Rangers. The nine-square grid program began at the University of Texas at Austin in the 1950s. Too radical for conservative University trustees, Hejduk, Slutzky, and company were eventually dismissed, and they migrated north. Texas' loss was Cooper Union's gain. At Cooper, the nine-square grid became the mainstay of the first-year architecture program for more than a decade.

Broadly speaking, the nine-square grid allowed young architects to explore abstract spatial and formal principles and to understand the properties of a seemingly neutral field. Without being reductive, it was also, on one level, an exercise in modular design. We students began by making a scale model, a white frame of painted quarter-inch basswood, divided into nine-equal squares, supported on sixteen quarter-inch square white columns resting on a black base. (If you are picturing a Sol Lewitt grid construction, that's no accident—Lewitt taught at Cooper in the 1960s and was influenced by the white grids he saw in the first-year architecture studio.) We then went on to fabricate a series of panels and Euclidean volumes of prescribed dimensions that were derived from ratios of the underlying grid dimensions. Using this kit of parts, we explored abstract compositions within the nine-square arrangement at increasing levels of complexity, presented each week in three-dimensional models and ruled ink drawings. Our individual development as young architects was inseparable from our shared discoveries. Our fluency in a common architectural and spatial language grew as we simultaneously learned to articulate that language verbally. The understanding we gained from the nine-square problem was a thread that wove through the rest of our Cooper Union education.

While the VUC bears no physical resemblance to the pure white geometry of the nine-square grid, and there is no pretense to architectural abstraction, there is in our system of intermodal modular architecture an underlying discipline that has much in common with my experience as a first-year student. The idea of a modular grid structure with myriad variations in the arrangement of subordinate parts is certainly a feature. But perhaps of the greatest importance is the potential of intermodal modular architecture to encourage architects to engage in a conversation within a common frame of reference.

The French word *charrette* for cart or wagon has a special meaning for architects. Architecture students at the 19th-century Ecole des Beaux-Arts wheeled their rolls of presentation drawings through the streets of Paris *en charrette* to the academy where their work was to be juried by their professors. At the end of an all-nighter, after meticulously applying the final ink washes, a Beaux-Arts student would load rolls of drawings onto their cart and race off to the jury hall. Over time, a charrette has come to mean an intensive group design session, especially during the conceptually formative stages of a project.

A socially networked vernacular, with participants speaking the lingua franca of intermodal modular, will connect architects across cultures, climates, and countries in an ongoing design charrette. A continual stream of variations within established dimensional standards will flow across the internet, much as open-source computer code is written and shared by programmers who never meet face to face. Online forums will emerge to discuss, debate, and critique the work, and the best ideas will rise to the top. Authorship will not disappear—contributors will be recognized, even celebrated—but in the aggregate, the work on the language of intermodal modular architecture will be a collaborative project.

Regional distinctions will emerge in response to climate and local preferences. Regional alliances of architects will focus on the development of novel stacking arrangements or componentry that, for example, might include climate-specific envelopes for improved energy performance. Others might develop built-in furniture or storage systems for interior fit-out. As new materials emerge, forms will appear that express old concepts in new ways. The work of these architects and designers will be to integrate new developments into the system—to write the code, so to speak, that ensures technical and dimensional compatibilities.

Architects will push the boundaries of the system, competing for recognition. The competitive instinct coupled with social networking will see to it that interesting, novel, or even outrageous proposals are passed around. While much of this activity will remain digital, building product manufacturers will seek out architects around the world as business partners with whom to develop and sell the most marketable components and catalog accessories.

9.6

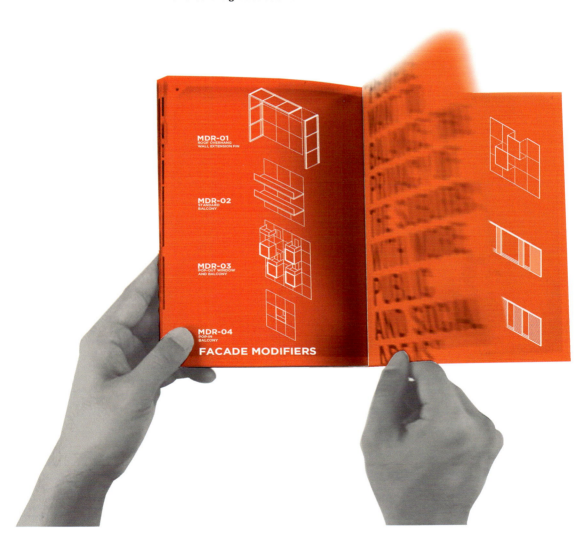

The intermodal modular manufacturer will ensure technical and dimensional conformance in the same way that Apple ensures that apps meet the technical standards of the iPhone operating system. The catalog will be a living document, continually growing and diversifying, making the widespread adoption of intermodal modular increasingly attractive. Architects will engage one another in a robust, even boisterous global design conversation that will spring from a common well of understanding. By breathing new life into everyday architecture, and by embracing the technical potential of manufacturing, everyday architecture and atelier architecture will enter a productive reciprocal relationship.

There remain unanswered questions. How will architectural practice change with the adoption of intermodal modular architecture? Can apartment-dwellers exercise meaningful agency in the design of their environments? How will everyday architecture evolve in our contemporary marketing-saturated culture? We will address these questions and others in the next chapter.

Notes

1 Kenneth Frampton, "Adolf Loos and the Crisis of Culture," quoted in *Modern Architecture: A Critical History* (New York and Toronto: Oxford University Press, 1980), 90–95.
2 *Merriam-Webster.com Dictionary*, s.v. "vernacular," accessed June 20, 2020, https://www.merriam-webster.com/dictionary/vernacular.
3 J.M Richards, "Is There a Modern Vernacular?" In *A Companion to Contemporary Architectural Thought*, ed. Michael Manser (New York and London: Routledge, 1993), 200.
4 Richards, 200.
5 Adolf Loos, *Ornament and Crime: Selected Essays* (Riverside, CA: Ariadne Press, 1998), 167.
6 Hilde Heynen, *Architecture and Modernity: A Critique* (Cambridge, MA and London: MIT Press, 2000), 94–95.
7 Heynen, 79.
8 Adolf Loos, "Architecture" (1910), quoted in Hilde Heynen, *Architecture and Modernity: A Critique* (Cambridge and London: MIT Press, 2000), 80.
9 Heynen, 76.
10 Richards, 198.
11 Adolf Loos, *Spoken into the Void: Collected Essays* (Cambridge, MA and London: MIT Press, Cambridge, 1982), 66.
12 Jennifer Winters, "Director's Column: 100 Years of Blocks: Why Blocks Continue to be a Conerstone in the Curriculum," Stanford, Bing Nursery School, last modified August 6, 2013, https://bingschool.stanford.edu/news/director-s-column-100-years-blocks-why-blocks-continue-be-cornerstone-curriculum.
13 Thomas O. Mason and James A. Lee, s.v. "Brick and Tile," *Encyclopedia Britannica* (Encyclopedia Britannica, inc, 2019), https://www.britannica.com/technology/brick-building-material.
14 Bernard Rudofsky, *Architecture Without Architects* (Garden City, NJ: Doubleday and Company, 1965), Preface.
15 Werner Blaser, *The Rock is My Home* (New York: Van Nostrand Reinhold Co., 1977).
16 Kent Kleinman and Leslie Van Duzer, *Mies van der Rohe: The Krefeld Villas* (New York: Princeton Architectural Press, 2006), 64–66.
17 Kenneth Frampton, *Studies in Tectonic Culture* (Cambridge, MA: MIT Press, 1995), 16.
18 Frampton, 191.
19 Denis De Lucca, *A Living Tradition? Maltese Vernacular Architecture* (New York and London: Routledge, 1993), 210–214.

20 Lindsey Asquith and Marcel Vellinga, *Vernacular Architecture in the Twenty First Century: Theory, Education and Practice* (New York and Ontario: Taylor & Francis, 2006), xvii.

21 Asquith and Vellinga, xvii.

22 Richards, 198.

23 Louis Kahn, "1973: Brooklyn, New York." *Perspecta 19* (1982): 92, accessed September 23, 2020. doi:10.2307/1567053.

24 De Lucca, 213.

25 N.J. Habraken and Jonathan Teicher, *Supports: An Alternative to Mass Housing* (London: Urban International Press, 2011), 106–107.

10   The Collaborative Open-Source Project

The architect as master builder is a stubborn trope. There are talented architects who design excellent, even extraordinary buildings; some are cultural influencers, and a handful are celebrities, but in contemporary practice, master builder is a term that has lost most of its meaning except as a metaphor. There are occasions when an architectural auteur integrates form and tectonics,[1] but as a rule the tectonic and technical development of buildings today is intensely collaborative. Specialists in myriad disciplines from structural engineering to energy modeling to facade consulting, to name just a few, each play a role in shaping a design concept into a constructed form. Architects adjudicate this collaborative process, and often create compelling architecture, but we do not drive the way buildings are built. Allowing for important exceptions, the architect is no longer a constructor.

In the previous chapter, we speculated on the possibility of a global vernacular based on intermodal modular architecture. In this chapter, we will explore the evolution of architectural practice into a collaborative, open-source project. Our hypothesis is that much of the work that architects and engineers do will shift from professional design firms to the design departments of intermodal modular enterprises and their supply chain partners. Some of that work may still be done by independent architects, either as design consultants to component manufacturers or as entrepreneurs marketing their own components. A new industrial ecosystem will emerge as the catalog of intermodal modular components grows and diversifies. The creation of the intermodal modular vernacular will be fostered by an online community of architects, designers, and manufacturers. Ideas will propagate via digital platforms and influencers.

The shift in architectural practice to open-source design will also bring about a change the way urban real estate is marketed. For the first time, the prospective apartment buyer will have an opportunity to shape their environment before it is built, by choosing from an array of plug-and-play components marketed by third-party app developers. Intermodal modular architecture could even facilitate vertical cooperative housing endeavors, along the lines of post-war suburban cooperatives such as Carl Koch's Conantum.

Even as contemporary architects have ceded the role of constructor to a collaborative process, architects retain cultural influence. Let's begin this chapter with a brief sketch of an architect who was both a constructor and a cultural figure at the beginning of the Modern Movement, to show by contrast how much has changed.

The Complete Architect

My earliest impression of the architect as maestro was formed by a stocky, balding sixty-ish man with a head somewhat too big for his body, and a voice similarly oversized. With a thick *Mittel European* accent and exaggerated formality, he would address me, seeming almost to bow with a hand flourish, as "my *dear* mister David". His name was Joseph Neufeld, but as a child I knew him affectionately as Munio, as did his friends and colleagues. He was one of my parent's oldest and closest friends, a frequent weekend guest when I was growing up. At our breakfast table, Munio would hold forth, very Germanic, with a wagging finger and strongly held opinions. He was a cosmopolitan European who had been a prominent architect in pre-World War II Israel before emigrating to the U.S. Neufeld's story gives us a glimpse of architectural practice during the early Modern Movement, and how architects at that time, as generalists, were much closer to the idea of the master builder.

Neufeld was born Galicia in 1899. Fearing pogroms at the beginning of World War I, he and his family emigrated to Vienna, where he attended high school before being inducted at the age of 16 into the Jewish Section of the Austrian Army. After the war, Neufeld embraced Zionism and left Vienna for Palestine, where he labored on a road-building gang. Eventually, he found employment in an engineering office and rose to construction supervisor. When the formwork for a concrete bridge he was overseeing collapsed, Neufeld realized that he should acquire some professional training. His first diploma was at The Private School of Architecture in Tel

Aviv, followed by the Scuola Superiore di Architettura in Rome, and then a graduate degree at the Akademie der Bildenden Kunst in Vienna on a scholarship in director Clemens Holzmeister's Meisterklasse.[2]

Neufeld was among the first generation of European modernists, just a decade or so younger than the group that included Le Corbusier and the other early masters. In the late 1920s, he worked in Erich Mendelsohn's office and later traveled to Moscow with Bruno Taut, another early modern luminary, to design the Inturist Hotel and other large projects. His stay in Moscow ended with Stalin's consolidation of power and crackdown on the avant-garde. In 1932, Neufeld made his way back to Palestine and established himself as an architect in Tel Aviv. Neufeld's strongly held opinions and his love of conversation quickly led to his forming an alliance with like-minded young architects.

> In a bohemian coffee house in Tel Aviv one evening in 1932, three architects argued until the wee hours over how to integrate avant-garde ideas into their building plans. Arieh Sharon, a former student of the Bauhaus school, Joseph Neufeld, from the Berlin firm of Erich Mendelsohn, and Ze'ev Rechter, a disciple of Le Corbusier, who had come from Paris, proclaimed themselves the 'circle of architects'.[3]

Neufeld and his colleagues in Tel Aviv were keen to transplant European architectural polemics to the Middle East. Emulating their mentors, they put out a manifesto, called "Building in the Near East, a Journal of the Circle of Architects in the Land of Israel". Neufeld, Rechter, and Sharon fought to have modernist principles incorporated into the Tel Aviv city plan during the 1930s. Ten issues of *Journal of the Circle of Architects* were published, and it had a substantial influence.[4] Today, Tel Aviv is recognized as a UNESCO World Heritage Site, sometimes called the "White City" for its extraordinary collection of International Style architecture.[5] Neufeld and his colleagues contributed worker's housing, schools, clinics, hospitals, cafés—representing the full panoply of modernist social programs. Through writing, urban planning, designing, and constructing, Neufeld's circle integrated the art of architecture with building technology, program, culture, history, climate, and place. Neufeld embodied the notion of the "complete architect". He was what an architect was expected to be in an earlier era, a bearer of many strands of knowledge, a generalist.

Architecture and Industrial Design

Even though architecture today is capable of sublime form, and even though we know a great deal more about building technology and building science than we did, say, in 1950, the everyday modern buildings that make up our built environment too often fail to satisfy our human need for well-proportioned, appropriately scaled, sensitively detailed, and well-crafted form. When it comes to the impact of manmade objects on our daily lives, industrial design—in which "everydayness" is deeply bound to the design ethos[6]—seems to do a much better job of meeting that need. Industrial design deals primarily with products that are meant to be used and to be used up. While products are disposed of or recycled at the end of their useful life, architecture is a comparatively permanent, site-specific, place-making art. Intermodal modular architecture is somewhere in between.

"The topos, the typos, and the tectonic" in Kenneth Frampton's conceptual scheme are the "three converging vectors" along which architects conceive the form of buildings.[7] In this schema, topos refers to site, place, landscape, and cityscape, the ground on which architecture is built; tectonic refers to the technical means by which we construct (and express the construction of) the building or superstructure; and typos refers to the tendency for architectural form to coalesce around certain patterns. The building site has always been and will always be local, irregular, and contingent. The buildings that we place on that site have become less and less place-specific, assembled from materials and products that can now be sourced from anywhere in the world. Housing, as a type, has largely been codified. Yet even with globally sourced materials and products, the methods we use to construct housing (and other building types, of course) remain site-based and woefully anachronistic. If we are going to reconcile this split, then the nature of architectural practice—along with architectural education and the architectural career—will have to change.

The "complete architect" as the synthesizing artist/technologist/humanist/planner, the archetype that I admired (and idealized) in Joseph Neufeld, is not extinct, but he or she today is a rare bird. The explosion of new fields of knowledge, and the scale and complexity of building projects has changed the practice of architecture the way it has changed, for example, the practice of medicine with its proliferation of specialties. If the thesis put forward in this book regarding intermodal architecture proves correct, architects must reorganize. A new corps of professionals will be needed to work on components of the superstructure—the products, or apps, in other words, that will flourish if the standards of intermodal architecture are widely adopted. Fewer architects will be needed in traditional practice because the technical demands of preparing construction documentation will be substantially reduced. Smaller, leaner firms will be capable of handling larger projects.

In looking forward to a future of practice based on intermodal architecture, we are talking about those building types—primarily housing—that are "utilitarian" in the Loosian sense. Architects will continue to design our public and cultural buildings—museums, libraries, sports arenas, etc.—which will be constructed mainly as site-specific one-off projects. Still, with a re-alignment of the way architecture is practiced, it is inevitable that there will be cross-pollination—a restoration, in other words, of a healthy relationship between vernacular and monumental architecture.

Industrial design and architecture have been overlapping disciplines going back to the Bauhaus. The first generation of modern architects—Mies van der Rohe, Le Corbusier, Alvar Aalto, and Marcel Breuer, among others—designed furniture for industrial production. These pieces are now appreciated as "classics", sold to a mass market through retailers such as Design Within Reach. Pioneering mid-century industrial designers of the 1950s like Charles Eames, Harry Bertoia, and George Nelson were trained as architects. Architect Eero Saarinen left a lasting mark on furniture design. A few contemporary architects—Norman Foster and Nicholas Grimshaw, for example—have industrial design practices within their firms. Philippe Starck is an architect perhaps better known for his faucets than for his buildings. Architects are now well-established design brands whose names lend marketing sizzle to attractive products.

When it comes to integrated systems design, the modern European system kitchen is unparalleled. Bulthaup, Poggenpohl, Valcucine, and other companies are continually advancing kitchen design and technology, with the introduction of new materials and finishes, inventive functional features, accessories, appliance integration, all with a sophisticated aesthetic. The European kitchen is invariably planned on a 60-centimeter (approximately 24-inch) cabinet module, which has made it possible for appliance manufacturers like Miele, Liebherr, Bosch, and others to design refrigerators, ovens, microwaves, cooktops, and dishwashers that integrate seamlessly with the cabinet module. Other European manufacturers, like Blum, market specialty subcomponents based on the 60-centimeter standard that offer limitless ways to organize kitchen drawers and cabinets for knives, flatware, spices, etc.

System kitchen design is done by a corps of highly skilled but largely anonymous industrial designers who dedicate themselves to continual product improvement, backed by corporate resources that allow for sufficient research and development to introduce, for example, lightweight aircraft plywood, customized aluminum extrusions, and innovative hardware that reduce resource consumption and allow for ingenious detailing, lighting, and operation. In the U.S., by contrast, kitchen design has been retarded by a fixation on period styles, faux craftsmanship, and the commercial-scale appliance as a status object, all of which go hand in hand with the bloated suburban house of the last 30 or 40 years.

In marketing the system kitchen, the consumer interacts directly with the manufacturer. System kitchen showrooms are staffed with designers who act as the factory liaison. Design drawings are rapidly priced out, with itemized options for upgrades as well as cost savings for the customer to select. Appliance integration, the most vexing aspect of custom kitchen design, is handled by the manufacturer, and appliances are included in the price. Once a design and price are agreed on, shop drawings and production are scheduled with predictable delivery dates. Where is the architect in all this? Mostly in the background, ensuring that the space is dimensioned and prepared to accommodate the kitchen, and perhaps advising the client on selections of finishes. In conventional construction, the disadvantage of the system kitchen is that there is often a mismatch between the modular kitchen layout and non-modular room dimensions, which are then taken up by custom filler pieces. With intermodal architecture, where the addressable grid governs the layout, system kitchens can be integrated seamlessly in varied arrangements into the larger whole. Why not system bathrooms, bedrooms, and living rooms?

The example of the European kitchen illustrates how a standard dimensional module can stimulate cross-industry coordination, technical advancement, predictable pricing, design variation, and stringent quality control. The principle of differentiation within standards is proven and well-established. Intermodal architecture may be a more complex undertaking, but that same principle applies.

PRINCIPLE #12 DIFFERENTIATION WITHIN STANDARDS

The Cultural Grid

George W.S. Trow, in *Within the Context of No Context*, observed the decline of bourgeois high culture in the age of television. In an oblique but evocative passage, Trow wrote:

> The middle distance fell away, so the grids (from small to large) that had supported the middle distance fell into disuse and ceased to be understandable. Two grids remained. The grid of two hundred million and the grid of intimacy. Everything else fell into disuse.[8]

The "middle distance"—the theater, music, and literature of the educated and privileged middle class of an earlier generation—had given way to pop culture. The market had replaced the critic as an arbiter.

The cultural flattening that began in the age of television continues unabated. Trow's book appeared 40 years ago, in its initial version filling a special issue of the *New Yorker*. It has proven durable, even prophetic.

In today's era of online cultural influencers, as recently noted in The Nation, Trow's book remains "relevant because everything he wrote about television applies doubly for social media".[9] The democratization of cultural authority, and along with it an explosion of niche offerings, has only leveled things further.

How does the discerning individual exercise meaningful choice and craft a cultural identity in this environment? In his book *Nobrow: The Culture of Marketing, The Marketing of Culture*,[10] another *New Yorker* writer, John Seabrook, reflected on his own cultural identity and lifestyle preferences, and extrapolated larger trends in contemporary marketing-saturated culture that exist outside of the traditional dichotomy of Highbrow/Lowbrow. He lifted the hood to expose the cultural and marketing machinery at work in pop music, magazine publishing, and big studio movie-making circa 2000. Seabrook wrote about the corrosive effect of commerce on culture in, for example, book publishing, and noted the decline of good mid-list writers who generate modest, but not blockbuster, sales. Nobrow is what remains after the erasure of the Highbrow/Lowbrow distinction, along with the waning of bourgeois culture situated somewhere between mass (popular) and marginal (avant-garde). You might experience this each time you look for a good film to watch on Netflix. Seabrook, amplifying Trow's observations, posits a conceptual scheme of Small Grids, where emergent, local, and authentic culture lives, and the Big Grid, where blockbuster content is marketed and mainstreamed by high-powered media corporations. Big Grid producers "strip mine" Small Grid talent to feed an insatiable demand for new product, the opposite of the old "trickle-down" theory that mass culture is a derivation of high culture.[11] In the end, Seabrook lets his question about meaningful choice linger unresolved. He concludes his book as he wanders through the new offices that the *New Yorker* magazine is about to occupy—a landscape of cubicles and windowless cells—and he seems defeated. Monotony and homogeneity have prevailed.

The internet has merged Small and Big Grids into one Grid. Today, cultural influencers operating out of their bedroom or kitchen using digital platforms (YouTube, Instagram, Twitter) appear to have bypassed the former gatekeepers of both marketing and culture. Street fashion influences high fashion. Influencers "amass a following by creating and posting some form of unpaid... original content that not only attracts the attention of other users but earns their trust and respect in some sense".[12] To be an influencer requires authenticity (or at least the appearance of it) which is a characteristic of Small Grid culture. At the same time, powerful entities on the old Big Grid, mainly corporations, but also colleges and universities, pay influencers with legions of loyal followers to do corporate and institutional marketing on digital platforms.

Successful influencers are:

> essentially one-person start-ups, and the best ones can spot trends, experiment relentlessly with new formats and platforms, build an authentic connection with an audience, pay close attention to their channel analytics, and figure out how to distinguish themselves in a crowded media environment – all while churning out a constant stream of new content.[13]

Influencers are not the same as celebrities, although some celebrities can be influencers. An influencer is perceived as an expert with whom a follower feels a personal connection.

> Users consider influencers more akin to a close friend than an advertiser or paid endorser, as the stream of content they produce – and the more casual way in which it is shared with the public – imbues influencers with an air of authenticity.[14]

There is something unseemly about this sleight of hand. The combination of the follower's perception of a relationship with the casual style of product placement that characterizes a skilled influencer shields the influencer from the appearance of pecuniary motive. Still, influencer culture, while problematic, is a part of our contemporary condition. In 2020, 4.6 billion people, or 55.8 percent of the global population, were online[15] Instagram has over a billion users;[16] there are more than 31 million YouTube channels;[17] and the top 50 influencers on TikTok have almost 500 million followers.[18]

Overcoming the Stigma of Modular

Our contemporary idea of subcultures was born in the counter-cultural era of the 1960s.[19] In 1971, the Italian avant-garde architectural firm Superstudio published a photocollage of a family of the future living a nomadic post-Woodstock existence on a clay-baked desert plain overlaid by an endless Cartesian grid vanishing toward distant mountains. The family, lacking material possessions other than a partly deflated tent bubble, appears primitive and yet nicely tanned, well-nourished, and happy. The unstated caption might be "in the future, the world will be flat, featureless, and monotonous, but we will be able to plug into the grid anywhere for all our needs and wants". Superstudio's cheerfully dystopic world on an endless grid compels us to reflect. The idea of utter monotony in a desert landscape as the endgame of industrialization and technology is the recurring nightmare of Modernism, which explains, perhaps, the persistent stigma associated with modular architecture.

10.1
Life, Education, Ceremony, Love, The Encampment, The Fundamental Acts. Photocollage by Superstudio, 1971–72 © CNAC/MNAM/Dist. RMN-Grand Palais/Art Resource, NY, permission from the Superstudio Archive.

Does the adoption of standards necessarily lead to repression of identity, as Seabrook experienced in the Conde Nast office landscape? The notion of a fecund blossoming of Small Grid subcultures making the jump to the Big Grid, or even bypassing the Big Grid, offers us a more hopeful way to think about the culture of intermodal modular architecture. Myriad architectural subcultures can coexist on the Small Grid. The authenticity of intermodal modular components created on the Small Grid satisfies our need for identity, and the variety of those components allows us to differentiate ourselves. Like discoverers of a cool new music genre or a quirky fashion accessory, as architects we can curate a building from the intermodal modular catalog. Or, if we are ambitious, we can design our own intermodal modular components. Architects can participate in a global design supply chain. Intermodal modular architecture will allow boutique firms on the Small Grid, as influencers, to establish peer-to-peer followings and bypass the Big Grid structures of large firms and the mainstream architectural media. As product manufacturers partner with intermodal modular content creators, the quantity and diversity of "apps" will expand. Like memes, in the sense of "an idea, behavior or style that spreads from person to person within a culture",[20] the best apps will propagate and find a market. The language of intermodal modular architecture will "evolve by natural selection in a manner analogous to that of biological evolution... through the processes of variation, mutation, competition and inheritance, each of which influences a meme's reproductive success".[21]

Does the Grid, in all its social, cultural, and technological manifestations – influencers and digital platforms, social networking, memes—offer a way forward? Distinctions in style, as an expression of the old High/Low dichotomy, are of little help in navigating the Grid. Any style is as good as any other. What we need are tools with which to work on architecture at a deeper level than style.

Joseph Neufeld and his small group of architects in 1930s Tel Aviv, consciously forming the geometric figure of a Circle, were emblematic of the old hierarchical interplay of cultural power centers that Nobrow deconstructs. A Circle of like-minded talents and personalities is both centrifugal and centripetal. It generates centripetal force by virtue of the intense internal debate among its closely linked members, who are associated by location, educational background, status, and outlook. Centripetal force compresses their argument into a pure state, a polemic. Then, seeking to impress that argument on the larger political and cultural landscape, the Circle propels its polemic outward through publication, lectures, and teaching. To propagate, the Circle has to rely on the brilliance of the polemic—its radiating influence—and to differentiate itself, the Circle argues that its values are higher than other Circles. The geography of Circles is hierarchical, a landscape of mountain peaks—some higher, some lower, some merely foothills.

Consider, in contrast with the Circle, the geographic properties the Grid: a flat, extensive, non-hierarchical field, a set of Cartesian coordinates in which no nodal intersection has any greater differential value than any other. Cultural differentiation, in the form of subcultures and sub-subcultures, thrives on the Grid, where everyone can network but no one can claim cultural hegemony. The only necessary condition is that the Grid functions properly as an infrastructure, operating according to a set of rules that everyone agrees on. The subcultural unit can be as small as one, but there can also be cultures of many. "Followers", "Friends", "Connections", and "User Groups" are some of the names of these larger, fluid cultural units held together by what sociologists call "weak ties". Location, background, and status are dissolved into the ether, and real names can even be hidden behind an alias. A few clicks and instantaneous contact across the Grid can be established, and just as quickly severed.

Architectural Practice on the Grid

A peer-to-peer community of architects and designers working on the intermodal modular platform will be comparatively small. It has no need for influencers with millions or even hundreds of thousands of followers.[22] The relationship of followers to influencers in a global peer-to-peer community will be much closer to the web forums that sprang up in the

1990s and early 2000s, where ideas and influence flow in all directions. It will have little to do with the hyped-up world of mega influencers.[23]

The Volumetric Unit of Construction is style-agnostic. As an architect, naturally I have my preferences, and while, like many architects, I've developed these preferences through what I believe is a personally valid creative journey, on the Grid all style preferences are of equal importance. With the market as an arbiter, as worrisome a proposition as that may be, culture can be democratized. Let's assume, for example, that there is a niche market out there for the kind of architecture that my practice represents. How would I reach that market in this new horizontal world? The question itself is radical from the standpoint of a profession based on the traditional client-architect relationship, analogous to haute-couture. Architecture on the Grid is pret-a-porter. Instead of thinking about the practice of architecture as the design of one building at a time for a singular client, we need to be thinking about designing integrated components that can be used for many buildings.

Maybe I am ambitious and want to create a kit (or write the code, in a manner of speaking) for an entire housing system using the VUC (the operating system) as my underlying chassis. I would develop a fully thought out set of components that can be put together in different arrangements—facades, interiors, kitchens, baths, and accessories like penthouses, balconies, sun shades—or maybe I want to focus more narrowly and redefine, say, the bathroom. I might decide to invest the time to design my product on spec, with the expectation that through design royalties earned through sales, I can generate an income stream. As an influencer, I attract interest from manufacturers with whom I partner to bring my kit to market. Much like the School Construction Systems Development (SCSD) project recounted in Chapter 5, the potential market is large enough that multiple manufacturers will invest in the necessary R&D to coordinate their systems with the standard VUC. Working with the VUC manufacturer's engineering department, I iron out any technical kinks, ensuring that my components are fully "plug and play". We are now traversing the Grid—very different from the traditional model of architectural practice.

Even so, context, climate, local regulations, community engagement, to name only a few local contingencies that bear on architectural projects, mean that every building is still site-specific. The atelier remains critically important.

Perhaps an architect in Los Angeles, designing a high-rise, has researched alternatives and decided that my kit has features that she likes. Working with standard VUCs, she develops a massing scheme, and then floor plans and elevations. She takes exterior and interior material and finishes selections from a standard palette. Let's suppose that there is some flexibility in the budget for a component that my kit doesn't include—say, for example, an exterior shading system to improve energy performance. Through my relationship with the VUC manufacturer, I receive an inquiry from the L.A. architect asking if we can add this one custom component. "Absolutely", I reply. "Just send a sketch of what you have in mind, and I'll work with the manufacturer to engineer it. We'll get back to you in two weeks with the cost". Eventually, the new shading system, having been prototyped and integrated into the building in Los Angeles, is added to the catalog as a standard component. An architect in Dubai then selects it from the catalog for his next project. And so on. A system of licensing rights in exchange for royalties incentivizes the development of new components that continually expand the catalog of apps. Through influencers and memes, compelling ideas propagate.

Later, bitten by the bug, the design architect decides that she can come up with a complete kit that is better than mine, and after six months of development, it's on the market. Architectural firms, in fact, have every reason to delve into intermodal modular product development as well as traditional site-specific building design. One reinforces the other.

Meanwhile, the developer, hoping to pre-sell as many units as possible, has set up a showroom in a leased warehouse. Floor models of apartments, arranged from actual VUC clusters, are displayed in the warehouse for prospective buyers to sample. A couple, young creative types, walk in one day. They are enamored by a two-bedroom unit, but something about the master bath seems wrong. Maybe it's too generic. After a conversation with the sales rep, they go back home to their cramped rental. They start surfing the web for VUCompatible™ bathroom kits, and there it is—an Accoya® lined bathroom just like the one they saw while browsing Houzz one evening.

It turned out that an architect in Brooklyn in a joint venture with a local woodworker, using capital raised on Kickstarter, had developed a bathroom kit called AccoyaSpa™, lined with Accoya® wall panels.[24] The kit is seamlessly integrated with the 4-inch addressable grid of the VUC, and it uses standard catalog riser cassettes. All the details were combed through the year before for technical compatibility by the VUC manufacturer's engineering staff. AccoyaSpa™ comes in several layouts to fit a range of apartment plans. The first year of business was encouraging, with sales of almost 500 units of AccoyaSpa™, and the next year's sales are expected to double. The price of AccoyaSpa™ is of course higher than the standard bathroom that the couple saw in the showroom, but they felt that they could afford it, and the following morning they called the showroom, who then contacted the intermodal modular manufacturer to confirm price and schedule. "Yes, we can include an AccoyaSpa™ bathroom for you". The sale closed.[25]

The design of apartment building facades might even begin to reflect how each occupant chooses to express their living space on the exterior. The rain screen façade technology used for VUCs easily accommodates interchangeable cladding materials, and like the example of the bathroom, façade differentiation is not a technical problem. It is only a question of supply chain and manufacturing logistics. Is it very different from choosing options for a car or a computer? Of course, this may be a little anxious making for design purists... but perhaps we need to loosen up. Some degree of aesthetic control might be exercised by curating a coordinated palette of exterior materials, ensuring that façades are an assemblage of related colors and patterns. Eventually, we might develop a collective design sensibility (sophisticated patchwork quilts were a collaborative—and modular—endeavor) and aesthetic control would then be internalized. And what if it weren't? We would still have attained an unheard-of degree of agency in determining the shape and style of our personal urban habitat.

10.2
Guanajuato, Mexico.

Dutch architect and theorist Nicholas Habraken in the early 1960s wrote a trenchant analysis of the intertwined complex of planning, design, and construction that he called, with capitalization, Mass Housing, abbreviated as MH.[26] Habraken contrasted MH with what he termed the Natural Relationship, a somewhat fanciful but still useful notion of an earlier era in which the inhabitant had a hand in, if not actually constructing his own habitation, at least instructing his builder as to his desires. Over time, dwellings were remodeled or expanded according to the needs of successive inhabitants. Mass Housing, which emerged in response to dire urban housing conditions during the early twentieth 20th century, did away with the agency of the inhabitant, who was now subjected to forces—the government authority, the planner, the developer, the architect – that were exerted from an invisible professional distance.

Urban dwellers have long since internalized MH with unquestioning acceptance, and so it remains an invisible force. From MH's beginnings in social housing, the problem that Habraken identified is today present in virtually all speculative developments at all income levels. MH even pervades in the high-end luxury market, but those who are wealthy enough simply tear out what the developer put in and replace it with an interior designed to custom specification.

In designing a speculative apartment building and lacking a client with whom to engage in a dialogue, the architect (whether consciously or not) invents a fictitious inhabitant for whom to design living spaces. Developers, seeking a predictable response from the market, and not trusting the architect's imagination, turn to real estate brokers to stand in lieu of the client, or more accurately, the buyer. A specialized profession of real estate marketing consultants who focus on the sale has emerged. The first impression of a potential buyer stepping into the apartment for the first time—the wow factor—is paramount.

Were we to fully embrace the Grid in all its potential, would a new form of urban housing based on intermodal modular architecture open the door to a technically viable, economical, and marketable solution to the problem of Mass Housing? For the first time, the middle-class urban apartment owner would be able to shape a living environment before it is built, with the satisfaction of an emotional need that comes from the exercise of personal choice.

The variations in what we might call the design supply chain are virtually limitless. Buildings might be sourced from a "one-stop" kit or assembled from different kits. A building sourced from various kits will be equally compatible and pre-engineered as a one-stop kit. The design process for urban apartment buildings will no longer interpose an insurmountable barrier between architects and inhabitants. It may seem counter-intuitive, but rationalized production based on a standard chassis, along with the flexibility that can be leveraged by information technology, can foster personal expression.

As briefly touched on in Chapter 5, it was not uncommon for cooperative suburban housing associations in the 1940s and 1950s to work with a progressive architect not just to design houses but to develop a community plan. As Carl Koch noted about Conantum—which he designed, built, and lived in—active involvement of home buyers in the planning and building process led to strong community bonds, stewardship of common space, and continual improvement of properties.[27] He observed the difference between a planned development for autoworkers in Detroit and cooperatively developed communities, noting with acuity about Detroit: "A sense of enclosure, passivity; the acceptance of tolerably comfortable circumstances; the use of energy towards conformity; the making of choices but not, in a way, decisions".[28] Without using Habraken's terminology, Koch was talking about the Natural Relationship in cooperative housing. Could this be a model for intermodal modular architecture in a vertical urban context?

We've already noted that intermodal modular architecture will make it possible for small firms to compete on an equal footing with larger firms. The staff and technical depth needed to produce the hundreds of working drawings for a conventional building will no longer be required to design a large multi-story urban building. It is not that jobs have been lost, but that the technical work is now done in a different place. It's more accurate, actually, to say that the technical work has been efficiently redistributed. Some of it is still done by the small design firm. Some of it is done by VUC/Compatible™ component suppliers, and some is done by the VUC manufacturer. There will be plenty of employment opportunities for professionals with architectural, industrial design, engineering, marketing, and other backgrounds. The difference is that design and technical development is no longer vertically integrated within the large architectural firm, but horizontally distributed on the Grid.

It's also worth noting that small firms often struggle to stay afloat financially. One of the reasons architects like to practice small is to be able to be involved hands-on in all aspects of the work, and to do projects that may not generate large fees but which may be creatively, intellectually, or socially motivated. Small firms, in fact, are often where the most culturally challenging and creative work is done. The revenue that a small firm could generate by participating in the design supply chain would support other work that is important but not sufficiently remunerative.

Does the Grid mean the end of excellence? Hardly. The emergence of modern technical complexes like the internet points the way toward a new open-source model for collaboration among peers who prize excellence. An operating system like Linux is created by anonymous programmers around the globe, each contributing a portion of code, critiquing, and correcting one another until the system is perfected. At the same time, open-source collaborations are living endeavors, in a perpetual state of evolution, and new contributors are continually entering the stream. Architecture can adopt this model, but only if the physical thing has a codifiable language – which means dimensionally standardized, addressable, with predictable quality that can only be achieved through industrial production.

• • •

Pritzker Prize winner Rafael Moneo has neatly summed up

> the role of an architect as still centering around the notion that the architect must assume responsibility for what is built… [including] the study of contemporary formal problems, the ability to build within a variety of urban mediums, the knowledge of new programs, a keen knowledge of technical issues, and, lastly, a deep investment in the world of culture while grasping the pregnancy of the moment.[29]

That is as close to a definition of a master builder as one can imagine in the 21st century. We want atelier architects who design our "monumental" buildings to meet Moneo's standard. However, we can't expect that the architects who design our everyday buildings will be Pritzker Prize winners. Everyday architecture can surely coexist with the atelier model— it always has—but for the first time a standard of excellence in everyday architecture will be attainable.

Beyond merely coexisting, a re-alignment of the design supply chain will in fact clear more space for architecture to achieve excellence in the public realm, in the cultural and institutional buildings that are the domain of the atelier architect. If the quality of everyday architecture rises to that of our best industrial design, then pressure will be brought to bear on site-built projects to attain a commensurate level by using more prefabrication and achieving better tolerances.

In closing this chapter, which began with the idea of the "complete architect", let's consider a counter-thesis to Moneo's definitive statement, one that addresses the new horizontal topography of the Grid. We might say that "only through peer collaboration can enough knowledge, talent, and skill be assembled to advance the art and technique of everyday building while answering to the market-driven pressures of cost and time". In the era of intermodal architecture, the atelier architect and the open-source everyday architect may in fact be one and the same, assuming the role of one or the other according to the requirements of each situation. Roles may be redefined, but architects will remain indispensable.

Notes

1 Robert Maulden, *Tectonics in Architecture: From the Physical to the Meta-Physical* (Cambridge, MA: MIT, 1986), 3. Tectonics in architecture is defined as "the science or art of construction, both in relation to use and artistic design". It refers not just to the "activity of making the materially requisite construction that answers certain needs, but rather to the activity that raises this construction to an art form".
2 Nir H. Buras, "Joseph Neufeld in Eretz Israel: Romanticism in Modernism" (doctoral thesis, Israel Institute of Technology, 2000), 148.
3 Catherine Weill-Rochant, "Myths and Buildings of Tel Aviv", Bulletin du Centre de recherche français à Jérusalem (English translations), published December 2003, https://journals.openedition.org/bcrfj/672?amp%3Bid=672.
4 Weill-Rochant, 2003.

5   "White City of Tel-Aviv – The Modern Movement," UNESCO, accessed June 20, 2020, https://whc.unesco.org/en/list/1096/.

6   "Dieter Rams: 10 Principles for Good Design," *Shuffle Magazine*, accessed June 20, 2020, https://readymag.com/shuffle/dieter-rams/.

7   Kenneth Frampton, *Studies in Tectonic Culture* (Cambridge, MA: MIT Press, 1995), 2.

8   George W.S. Trow, *Within the Context of No Context* (Boston, MA: Little, Brown and Company, 1997), 47.

9   Kyle Chayka, "What's the Deal with George W.S. Trow," Culture, *Nation*, April 17, 2019, https://www.thenation.com/article/archive/george-trow-context-no-context-book-harpers-reviewing-social-media/

10 John Seabrook, *Nobrow: The Culture of Marketing, The Marketing of Culture* (New York: Random House, 2001).

11 John Seabrook, interview by PBS affiliate WGBH, *Frontline*, Channel Thirteen, November 18, 2015.

12 Paris Martineau, "The Wired Guide to Influencers," Business, *Wired*, December 6, 2019, https://www.wired.com/story/what-is-an-influencer/.

13 Kevin Roose, "Don't Scoff at Influencers. They're Taking Over the World," Technology, *New York Times*, July 16, 2019, https://www.nytimes.com/2019/07/16/technology/vidcon-social-media-influencers.html.

14 Martineau, 2019.

15 "Internet Usage Statistics: The Internet Big Picture," Internet World Stats, last modified June 12, 2020, https://www.internetworldstats.com/stats.htm.

16 "Instagram by the Numbers: Stats, Demographics & Fun Facts," OmnicoreAgency.com, last modified February 10, 2020, https://www.omnicoreagency.com/instagram-statistics/.

17 Matthias Funk, "How Many YouTube Channels Are There?" *Tubics* (blog), last modified January 31, 2020, https://www.tubics.com/blog/number-of-youtube-channels/.

18 "TikTok Statistics," *99 Firms* (blog), accessed June 20, 2020, https://99firms.com/blog/tiktok-statistics/#gref.

19 See for example, Tom Wolfe's *Electric Kool Aid Acid Test*, or Gay Talese's *Thy Neighbor's Wife*.

20 Wikipedia, s.v. "Meme," last modified May 30, 2020, 06:05, https://en.wikipedia.org/wiki/Meme.

21 Wikipedia, s.v. "Meme."

22 Bella Foxwell, "A Guide to Social Media Influencers: Mega, Macro, Micro, and Nano," *Iconosquare* (blog), last modified February 17, 2020, https://blog.iconosquare.com/guide-to-social-media-influencers/.

23 Foxwell, 2020. In the hierarchy of influencers: Mega (over 1 million followers Macro (100,000–1 million), Micro (10,000–100,000), and Nano (Under 10,000).

24 Accoya® is a sustainably harvested, non-toxic, and extremely water resistant composite hardwood product.

25 If you haven't caught on yet, or aren't sure, the foregoing are hypothetical scenarios. The notion of VUC/Compatible™ is still a concept and has not yet been put into practice.

26 N.J. Habraken and Jonathan Teicher, *Supports: An Alternative to Mass Housing* (London: Urban International Press, 2011).

27 Carl Koch, *At Home with Tomorrow* (New York and Toronto: Rinehart and Company, 1958), 145.

28 Koch, 193.

29 Rafael Moneo, "A Talk with Rafael Moneo: The Beck's Architect Finds in Houston a Plane Truth," interview by Carlos Jiménez, *Cite*, no. 24 (Spring 2000): 23.

11 The Place of Intermodal Modular Architecture

What This Book Has Been About

The world's cities are growing at the rate of a million people a week. The global middle class is projected to reach nearly five billion people by 2030. Urban surface area worldwide is increasing at twice the rate of urban population growth. If there is a sustainable solution to the problem of "housing every two seconds", it is a solution in which three things matter above all else. Number one is scale, and... well... I can't recall what the other two are. Okay, scale is the *one* thing that matters before anything else. Principle #1: Economies of Scale.

Scale is the driver, and from scale, everything else is derived. Scale drives industrialization, interchangeable parts manufacturing, modern quality control techniques. Manufacturing, which entails significant capital investment in plant and equipment, is about economies of scale.

But the legacy modular industry is unable to scale. National, if not global, markets are required to achieve scale in manufacturing, and legacy modular manufacturers are locked in a regional trap of 125-mile trucking. The key to escaping the regional trap lies in Principle #2: Economical Long-Distance Transportation. That key, hidden in plain sight, is intermodal transportation, the system by which tens of millions of shipping containers are moved inexpensively around the globe each year by ship, rail, and truck, all seamlessly interchanged, coordinated, and tracked.

Intermodal modular architecture, like containerization, relies on Principle #3: Intermodal Standards. And economical long-distance transportation, in turn, leads to Principle #4: Global Supply Chains.

The history of prefabricated and modular architecture as commercial enterprises offers lessons for contemporary endeavors. The Sears Modern Homes program, Lustron, Techbuilt, and the School Construction Systems Development (SCSD) project each in their own way adhered to Principle #5: Leverage Existing Infrastructures. Sears built its catalog house business on its pre-existing network of lumber and building supply wholesalers and transported its kit homes by railroad. The Lustron Corporation, previously a manufacturer of porcelain-enameled sheet metal products, created a factory capable of producing 100 porcelain-enameled steel homes a day to meet the post-World War II housing shortage. Techbuilt, the manufacturer of America's best-known Mid-century Modern house, partnered with lumber and millwork suppliers across the U.S. to prefabricate and distribute their post-and-beam frames and infill panels. SCSD, by establishing rigorous design and performance standards along with a guaranteed volume of production, was able to leverage industry partners to do the necessary technical innovation for an economical system of prefabricated schools.

The introduction of containerized shipping more than 60 years ago led to a revolution in global trade, but until now a shipping container was a metal box stuffed with products—it was not the product itself. Starting from a well-intentioned but fruitless effort to develop a scalable method for turning shipping containers into building modules, my team at GBM arrived at Principle #6: Use Intermodal Standards, But Don't Use Shipping Containers. We leveraged the existing intermodal infrastructure to create the Volumetric Unit of Construction, or VUC. The VUC retains the advantages of shipping containers for transportation, but unlike a shipping container the VUC is purpose-engineered to meet the specific and stringent requirements of mid- and high-rise building construction. Principle #7: Spatially Indeterminate Modular Planning is a new approach to designing modular buildings which, with technical innovations such as beam stitching, makes it possible to transform 8-foot-wide VUCs into a boundless variety of living spaces. With Principle #8: Component Assembly, we can manufacture VUCs using on-demand supply-chain methods to bring housing construction up to date with other 21st-century industries.

It seems counter-intuitive that long-distance transportation of VUCs is sustainable, but with Life Cycle Assessment (LCA), we discovered that transportation energy and greenhouse gas impacts are negligible. At the same time, the environmental benefits of economical multi-story housing constructed with VUCs are significant when considered in the context of "location efficiency". This is where we part company with the conventional wisdom that locally sourced building products are inherently sustainable.

Our LCA study established Principle #9: Location Efficiency Matters. Local Sourcing Does Not.

Efficiency in construction has been stagnant for 60 years. Construction culture, rooted in outmoded trade divisions, is resistant to innovation. The history of technology suggests that change is inevitable, but technical innovation is the easy part. Cultural change is difficult. Through the application of Principle #10: Design Thinking, we can address the "wicked problem" of cultural change. Like all wicked problems, cultural change requires the engagement of multiple stakeholders in an ongoing process. Design thinking is a method for reconciling conflicting values through an awareness that any given solution is provisional and always open to "re-solution".

Principle #11: Open Source is the basis on which a new global vernacular will emerge, which will enable stakeholders to write the code, so to speak, of intermodal modular architecture. The internet and social media will link a diverse community of users that will multiply the power of distributed intelligence. The dimensional standards of the VUC, the addressable grid, and rules that govern the arrangement of components—an architectural operating system—will provide behind-the-scenes support for a continually expanding catalog of apps. A web of connections among influencers, entrepreneurs, and stakeholders will ignite a global architectural conversation. Regional differences—cultural, environmental, historical—will find expression within a system of broadly accepted technical standards. Finally, with Principle #12: Differentiation Within Standards, intermodal modular architecture can achieve climate adaptation, regional diversity, and cultural acceptance.

Based on the principles of intermodal modular architecture, the VUC will be the backbone of a coordinated housing system that will spawn a new industrial ecology, an interdependent network of architects, designers, engineers, entrepreneurs, and building product manufacturers that will flourish in a global marketplace. The intermodal modular industry will manufacture a product—multi-story urban housing—that will be both affordable and desirable. By bringing construction costs down to a point where city living is a viable alternative to "drive 'till you qualify", intermodal modular architecture will contribute to an equitable and economically diverse urbanism.

• • •

While this book has largely been devoted to a discussion of what intermodal modular architecture is and what it might become, this final chapter will situate it in a broader context by tracing the boundaries of intermodal modular and exploring what it is not.

We already know that intermodal modular architecture is not traditional construction. How does that affect our emotional connection to our built environment? We are accustomed to thinking of our living spaces as constructed, not as manufactured, with associations to a world of "hand-made" goods. We'll take a clear-eyed look at the nature of manufacturing and the bargain we strike when we exchange a building culture that is craft-based, however anachronistic it might be, for one that is industrial. The word "home" is freighted with personal meaning, while the word "housing" is impersonal. Manufactured housing is associated with the stigma of trailers and trailer parks. As consumers, we purchase goods that come from local as well as global sources. Can we become accustomed to making our home in urban housing that is a product?

Intermodal modular architecture is intended for differentiation, but it is not "made-to-measure". We might say that it is "mass-customized", but we need to understand precisely what that means when it comes to the technical complexities of architecture. We'll interrogate those concepts to understand the essential distinctions between mass-customized and made-to-measure.

Intermodal modular architecture is not a theory of everything. In advocating for the industrialization of urban housing, I would draw a boundary that separates it from the way we furnish and decorate our interior spaces. I would also draw a boundary between intermodal modular architecture as an industrial product and the site. The site—broadly considered as the ground on which buildings are placed, and the public space between buildings— is local, irregular, and contingent on made-to-measure workmanship. By maintaining the distinction with our private interiors on the one hand, and the public realm on the other, intermodal modular architecture can exist in a healthy balance with local craft and building culture.

One further point: intermodal modular architecture is not a housing policy. Rather, it is a design and technical solution to the problems of cost, scale, and sustainability in urban housing production. The private sector can raise capital and organize the production process, but the public sector must ensure that the benefits of intermodal modular architecture are equitably distributed. An impetus in writing this book is my hope that others with expertise in housing policy will see intermodal modular architecture as a tool to achieve beneficial social, environmental, and economic goals.

Finally, intermodal modular architecture is relevant to climate resilience. We'll touch briefly on that topic later in the chapter.

Craft Is a Mentality

At its root craftsmanship is a mentality. It has nothing to do with complexity or fancy ornament, nor is it necessarily a matter of handwork. Judgment, however, is a critical aspect of craftsmanship. Starting with the selection of materials—for example, the knowledge of the behavior of different wood species under various environmental conditions, or the understanding of a particular grain pattern and how to work with it—a woodworker makes continual judgments. At its highest level, judgment becomes an art form. A George Nakashima piece merges the personal sensibility of the craftsman with a profound understanding of the nature of wood.

Synthetic materials with a predictable and uniform consistency are better for digital machining or for 3D printing than materials with inherent flaws or anomalies, because once the machine is set in motion, there is no opportunity for further judgment and response. The translation from an intricately conceived digital model to a computer algorithm that guides a five-axis milling machine or a 3D printer is a bloodless process. When the intention is to invest material with the *simulation* of skill, the results are on some level always inert.

All is not lost, though. If craft touches our emotions, there are also emotional compensations in thoughtfully designed and smartly executed industrial products. We find unexpected affirmation of this in a *New York Times Magazine* article profiling the comedian Jerry Seinfeld. The author quotes Seinfeld: "I have this old 1957 Porsche Speedster, and the way the door closes, I'll just sit there and listen to the sound of the latch going 'cluh-CLICK-click', Seinfeld said. That door! I live for that door. Whatever the opposite of planned obsolescence is, that's what I'm into".[1] In adapting emotionally to an industrial architecture, why shouldn't we experience moments of rapture like the one Seinfeld reports upon closing the door of his vintage Porsche?

What Is Mass-Customization?

Let's take a moment to consider the notion of "mass-customization". What exactly is it? We often hear the phrase used to imply a new design freedom that comes with the digital/industrial revolution, but there seems to be no clear idea of what it means when architects talk about it. To bring some clarity, we'll start by analyzing the two halves of the term, "mass" and "customization", separately.

We understand mass production as having something to do with interchangeable parts manufacturing, along with the concept of tolerance, in which jigs, templates, gauges, and now computer algorithms are used. Mass production replaces the "workmanship of risk" with the "workmanship of certainty".[2] Even so, errors occur, and iterative quality control methods have been devised to manage risk and confine those errors to a low statistical probability. Economies of scale are made possible by replacing risk with a predictable degree of certainty.

Customization, like bespoke tailoring, means things made-to-measure. Each piece is cut to fit, and fitting may require more than one trial to get it right. Made-to-measure is the antithesis of interchangeable parts, and customization in its true sense aims toward a one-off, non-repeatable, and definitive product. In customization, quality is not externalized as a set of objective procedures and standards, like tolerance or six sigma, but is, rather, an internalized and personal ethic, a striving by the craftsman to come as close to an ideal as humanly possible.

Has information technology really changed the nature of things to make a mash-up of these two seemingly opposed concepts possible? Does the computer enable bespoke tailoring at lightning speed to produce goods— each item different, each measured and cut to fit everyone—on a mass scale? Yes, to some extent. Mass-customized jeans, for example, are indeed available and could conceivably become the norm. At the same time, the computer has also made bespoke tailoring more sophisticated. Working at the cutting edge, industrial designer Scott Summit has created highly customized prosthetic limbs,[3] each exquisitely designed and fitted to the body as well as expressive of the personality of each of his clients. Like Summit, many architects today are using the computer to generate complex sculptural forms and richly textured patterns to be milled or 3D-printed by Computer Numerical Control (CNC).

Ordinary mass production entails a cycle of design, prototyping, process engineering, tooling, production start-up, and quality control. In simple CNC operations, it is certainly possible to introduce variations without going through that full production cycle. CNC technology can be used to cut patterns in sheet materials and to mill sculptural forms out of blocks. 3D printing accomplishes this with less waste, and as it becomes scalable, 3D printing will likely play an increasingly important role in many aspects of construction.

Buildings, however, are comprised of multiple interdependent and interpenetrating systems made of widely varied materials and products. Dimensional changes to one system ripple throughout, affecting dimensions, details, and performance, and even code compliance of the entire painstakingly designed arrangement. When it comes to buildings, the argument that there is a short cut to the product cycle—the promise of "mass-customization"—presumes that an algorithm can be written for custom manufacturing a complex object like a building. Perhaps mass-customized housing is theoretically possible, with as yet unrealized computational power and artificial intelligence. Applied to buildings—or even building modules—the notion of mass-customization is at present, however, an oxymoron, at best a rhetorical figure of speech.

Maybe we should think of mass-customization in architecture as a useful illusion. In cinema, the illusion of motion is created by 24 still frames a second. As in cinema, the illusion of mass-customization can be created by a menu of pre-set options extensive and varied enough to trick us into thinking that each choice on the menu was tailored to suit each individual desire. Let's call each menu item a "unit of choice" and each individual desire a "unit of desire". If choices could be infinitely varied, there would be a unit of choice that would match each unit of desire, and we would have true mass-customization. In buildings, however, there will always be far fewer units of choice available (by many orders of magnitude) than there will be units of desire. We must accept that the closest thing to mass-customization in architecture is nothing more than an increased (but always finite) number of choices. That the application of computer power enables a significant increase in the number of those choices is no small thing. Intermodal modular architecture harnessed to information technology and operating on a global scale would offer unprecedented choice in the way our everyday buildings are designed.

The Private Domain and the Public Realm

Housing occupies a middle realm where the private domain of our interior environment meets the outer, public realm of the urban landscape which we share with others in our daily comings and goings. Reflecting on the "world of things", Hannah Arendt wrote:

> To live together in the world means essentially that a world of things is between those who have it in common, as a table is located between those who sit around it; the world, like every in-between, relates and separates men at the same time. The public realm, as the common world, gathers us together and yet prevents our falling over each other, so to speak. What makes mass society so difficult to bear is not the number of people involved, or at least not primarily, but the fact that the world between them has lost its power to gather them together, to relate and to separate them.[4]

If housing made in factories mediates between our inner private domain and the outer public realm, is there still a place for local craft culture? What does a shift from the one-off, site-constructed building to an industrialized solution mean when it comes to our interior and exterior environments?

We populate our interior spaces with furniture, fabrics, accessories, books, gear, and all manner of quirky knick-knacks. Factory-made housing will not address our yearning for the connection to the world that we make through handmade objects or locally grown food. Still, we can look forward to an industrialized architecture that resonates like a well-designed and manufactured automobile while at the same time we can furnish our living spaces with our personal collection of craft, art, and sentimental objects. While craft skills in the building trades have been in steady decline for a century or more, local and regional craft production and small-scale manufacturing in furniture, fiber arts, ceramics, glass, and metalwork have remained vital, even enjoying a renaissance over the last several decades. Recent trends in local artisanal foods and beverages spring from the same appreciation for the handmade and the personal. Craft, defined as "will and skill—the will to take pains and the skill and resourcefulness to take pains creatively and effectively",[5] is as necessary and urgent now and for the future as it ever was.

American crafts are firmly ensconced in higher education at institutions like the Rhode Island School of Design or Alfred University. Young graduates of these schools set up shop where space can be had at low cost, establish small-scale internet-based companies, and show their work at crafts fairs or in galleries. Aggregators like Etsy have created global marketing platforms for locally made crafts. In this arena, design and skill in crafts are alive and well. The attraction to crafts answers to a human "instinct for workmanship", a need to exercise agency over the material world that is deeply rooted in our psyche.

If the continuity and vitality of craft/design traditions allow us to invest our industrially made interior spaces with personal meaning, local, site-based craft is equally irreplaceable in the construction of the public realm, the ground on which our buildings are placed and the surrounding urban landscape. The irregular contours of each site call for a unique response that mediates the relationship of constructed geometry to that irregularity. Irregularity requires the use of measure, cut, and fit construction methods. Even with laser scanning technology and digital fabrication, final fitting must be done in place. Craft skills, aided by technology, will always be required to shape and join materials in contact with the earth—the cutting and setting of stone masonry, or the integration of metalwork in the form of gates, balustrades, lamp posts, and the like.

Projects like New York's High Line point the way toward a re-vitalized public realm, and the public shows its appreciation by flocking to it in droves. But too many of our public spaces are visually impoverished, with unimaginative design, poor materials, and crude details. There is plenty of work to do. Building public space requires skills and attitudes that go hand in hand with craft traditions. Investment in our public spaces, along with a commitment to excellence in design and construction, would offer an inexhaustible opportunity to make improvements to streets, plazas, and parks. The definition of "infrastructure" should be broadened to include the public realm.

Far from being a call to abandon traditional workmanship, the industrialization of housing is an opportunity to reallocate resources and to use traditional workmanship more effectively. By investing in the public realm, where there is an appropriate match between the contingent nature of irregular site conditions and measure-to-fit techniques, we can support traditional building trades. Even as we transform housing with the adoption of advanced manufacturing technology, it should be our national mission to develop and maintain a manually skilled workforce. By investing in our local public spaces, we can simultaneously create lasting and beautiful works and renew our confidence that we possess the agency to shape our world.

Resilience and Climate Adaptation

In the last decade or so, we have become increasingly aware that urban development is inseparable from resilience. According to the World Health Organization, natural disasters kill 90,000 people each year, and affect another 160 million.[6] In terms of economic cost, in 2019, there were 40 disasters that cost $1 billion or more, and the decade 2010–2019 had the highest dollar cost of the last three decades.[7] Increased frequency and intensity of weather-related disasters are anticipated due to climate change.[8] Catastrophic damage resulting from non-weather-related events, such as earthquakes and tsunamis affecting Haiti in 2010, Fukushima in 2011, and New Zealand in 2011, also affects vulnerable urban populations. As urban populations continue to increase, the scale of human suffering from natural disasters will be magnified.

While the application of intermodal modular architecture as a solution for urban resilience is worthy of further study, it is beyond the scope of this book. Even so, we can still mention some general concepts that suggest an outline for exploration in greater depth.

The problem of disaster relief housing is the problem of scale multiplied by urgency. Tens of thousands of people are suddenly without shelter, and days stretch into weeks and months during which sorely strained temporary facilities or improvised shelters become the new normal for families. In the wake of Hurricane Katrina in 2005, FEMA ordered 140,000[9] travel trailers. By comparison, the annual output of the entire U.S.-manufactured homes industry (modular housing built to HUD standards) is about 90,000 units.[10] Aside from inadequate industry capacity, manufactured homes are oversize modules that are more difficult to transport than trailers. FEMA, lacking other prefabricated alternatives, haplessly turned to trailers, which met the requirements of scale and speed.

In the wake of a disaster, once the basics of food, water, shelter, and sanitation are provided, the ability for people to interact socially along with the expectation that they will soon return to reconstructed neighborhoods is essential to make the condition of displacement bearable. The FEMA trailers were parked in vast fields, leaving people isolated and cut off from their communities. Reconstruction took years. Meanwhile, families without other options saw no choice but to leave New Orleans and relocate elsewhere. The FEMA trailer was a poor solution for community building.

The planning of temporary settlements with an eye toward reconstruction can surely make a difference. Ideally, the temporary solution should contain within it the seeds to grow organically into permanent neighborhoods that will flourish soon after the initial emergency subsides. Beyond the provision of basic shelter, the rapid deployment of VUCs can be the first phase of a comprehensive approach to post-disaster community building. VUCs can be mobilized at the scale and speed required, while allowing for the variation and flexibility needed to create diverse, human-scale neighborhoods.

VUCs for emergency housing, manufactured around the world to a common standard, could be stockpiled in large quantities for rapid deployment on the intermodal transportation system. The first VUCs to arrive on site would contain core elements—kitchens and bathrooms—placed on temporary foundations and connected to temporary infrastructure. Initially supplemented by tents, additional VUCs comprising sleeping rooms would arrive afterward to aggregate with cores into larger living units. Arrangements of emergency VUCs should include space for social and cultural life.

Meanwhile, planners and architects working with displaced property owners and community stakeholders can be designing new resilient communities. New housing, based on VUC dimensions, could be multi-story or low-rise, whichever makes sense. In low-lying coastal areas, reconstructed neighborhoods should, if feasible, be relocated to higher ground.[11] Once infrastructure is in place, the initially deployed VUCs can be picked up and quickly reassembled into new neighborhood configurations. Extra VUCs would be provided to enable phased occupancy directly from temporary to permanent housing. At the end of the reconstruction cycle, these surplus units would be returned to the emergency stockpile.

Supply lines are severed when hurricanes, typhoons, and tsunamis strike coastal regions. Damaged roads and bridges, downed power lines, and loss of fuel supply can prevent or impede recovery efforts. Disrupted overland supply lines need not prevent rapid delivery of VUCs. Container ships anchored in deep water can offload to shallow-draft barges to carry VUCs ashore.

The VUC is an easily transported steel-framed module. It is engineered to the stringent requirements of contemporary building codes, including the structural capability to withstand hurricanes and earthquakes. Resilience is built into intermodal modular architecture.

A Few Words on Policy

A detailed discussion of housing policy is beyond the author's expertise, but a few words are in order. Housing policy encompasses issues—social, political, financial—that are intertwined with architecture but are not determined by it. Without good policies, an architectural solution that brings down the cost of housing production will not necessarily bring affordability to a market economy. Market-driven land values in urban cores will remain a significant housing cost driver. Developers will have no incentive to bring the price of housing down and unless constrained will pocket the construction cost savings that come from selling or renting lower cost intermodal modular housing at market rates. Housing for the homeless, the poor, and the working poor will always require subsidies, and while intermodal modular architecture may enable subsidies to be reduced, they will not disappear. Gentrification is driven by market forces and will only be remedied through urban regeneration policies that protect the rights of poorer residents. To foster the equitable distribution economic benefits, shift to an industrialized system of housing will have to be accompanied by policies that strike the right balance between profit and affordability.

Because industrialized housing begins with scale, there is no New York solution, or San Francisco solution, or London, Sydney, Mumbai, or Seoul solution to the problem of housing construction cost and quality. We must abandon the idea of locally manufactured modular buildings and turn instead to a global, open-source solution. Urban cores—with high real estate costs, high labor costs, and congested streets—are the least cost-effective places for large-scale manufacturing. VUCs should be manufactured where it makes economic sense. They can be transported anywhere.

There it is—the unsentimental, remorseless logic of global capitalism. Is that necessarily bad? It depends on whether market forces are held in check by countervailing policies that channel capitalism's productive capability toward socially constructive purposes and toward the equitable distribution of wealth. We must not make the error of confusing means with ends. Intermodal modular architecture is a technology, a tool. How that tool is managed, and who it benefits, is a matter of policy. Technology won't tell us what to do.

• • •

The pace at which the world is changing calls for world-changing ideas. The acceleration of urban population growth, of climate change, of resource depletion are all problems of scale, and without commensurate scale our responses to those problems will fall short. Scale has always been the dark side of modernity. It is disorienting, overwhelming, and alienating. The malaise of scale tempts us to seek reassurance in local, place-specific pleasures. But we must do more than find ameliorating pleasures while letting scale permeate thoughtlessly as we cede open space to the sprawling megalopolis and the implacable demands of the automobile.

The challenge, then, is how to manage scale through diversity, differentiation, and local adaptation, and critically, with urban density. Architecture as an art form remains essential, but it is not scalable. The artist's vision magnified to urban scale has proven a disaster. I was educated to think that Le Corbusier unfairly took the blame for the brutal tower-in-the-park public housing of the Robert Moses era, but like many architects I've come to reject total visions of the world, whether it is the rational vision embodied in Le Corbusier's Radiant City or the pastoral vision of Frank Lloyd Wright's Broadacre City. At the highest level, this book aims for a synthesis of Moses' impact with the organic, circumstantial, and small-scale contributions of myriad individuals that Jane Jacobs celebrated as the ingredients of successful cities.

Intermodal modular architecture is ultimately about differentiation. To borrow the ancient parable,[12] it is a system designed with a hedgehog's singular focus on which foxes will play innumerable riffs and inventions. The global flow of information in digital form will have its physical counterpart embodied in the VUC, the byte of a steel-framed architecture gliding across oceans on the intermodal shipping network. Open-source design will release a torrent of ideas, experiments, and enterprises. There will be no controlling vision, only a set of well thought out rules.

The artistically conceived building or ensemble of buildings will always be an indispensable form of architectural expression, but if we are to manage global scale without sacrificing human scale, we must broaden our definitions and shake ourselves loose from a fixation on *all* architecture as "art". The future of modular architecture is an "artless" everyday architecture—a building culture that scales itself and at the same time differentiates itself, in the way that spoken language evolves over time and with popular usage. Intermodal modular architecture is a scalable, shared, open-source language of industrialized construction—a global vernacular. That is a world-changing idea.

Notes

1 Jonah Weiner, "Jerry Seinfeld Intends to Die Standing Up," *New York Times Magazine*, December 23, 2012, 27.
2 David Pye, *The Nature and Art of Workmanship* (London: Cambridge University Press, 1968), 4–8.
3 "Work," Summit ID Industrial Design, accessed June 22, 2020, http://www.summitid. com/.

4 Hannah Arendt, *The Human Condition* (Chicago, IL: University of Chicago Press, 1956), 52–53.

5 Don Wallance, *Shaping America's Products* (New York: Rhineholt, 1956), 10. Don Wallance, 1909–1990, was the author's father.

6 "Environmental Health in Emergencies," World Health Organization, accessed June 22, 2020, https://www.who.int/environmental_health_emergencies/natural_events/en/.

7 Jeff Masters, "Earth's 40 Billion-Dollar Weather Disasters of 2019: 4th Most Billion-Dollar Events on Record," Opinion, *Scientific American*, January 22, 2020, https://blogs.scientificamerican.com/eye-of-the-storm/earths-40-billion-dollar-weather-disasters-of-2019-4th-most-billion-dollar-events-on-record/#:~:text=In%20the%20U.S.%2C%20there%20were,to%20both%20Aon%20and%20NOAA.&text=The%201980%E2%80%932019%20annual%20inflation,than%20doubled%2C%20to%2013.8%20events.

8 "New Approaches to Help Businesses Tackle Climate Change," Research News, *University of Cambridge*, February 22, 2020, https://www.cam.ac.uk/research/news/new-approaches-to-help-businesses-tackle-climate-change.

9 Michael Kunzelman and Michael Biesecker, "Lessons learned from Katrina, FEMA says it won't rely on trailers for Irma, Harvey victims," News, *Advocate*, September 19, 2017, https://www.theadvocate.com/baton_rouge/news/article_19ecca5c-9d4c-11e7-845b-7f0edcb8d0a7.html#:~:text=FEMA%20purchased%20more%20than%20140%2C000,or%20in%20makeshift%20trailer%20parks.

10 "Who We Are," MHI Manufactured Housing Institute, accessed June 22, 2020, https://www.manufacturedhousing.org/who-we-are/. The distinction between travel trailers and manufactured homes is commonly misunderstood. Trailers are a recreational product not meant for permanent habitation.

11 Christopher Flavelle, "U.S. Flood Strategy Shifts to 'Unavoidable' Relocation of Entire Neighborhoods," *New York Times*, August 26, 2020, accessed August 28, 2020, https://www.nytimes.com/2020/08/26/climate/flooding-relocation-managed-retreat.html?action=click&module=Top%20Stories&pgtype=Homepage

12 Isaiah Berlin, *The Hedgehog and the Fox* (London: Weidenfeld & Nicolson, 1963).

Glossary

Beam Stitching A method of bolting the floor rails of a VUC to the roof rails of the VUC below, to create a composite beam and thereby increase floor stiffness. (See Volumetric Unit of Construction.)

Building Information Model (BIM) A three-dimensional computer model that, in addition to representing the geometry of a building, contains data that describe the building and its various parts. Used for managing the design, construction, and operation of a building throughout its life cycle.

Building Services The mechanical, electrical, plumbing, fire protection, and information technology systems of a building.

Building Typologies Classifications of buildings, based on their form and function as derived from the organization of space, structure, cores, and services.

Cold-formed steel Steel sheet or plate that has been formed into a bent shape without heat, useful for comparatively thin cross-sections and custom profiles.

Column Stitching A method of bolting adjoining corner posts of VUCs to create a composite column and thereby increase resistance to buckling. (See Volumetric Unit of Construction.)

Continuous Insulation Building insulation that is uninterrupted by studs or structural framing, resulting in improved thermal performance.

Cores The vertical systems of a building that include elevators, egress stairs, and building service risers.

Dead Load The permanent weight of a building structure, exclusive of live loads and superimposed dead loads. (See Live Loads and Superimposed Dead Loads.)

Greenhouse Gas (GHG) Gaseous compounds generated by human activity, including carbon dioxide, methane, nitrous oxide, ozone, and water vapor, which contribute to climate change by absorbing infrared radiation and trapping heat in the Earth's atmosphere.

Hot-rolled steel Steel that has been formed by moving a red-hot billet (a thick bar) between pairs of rollers to form it into a structural cross-section such as an I-beam, used for the primary structural members of buildings.

Inclusionary Housing A mandatory requirement or zoning incentive to create a certain percentage of low-income housing as part of a new or substantially rehabilitated housing development.

Intermodal Modular Architecture Modular architecture based on the dimensions and automated freight handling requirements of intermodal shipping but designed and engineered expressly for building construction.

Life Cycle Assessment (LCA) A method of accounting for the environmental impacts over the cradle-to-grave or cradle-to-cradle life of a product, process, or service, including buildings.

Lateral Load A horizontal load imposed on a building by wind or seismic forces.

Live Load A non-permanent load on a building or structure exclusive of the structure itself. Live loads may include people, furniture, equipment, etc., and may be fixed or moveable.

Manufacturing The industrial process by which goods are produced in large quantities from raw materials. Manufacturing is economical, and allows for high degree of quality control.

Mateline(s) The joint(s) between two adjacent building modules after they have been craned into place, which must then be patched and finished.

MEPF Mechanical, electrical, plumbing, and fire protection systems.

Modular Merriam Webster offers an excellent definition of modular, quoted here: "constructed with standardized units or dimensions for flexibility and variety in use."

Nodes The steel corner blocks of a VUC, which conform to international shipping container standards. (See Volumetric Unit of Construction.)

Podium A low-rise base of a high-rise building that may contain uses such as retail, educational, cultural, etc.

Post-tensioning A method of reinforcing a structural member by inserting a rod or cable through the member and then tensioning it, which creates an internal force that counteracts external forces.

Prefabrication Off-site fabrication, often to a custom specification, of building components that may comprise all or part of a completed building.

Rails The structural members that stiffen the top and bottom edges of a VUC (from shipping container terminology). (See Volumetric Unit of Construction.)

Rain Screen A type of building façade comprised of open-jointed panels mounted in front of an air- and water-tight barrier, which accepts the intrusion of rainwater into a drained and ventilated cavity.

Spatially Determinate Modular architecture in which each building module is a room, the dimension of a single module, with openings between modules to connect one room to another.

Spatially Indeterminate Modular architecture in which two or more modules can be joined to create rooms larger than the dimension of a single module.

Stack Joint The horizontal joint between adjoining units of curtain wall or building modules.

Stressed-skin A type of strong and lightweight structural panel comprised of thin sheets of plywood, metal, or other material bonded to a lightweight core.

Superimposed Dead Load A secondary permanent load that is added to the primary structure of a building, including the weight of partitions, facades, roofing, air conditioning systems, etc. (See Dead Load and Live Load.)

Tectonics The architectural expression of structure raised to the level of art.

Thermal Bridging The interruption of a layer of building insulation by thermally conductive materials, such as studs or structural framing, which reduce its thermal performance.

Thermal Envelope The thermally resistive layer, generally comprised of insulation or insulated glass, in a wall, roof, or floor assembly.

Tolerance An allowance made to accommodate the inevitable discrepancy between theoretical and actual dimensions in joining two or more fabricated or constructed elements.

Twenty-foot Equivalent Unit (TEU) The standard measure of shipping container quantity used for statistical purposes. A 40-foot container equals 2 TEU.

Unitized Curtain Wall Prefabricated non-load bearing façade panels, often comprised primarily of glass set in an aluminum frame, that span from floor to floor of a multi-story building.

Urban Overbuild Urban development constructed on platforms spanning over open infrastructure such as rail yards or expressways.

Volumetric Unit of Construction (VUC) A building module conforming to standards for intermodal shipping, designed and engineered expressly for building construction; the fundamental element of intermodal modular architecture. (See Intermodal Modular Architecture.)

Bibliography

Chapter 1

"Nomadic Museum." World-Architects.com. Accessed July 20, 2020. https://www.world-architects.com/en/shigeru-ban-architects-tokyo/project/nomadic-museum.

Castonguay, James. "International Shipping: Globalization in Crisis." *Witness*. Accessed July 20, 2020. https://www.visionproject.org/images/img_magazine/pdfs/international_shipping.pdf.

Irwin, Douglas A. "The False Promise of Protectionism." *Foreign Affairs*, May/June 2017. https://www.foreignaffairs.com/articles/united-states/2017-04-17/false-promise-protectionism.

Muschamp, Herbert. "It's Something New under the Stars (And Looking Up)." *New York Times*, February 13, 2000.

Putzier, Konrad. "Momentum Builds for Automation in Construction." *Wall Street Journal*, July 2, 2019. https://www.wsj.com/articles/momentum-builds-for-automation-in-construction-11562073426.

Rudofsky, Bernard. *Architecture without Architects*. Garden City, NJ: Doubleday, 1964.

Chapter 2

"68% of the World Population Projected to Live in Urban Areas by 2050, Says UN." United Nations Department of Economic and Social Affairs. Published May 16, 2018. https://www.un.org/development/desa/en/news/population/2018-revision-of-world-urbanization-prospects.html.

"What Is Inclusionary Housing?" Inclusionary Housing. Accessed July 4, 2020. https://inclusionaryhousing.org/inclusionary-housing-explained/what-is-inclusionary-housing/#:~:text=Inclusionary%20housing%20programs%20are%20local,units%20to%20lower%2Dincome%20residents.

Ali, Shimelse and Uri Dadush. "The Global Middle Class is Bigger than We Thought." Argument. *Foreign Policy*, May 16, 2012. https://foreignpolicy.com/2012/05/16/the-global-middle-class-is-bigger-than-we-thought/.

Bassett, Mary T. "Just Because You Can Afford to Leave the City Doesn't Mean You Should." Opinion. *New York Times*, May 15, 2020. https://www.nytimes.com/2020/05/15/opinion/sunday/coronavirus-cities-density.html.

Bongaarts, John. "Household Size and Composition in the Developing World in the 1990s." *Population Studies* 55, no. 3 (2001): 263–279.

Chetty, Raj, Nathaniel Hendren, Patrick Kline and Emmanuel Saez. "The Equality of Opportunity Project." Harvard University, University of California Berkley, 2013.

Cukar, Tyler. "Orchestrated Urbanism: The Race Built City." *FXCollaborative Podium*. Published November 29, 2017. http://www.fxcollaborative.com/activity/publications/13/orchestrated-urbanism/.

Dash, Uri and Shimelse Ali. "In Search of the Global Middle Class: A New Index." Carnegie Endowment for International Peace. Published July 23, 2012. https://carnegieendowment.org/2012/07/23/in-search-of-global-middle-class-new-index-pub-48908.

Dudley, Michael Quinn. "Sprawl As Strategy: City Planners Face the Bomb." *Journal of Planning Education and Research* 21, no. 1 (2001): 52–63.

Editorial Board. "The Cities We Need." Opinion. *New York Times*, May 11, 2020. https://www.nytimes.com/2020/05/11/opinion/sunday/coronavirus-us-cities-inequality.html.

Florida, Richard. *The New Urban Crisis: How Our Cities Are Increasing Inequality, Deepening Segregation, And Failing The Middle Class – And What We Can Do About It*. New York: Basic Books, 2017.

Freidrichs, Chad, dir. *The Pruitt-Igoe Myth*. 2011; St. Louis, MO: Unicorn Stencil. DVD.

Friedman, Thomas. "India vs. China vs. Egypt." Opinion. *New York Times*, February 6, 2013. https://www.nytimes.com/2013/02/06/opinion/friedman-india-vs-china-vs-egypt.html.

Frumkin, Howard. "Urban Sprawl and Public Health." *Public Health Reports* 117, no. 3 (2002): 201–217. Accessed August 9, 2020. https://doi.org/10.1093/phr/117.3.201.

Hickey, Robert, Jeffrey Lubell, Peter Haas and Stephanie Morse. "Losing Ground: The Struggle of Moderate-Income Households to Afford the Rising Costs of Housing and Transportation." *Center for Housing Policy* and *Center for Neighborhood Technology*, 2012. https://www.novoco.com/sites/default/files/atoms/files/nhc_losing_ground_101812.pdf.

Isaacs, Julia B. "International Comparisons of Economic Mobility." *The Brookings Institution*, (2016): 6. https://www.brookings.edu/wp-content/uploads/2016/07/02_economic_mobility_sawhill_ch3.pdf.

Kimmelman, Michael. "Towers of Dreams: One Ended in Nightmare." Critic's Notebook. *New York Times*, January 25, 2012. https://www.nytimes.com/2012/01/26/arts/design/penn-south-and-pruitt-igoe-starkly-different-housing-plans.html.

Krugman, Paul. "Stranded by Sprawl." Opinion. *New York Times*, July 28, 2013. https://www.nytimes.com/2013/07/29/opinion/krugman-stranded-by-sprawl.html.

Leonhardt, Dave. "In Climbing Income Ladder, Location Matters." *New York Times*, July 22, 2013. https://www.nytimes.com/2013/07/22/business/in-climbing-income-ladder-location-matters.html.

Semuels, Alana. "Why Are Developers Still Building Sprawl?" Business. *Atlantic*, February 24, 2015. https://www.theatlantic.com/business/archive/2015/02/why-are-people-still-building-sprawl/385741/.

Seto, Karen C., Burak Güneralp and Lucy R. Hutyra. "Global Forecasts of Urban Expansion to 2030 and Direct Impacts on Biodiversity and Carbon Pools." *Proceedings of the National Academy of Sciences of the United States of America* 109, no. 4 (2012): 16083.

Stromberg, Joseph. "The Real Story behind the Demise of America's Once-mighty Streetcars." *Vox*, May 7, 2015. https://www.vox.com/2015/5/7/8562007/streetcar-history-demise.

Tomer, Adie, Elizabeth Kneebone, Robert Puentes and Alan Berube. "Metropolitan Opportunity: Transit and Jobs in Metropolitan America." *Metropolitan Infrastructure Initiative Series and Metropolitan Opportunity Series*, 2011. https://www.brookings.edu/wp-content/uploads/2016/06/0512_jobs_transit.pdf.

Vassigh, Alidad and Tab vom Hove. "Urban Population Growth between 1950 and 2030." Last modified August 7, 2012. http://www.citymayors.com/statistics/urban-population-intro.html.

Wallance, David and Austin Sakong. "Boundary Issues: Building Form, Site Form, Urban Form." *FXCollaborative Podium*, 2020. Accessed July 4, 2020. https://issuu.com/fxfowle/docs/190220_boundaryissues.

Woetzel, Jonathan, Jan Mischke and Sangeeth Ram. "The World's Housing Crisis Doesn't Need a Revolutionary Solution." Policy. *Harvard Business Review*, December 25, 2014. https://hbr.org/2014/12/the-worlds-housing-crisis-doesnt-need-a-revolutionary-solution.

Yapp, Jimmy. "Singaporean Former Diplomat Kishore Mahbubani on Why He Is Optimistic about the Future." ACCA. Published October 1, 2016. https://www.accaglobal.com/in/en/member/member/accounting-business/2016/10/interviews/kishore-mahbubani.html.

Chapter 3

"Auction of Kullman Building Corp. Assets Set for Tuesday, Dec. 13 Under Direction of Alco Capital, Assignee for Benefit Creditors." Cision PR Newswire. Published December 7, 2011. https://www.prnewswire.com/news-releases/auction-of-kullman-building-corp-assets-set-for-tuesday-dec-13-under-direction-of-alco-capital-assignee-for-benefit-of-creditors-135182808.html.

"Facts about Manufactured Housing." Prosperity Now. Published June 2019. https://prosperitynow.org/resources/facts-about-manufactured-housing-2019.

"Home." BTEA. Accessed July 5, 2020. https://www.bteany.com/home/.

"Modular Homes." Dwellito. Accessed July 5, 2020. https://www.dwellito.com/modular-homes.

"Permanent Modular Construction Annual Report 2019." Modular Building Institute, 2019. https://www.modular.org/documents/public/images/2019-PMC-Report-reduced.pdf.

Bertram, Nick, Steffen Fuchs, Jan Mischke, Robert Palter, Gernot Strube and Jonathan Woetzel, "Modular Construction: From Projects to Products." McKinsey & Company. Published June 18, 2019. https://www.mckinsey.com/industries/capital-projects-and-infrastructure/our-insights/modular-construction-from-projects-to-products#.

Frishberg, Hannah. "Rising Rents in Brooklyn Force Navy Yard Modular Factory Capsys to Close." Brownstoner. Published October 20, 2015. https://www.brownstoner.com/real-estate-market/capsys-brooklyn-navy-yard-factory-closes-due-to-rising-rents/.

Jackson, Kenneth T. *Crabgrass Frontier: The Suburbanization of America*. New York: Oxford University Press, 1985.

Kieran, Stephen and James Timberlake. *Refabricating Architecture*. New York: McGraw-Hill, 2004. (Also Chapters 6, 8.)

Oder, Norman. "STV_8/15/14 with Highlights." Scribd (August, 2017). https://www.scribd.com/document/276397805/STV-8-15-14-With-Highlights.

Rudden, Jennifer. "Number of Multifamily Housing Start in the U.S. 2000–2018." Statista. Published June 29, 2020. https://www.statista.com/statistics/184845/multifamily-house-starts-in-the-united-states-since-2000/.

Smith, Ryan E. *Prefab Architecture: A Guide for Architects and Construction Professionals*. Hoboken, NJ: John Wiley & Sons, 2011. (Also Chapter 6.)

Teicholz, Paul. "Labor-Productivity Declines in the Construction Industry: Causes and Remedies (Another Look)." *AECbytes*. Published March 14, 2013. http://www.aecbytes.com/viewpoint/2013/issue_67.html.

Turi, Attila, Marian Mocan, Larisa Ivascu, Gilles Goncalves and Sorin Maistor. "From Fordism to Lean Management: Main Shifts in Automotive Industry Evolution within the Last Century." Paper presented at the Proceedings of the MakeLearn and TIM Joint International Conference 2, Bari, Italy, May 27–29, 2015. http://www.toknowpress.net/ISBN/978-961-6914-13-0/papers/ML15-098.pdf.

Urie, Daniel. "Thousands Laid Off in 2017 at Companies Throughout Pa." Penn Live Patriot-News. Last modified May 22, 2019. https://www.pennlive.com/business/2018/01/warn.html.

Vitullo-Martin, Julia and Hope Cohen. *Construction Labor Costs in New York City: A Moment of Opportunity*, report. New York: Regional Plan Association, June 2011. https://rpa.org/uploads/pdfs/RPA-CUI-Construction-Costs.pdf.

Winters Downey, Erika and Jason Ericksen. "Tolerance Illustrated." *SteelWise*. Published October 2006. https://www.aisc.org/globalassets/modern-steel/steelwise/102006_30758_steelwise_tolerances.pdf.

Chapter 4

"7 Ships Proposed to Take Trailers." *New York Times*, June 17, 1955.

"America on the Move, Transforming the Waterfront." National Museum of American History Behring Center. Accessed July 9, 2020. https://americanhistory.si.edu/america-on-the-move/transforming-waterfront.

"Container Port Traffic (TEU: 20 foot equivalent units)." The World Bank. Accessed July 9 2020. https://data.worldbank.org/indicator/IS.SHP.GOOD.TU.

"History." Waterfront Commission of New York Harbor. Accessed July 9, 2020. http://www.wcnyh.gov/history.htm.

"Interstate Commerce Commission." U.S. Government Manual. July 1, 1995. https://www.govinfo.gov/content/pkg/GOVMAN-1995-07-01/pdf/GOVMAN-1995-07-01-Pg596.pdf.

"Malaccamax." Maritime Connector. Accessed July 9, 2020. http://maritime-connector.com/wiki/malaccamax/.

"Number Search." USPTO Patent Full-Text and Image Database. Accessed July 11, 2020. http://patft.uspto.gov/netahtml/PTO/srchnum.htm.

"Pier Strike Terms Reached; Pay Increased by 13 Cents; Union to Vote on Saturday." *New York Times*, November 25, 1948.

"The ILWU Story." ILWU. Accessed July 9, 2020. https://www.ilwu.org/history/the-ilwu-story/.

"Total Value of Exports and Imports (1950-) – Trade Statistics of Japan." Trade Statistics of Japan. Accessed July 9, 2020. https://www.customs.go.jp/toukei/suii/html/nenbet_e.htm.

"Triple-E Class Container Ship, Denmark." Ship Technology. Accessed July 9, 2020. https://www.ship-technology.com/projects/triple-e-class-container-ship/.

"Wildcat Strikers Make 15 Piers Idle." *New York Times*, October 16, 1951.

"WLB Orders Strike Ended." *New York Times*, April 28, 1945.

Barnes, Charles B. *The Longshoremen.* New York: Russell Sages Foundation, 1915.

Davis, Collins J. "'Shape or Fight?': New York's Black Longshoremen, 1945–1961." *International Labor and Working-Class History* 62, no. 1 (2002): 143–163. Accessed July 2, 2020. www.jstor.org/stable/27672812.

Donovan, Arthur. "Longshoremen and Mechanization." *Journal for Maritime Research* 1, no. 1 (1999): 66–75.

Donovan, Arthur and Joseph Bonney. *The Box That Changed the World: Fifty Years of Container Shipping – An Illustrated History*. East Windsor, NJ: Commonwealth Business Media, 2006.

Horne, George. "4,000 Pier Workers in Wildcat Strike Delay 11 Sailings." *New York Times*, August 21, 1947.

Irwin, Douglas A. Irwin. "The False Promise of Protectionism." *Foreign Affairs*. May/June 2017. https://www.foreignaffairs.com/articles/united-states/2017-04-17/false-promise-protectionism.

Leonhardt, David. "Keith W. Tantlinger, b. 1919." The Lives They Lived. *New York Times Magazine*, December 22, 2011.

Levinson, Marc. *The Box: How the Shipping Container Made the World Smaller and the World Economy Bigger*. Princeton, NJ: Princeton University Press, 2006.

Maritime Transportation Research Board. *Case Studies in Maritime Innovation*. Washington, DC: National Academy of Sciences, 1978.

Mumford, Lewis. *Technics and Civilization*. New York: Harcourt Brace & Company, 1934.

Raskin, A.H. "I.L.A. Leaders Ask Pact Acceptance." *New York Times*, December 31, 1954.

Raskin, A.H. "Union Head Backs 'Sea-Land' Trucks: Beck Approves A Coastwise Trailer-Transport Service to Help the Industry." *New York Times*, February 17, 1954.

Van Ham, Hans, J. C. van Ham and Joan Rijsenbrij. *Development of Containerization: Success through Vision, Drive and Technology*. Amsterdam: IOS Press, 2012.

Chapter 5

"Albert Carl Koch and NC Techbuilt Houses." NCModernist. Accessed July 12, 2020. https://ncmodernist.org/techbuilt.htm.

"Chronology of the Sears Modern Homes Program." Sears Archives. Last modified March 21, 2012. http://www.searsarchives.com/homes/chronology.htm.

"General Panel System House, Los Angeles, CA (1949–1950)." PCAD. Accessed July 12, 2020. http://pcad.lib.washington.edu/building/6938/.

"How Much Cost It Cost to Build a House?" HomeGuide. Accessed July 12, 2020. https://homeguide.com/costs/cost-to-build-a-house.

"Measuring Worth Is a Complicated Question." MeasuringWorth.com. Accessed July 12, 2020. https://www.measuringworth.com/.

"Meet Carl Strandlund." Ohio History Collection. Accessed July 12, 2020. https://www.ohiohistory.org/visit/exhibits/ohio-history-center-exhibits/1950s-building-the-american-dream/lustron-about/help-for-lustrons/meet-the-lustrons/meet-history/meet-carl-strandlund.

"New Techbuilt Shares to Finance Expansion." *Democrat and Chronicle*, September 8, 1954.

"Post-war Housing Crisis." Ohio History Collection. Accessed July 12, 2020. https://www.ohiohistory.org/visit/exhibits/ohio-history-center-exhibits/1950s-building-the-american-dream/lustron-about/help-for-lustrons/meet-the-lustrons/meet-history/meet-history-post-war-housing-crisis.

"Progress Report: The Work of Carl Koch & Associates." *Progressive Architecture*, December 1958.

"Steel House Goes on Display Here." *New York Times*, April 14, 1948.

"What is a Sears Modern Home." Sears Archives. Last modified March 21, 2012. http://www.searsarchives.com/homes/.

Armsey, James W. "A Commentary on a Series of Grants by the Ford Foundation to the Educational Facilities Laboratories, Inc. 1958–1975, 1976 Sept. (Reports 012263)." 1976. Box 587. Ford Foundation Records, Catalogued Reports, Reports 11775-13948 (FA739E). Rockefeller Archive Center, Sleepy Hollow NY.

Benet, James, Christopher Arnold, Jonathan King and James W. Robertson. *SCSD: The Project and the Schools, a Report from the Educational Facilities Laboratories*. New York: Educational Facilities Laboratories, 1967.

Boice, John. *School Construction Systems Development Project*. Publisher unknown; reproduced by the U.S. Office of Health Education and Welfare, Office of Education, 1965.

Brenzel, Kathryn and David Jeans. "Warped Lumber, Failed Projects: TRD Investigates Katerra, SoftBank's $4B Construction Startup." *The Real Deal*. December 16, 2019. https://therealdeal.com/2019/12/16/softbank-funded-construction-startup-katerra-promised-a-tech-revolution-its-struggling-to-deliver/.

Cole, Regina. "The Sears House was the American Dream That Came in a Box." *Forbes*. October 23, 2018. https://www.forbes.com/sites/reginacole/2018/10/23/the-sears-house-was-the-american-dream-that-came-in-a-box/#7defaad9731b.

Doezema, Marie. "Time Is Running Out for Tokyo's Nagakin Capsule Tower." *Bloomberg*. August 26, 2019. https://www.bloomberg.com/news/articles/2019-08-26/tokyo-s-famous-capsule-tower-may-not-be-doomed.

Educational Facilities Laboratories. *SCSD, An Interim Report*. New York: Educational Facilities Laboratories, 1965.

Ehrenkranz, Ezra. "What's Happening to SCSD and Why." *Nation's Schools* 83, no. 4 (1969): 55–57.

Fetters, Thomas T. and Vincent Kohler. *The Lustron Home: The History of a Postwar Prefabricated Housing Experiment*. Jefferson, NC: McFarland, 2002.

Ford, Carmel. "Cost of Constructing a Home." NAHB Economics and Housing Policy Group. Published December 1, 2017. https://www.nahbclassic.org/fileUpload_details.aspx?contentTypeID=3&contentID=260013&subContentID=707961.

Ford Foundation TV Radio Workshop. "Excursion." Aired on February 14, 1954.

Freidrichs, Chad, dir. *The Pruitt-Igoe Myth*. St. Louis, MO: Unicorn Stencil, 2011. DVD.

Hearing Before a Subcommittee on Banking and Currency, First Session on the Proposed Disposition of the Lustron Corp. Prefabricated Housing Plant at Columbus, Ohio. 82nd Cong. 5. (1951).

Hoag, Malcolm W. *An Introduction to Systems Analysis*. Santa Monica, CA: RAND Corporation, 1956.

Jackson, Kenneth T. *Crabgrass Frontier: The Suburbanization of the United States*. New York: Oxford University Press, 1985.

Keaton, Buster and Edward F. Cline, dir. *One Week*. 1920; Los Angeles, CA: Metro Studios, 2019. Internet resource.

Knerr, Douglas. *Suburban Steel: The Magnificent Failure of the Lustron Corporation, 1945-1951*. Columbus: Ohio State University Press, 2004.

Koch, Carl. *At Home with Tomorrow*. New York: Rinehart, 1958. (Also Chapter 10.)

Koch, Carl and Roger K. Lewis. *Roadblocks to Innovation in the Housing Industry: A Report to the National Commission on Urban Problems*. Washington, DC: National Commission on Urban Problems, 1969.

Lee, Joshua David. "Questioning Modern Approaches to Flexibility: 50 Years of Learning from the School Construction Systems Development (SCSD) Project." Ph.D. dissertation, University of Texas at Austin, 2016.

Marks, Judy. "A History of Educational Facilities Laboratories (EFL)." *National Clearinghouse for Educational Facilities*. Last modified 2009.

Mumford, Eric Paul. *The CIAM Discourse on Urbanism, 1928–1960*. Cambridge, MA: MIT Press, 2002.

Omnibus. "Ford Foundation's TV Radio Workshop Techbuilt Show." 1954; Ford Foundation. Internet Resource. https://thetechbuilthouse.com/.

Pepis, Betty. "The People's Choice." *New York Times*, January 2, 1955.

Rand, George and Chris Arnold. "Evaluation: A Look Back at the 60's Sexiest System." *AIA Journal* 68, no. 4 (1979).

Rowe, Colin and Robert Slutzky. "Transparency: Literal and Phenomenal." *Perspecta* 8 (1963): 45–54.

Sadler, Simon. *Archigram: Architecture without Architecture*. Cambridge: MIT Press, 2005.

Stevenseon, Katherine H. and H. Ward Jandl. *Houses by Mail: A Guide to Houses from Sears, Roebuck and Company*. Washington, DC: Preservation Press, 1986.

Wallance, Don. *Shaping America's Products*. New York: Reinhold Publishing Corporation, 1956. (Also Chapter 11.)

Weiss, Daniel, Gregor Harbusch and Bruno Maurer. "CIAM 4 and the 'Unanimous' Origins of Modernist Urban Planning." ArchDaily. Published February 7, 2015. https://www.archdaily.com/596081/ciam-4-and-the-unanimous-origins-of-modernist-urban-planning.

Chapter 6

"Containers." CIMC. Accessed August 8, 2020. http://www.cimc.com/en/index.php?m=content&c=index&a=show&catid=36&id=1.

Kahn, Louis I. *World Architecture One*. London: Studio Vista, 1964. Quoted in Dean Hawkes. *The Environmental Tradition: Studies in the Architecture of Environment*. London: Taylor & Francis, 1996.

Kirk, Mimi. "Will the Advent of Artificial Intelligence Affect Small Firms?" AIA. *Architect Magazine*, February 1, 2019. https://www.architectmagazine.com/aia-architect/aiafeature/will-the-advent-of-artificial-intelligence-affect-small-firms_o.

Wall, Christene. *An Architecture of Parts: Architects, Building Workers and Industrialization in Britain, 1940–1970*. London and New York: Routledge, 2013.

Chapter 7

"Autonomous Ship Project, Key Facts about Yara Birkeland." *Kongsberg*. Accessed June 22. 2020. https://www.kongsberg.com/maritime/support/themes/autonomous-ship-project-key-facts-about-yara-birkeland/.

"Calculation." EcoTransIT World. Accessed June 22, 2020. https://www.ecotransit.org/calculation.en.html.

"Clean by Design: Transportation." Table 1, Natural Resources Defense Council. Published April 2013.

"Construction Costs." New York Building Congress. February 2019. https://www.buildingcongress.com/advocacy-and-reports/reports-and-analysis/construction-outlook-update/Construction-Costs.html.

"DOE Releases Common Definition for Zero Energy Building, Campuses, and Community." Office of Energy Efficiency & Renewable Energy. Energy.gov. Published September 16, 2015. https://www.energy.gov/eere/buildings/articles/doe-releases-common-definition-zero-energy-buildings-campuses-and.

"History." GHG Management Institute. Accessed June 22, 2020. https://ghginstitute.org/history/.

"Home." Athena Sustainable Materials Institute. Accessed June 22, 2020. http://www.athenasmi.org/.

"LEED v4 for Building Design and Construction." *U.S. Green Building Council*. 2019. https://www.usgbc.org/sites/default/files/LEED%20v4%20BDC_07.25.19_current.pdf.

"Steel is the World's Most Recycled Material." Steel Recycling Institute. Accessed June 22, 2020. https://www.steelsustainability.org/recycling.

"Sustainable Management of Construction and Demolition Materials." EPA. Accessed June 24, 2020. https://www.epa.gov/smm/sustainable-management-construction-and-demolition-materials.

"The Difference between Source and Site Energy." Energy Star. Accessed June 22, 2020. https://www.energystar.gov/buildings/facility-owners-and-managers/existing-buildings/use-portfolio-manager/understand-metrics/difference.

"The World's Tallest and Largest Residential Passive House." *Burohappold Engineering*. 2016. https://www.burohappold.com/wp-content/uploads/2016/05/bhe-cornell-tech-casestudy-web2.pdf.

"Will electric vehicles really create a cleaner planet?" Thompson Reuters, accessed December 11, 2020. https://www.thomsonreuters.com/en/reports/electric-vehicles.html.

Andrew, Peter. "Is Your House the 'Typical American Home'?" HSH. Last modified January 26, 2020. https://www.hsh.com/homeowner/average-american-home.html.

Athena Sustainable Materials Institute. *Athena Impact Estimator for Buildings: User Manual and Transparency Document*. Ottawa: Athena Sustainable Materials Institute, 2019. https://calculatelca.com/wp-content/uploads/2019/05/IE4B_v5.4_User_Guide_May_2019.pdf.

Brander, Matthew. "Greenhouse Gases, CO2, CO2e, and Carbon: What Do All These Terms Mean?" White Pages. *Ecometrica*, September 4, 2012. https://ecometrica.com/white-papers/greenhouse-gases-co2-co2e-and-carbon-what-do-all-these-terms-mean.

Broughel, James and Emily Hamilton. "Op-Ed: One Reason for the High Cost of Housing in California may Surprise You—Overregulation." Opinion. *Los Angeles Times*, July 3, 2019. https://www.latimes.com/opinion/op-ed/la-oe-broughel-hamilton-overregulation-housing-california-20190703-story.html.

Buhayar, Noah and Christopher Cannon. "How California Became America's Housing Market Nightmare." *Bloomberg*. November 6, 2019. https://www.bloomberg.com/graphics/2019-california-housing-crisis/.

Economy, Elizabeth. Council on Foreign Relations. Quoted in Neil Irwin. "It's the End of the World Economy as We Know It." *New York Times*, April 16, 2020.

Friedman, Thomas. "China and America Are Heading toward Divorce." *New York Times*, June 23, 2020.

Fuller, Thomas. "Why Does It Cost $750,000 to Build Affordable Housing in San Francisco." *New York Times*, February 20, 2020. https://www.nytimes.com/2020/02/20/us/California-housing-costs.html.

Gates, Moses, Sarah Serpas, Kellan Cantrell and Ben Oldenburg. "Creating more affordable housing in New York City's high-rise areas." Regional Plan Association. February 2018. https://rpa.org/uploads/pdfs/RPA-12-FAR.pdf.

Glaeser, Edward L. "Green Cities, Brown Suburbs." *City Journal*, Winter 2009. https://www.city-journal.org/html/green-cities-brown-suburbs-13143.html.

Glaeser, Edward L. *The Triumph of the City*. New York: Penguin, 2011.

Goldstein, David and Jamy Bacchus. "A New Net Zero Definition: Thinking outside the Box." Paper presented at the ACEE Summer Study on Energy Efficiency in Buildings, Pacific Grove, CA, August 2012.

Grant, Aneurin and Robert Ries. "Impact of Building Service Life Models on Life Cycle Assessment." *Building Research & Information* 41, no. 2 (2013): 168–186. doi:10.1080/09613218.2012.730735.

Hernandez, Daniel, Matthew Lister, and Celine Suarez. "Location Efficiency and Housing Type: Boiling it Down to BTUs." EPA. Published March 2011. https://www.epa.gov/sites/production/files/2014-03/documents/location_efficiency_btu.pdf.

Holusha, John. "Consumer's World; Diaper Debate: Cloth or Disposable?" *New York Times*, July 14, 1990.

Larson, William, Jessica Shui, Morris Davis and Stephen Oliner. "Working Paper 19-01: The Price of Residential Land for Countries, ZIP codes, Census Tracts in the United States." Federal Housing Finance Agency. Last modified February, 2020. https://www.fhfa.gov/PolicyProgramsResearch/Research/PaperDocuments/wp1901.pdf.

Lechner, Norbert. *Heating, Cooling, Lighting: Sustainable Design Methods for Architects.* Hoboken, NJ: John Wiley & Sons, 2014.

Lehne, Johanna and Felix Preston. "Making Concrete Change: Innovation in Low-Carbon Cement and Concrete." *Chatham House Report*. London: The Royal Institute of International Affairs, 2018. https://www.chathamhouse.org/sites/default/files/publications/2018-06-13-making-concrete-change-cement-lehne-preston-final.pdf.

LERA Consulting Structural Engineers. Paper presented at the Council on Tall Buildings and Urban Habitat, New York, January 21, 2017.

McDonald, Jessica. "How Potent is Methane?" *FactCheck.org*. Last modified September 24, 2018. https://www.factcheck.org/2018/09/how-potent-is-methane/.

McKinnon, Alan. "Freight Transport in a Low-Carbon World: Assessing Opportunities for Cutting Emissions." *TR News* November/December 2016, no. 306 (2016): 8–15.

Mehlman, Bruce. "De-Global: 10 Trends Defining the New World." *Mehlman Castagnetti Rosen & Thomas*. Last modified November 13, 2019. https://mehlmancastagnetti.com/wp-content/uploads/De-Global-2019.pdf.

Rios, Fernanda Cruz and David Grau. "Circular Economy in the Built Environment: Designing, Deconstructing, and Leasing Reusable Products." *Reference Module in Materials Science and Engineering*, 2019. doi:10.1016/B978-0-12-803581-8.11494-8.

Tooze, Adam. Columbia University. Quoted in Neil Irwin. "It's the End of the World Economy as We Know It." *New York Times*, April 16, 2020.

United Nations Environmental Programme. *Sand and Sustainability: Finding new solutions for environmental governance of global sand resources*. Geneva: GRID-Geneva, 2019. https://wedocs.unep.org/bitstream/handle/20.500.11822/28163/SandSust.pdf?sequence=1&isAllowed=y.

Valentine, Harry. "Improved Prospects for Container Ships on the St. Lawrence Seaway." Editorials. *The Maritime Executive*, October 6, 2018. https://www.maritime-executive.com/editorials/improved-prospects-for-container-ships-on-the-st-lawrence-seaway.

Van Damm, Andrew. "Detailed Data Show the Value of Land under Homes across the Country." Economic Policy. *Washington Post*, January 23, 2019. https://www.washingtonpost.com/us-policy/2019/01/23/why-its-problem-that-dirt-brooklyn-is-so-much-more-expensive-than-dirt-arkansas/.

Wallance, David, Jamy Bacchus and Jeffrey Ravn. "Moving Parts: Modular Architecture in a Flat World." Paper presented at the Greenbuild International Conference and Expo, Washington, DC, 2015.

Widdicks, Mary. "Are Cloth Diapers Really Any Better for the Environment, Your Wallet, or Your Baby?" The Goods. *Vox*, October 15, 2019. https://www.vox.com/the-goods/2019/10/15/20892011/cloth-diapers-debate-parenting-advice.

Wiener, Scott and Daniel Kammen. "Why Housing Policy is Climate Policy." Opinion. *New York Times*, March 25, 2019. https://www.nytimes.com/2019/03/25/opinion/california-home-prices-climate.html.

Zientara, Ben. "How Much Electricity Does a Solar Panel Produce?" Solar Power Rocks. Last modified April 2, 2020. https://www.solarpowerrocks.com/solar-basics/how-much-electricity-does-a-solar-panel-produce/.

Chapter 8

"Chart Book (6th edition): OSHA Enforcement and Injury Costs – Workers' Compensation in Construction and Other Industries." The Center for Construction Research and Training. Accessed June 23, 2020. https://www.cpwr.com/chart-book-6th-edition-osha-enforcement-and-injury-costs-workers%E2%80%99-compensation-construction-and.

"Employments by Major Industry Sector." U.S. Bureau of Labor Statistics. Last modified September 4, 2019. https://www.bls.gov/emp/tables/employment-by-major-industry-sector.htm.

"Empowering Workers through Accountable Capitalism." Warren Democrats. Accessed June 23, 2020. https://elizabethwarren.com/plans/accountable-capitalism.

"Lean Thinking and Methods – Kaizen." EPA. Last modified September 12, 2019. https://www.epa.gov/sustainability/lean-thinking-and-methods-kaizen.

"The Define, Measure, Analyze, Improve, Control (DMAIC) Process." ASQ. Accessed June 23, 2020. https://asq.org/quality-resources/dmaic.

Alder, Ken. "Innovation and Amnesia: Engineering Rationality and the Fate of Interchangeable Parts Manufacturing in France." *Technology and Culture* 38, no. 2 (April 1997): 273–311.

Brenzel, Kathryn and David Jeans. "Warped Lumber, Failed Projects: TRD Investigates Katerra, SoftBank's $4B Construction Startup." *The Real Deal*, December 16, 2019. https://therealdeal.com/2019/12/16/softbank-funded-construction-startup-katerra-promised-a-tech-revolution-its-struggling-to-deliver/.

Brooks, David. "What Machines Can't Do." Opinion. *New York Times*, February 3, 2014. https://www.nytimes.com/2014/02/04/opinion/brooks-what-machines-cant-do.html.

Dam, Rikke Friis and Teo Yu Siang. "5 Stages in the Design Thinking Process." Interaction Design Foundation. Last modified May 2020. https://www.interaction-design.org/literature/article/5-stages-in-the-design-thinking-process.

Denning, Steve. "How Not to Fix US Health Care: Copy the Cheesecake Factory." Leadership. *Forbes*, August 13, 2012. https://www.forbes.com/sites/stevedenning/2012/08/13/how-not-to-fix-us-health-care-copy-the-cheesecake-factory/#79d5a9ec2bd2.

DiMento, Joseph F.C. "Stent (or Dagger?) in the Heart of Town: Urban Freeways in Syracuse, 1944–1967." *Journal of Planning History* 8, no. 2 (2009): 133–161. doi:10.1177/1538513208330768.

Gawande, Atul. "Big Med." Annals of Health Care. *New Yorker*, August 6, 2012. https://www.newyorker.com/magazine/2012/08/13/big-med.

Gillispie, Charles Coulston and Ken Alder. "Engineering the Revolution." *Technology and Culture* 39, no. 4 (1998): 733–754. doi:10.1353/tech.1998.0094.

Goehle, Brad and Robert Chwalik. "The Global Innovation 1000 study," last modified December 17, 2019, https://www.strategyand.pwc.com/gx/en/insights/innovation1000.html.

Jaruzelski, Barry, Robert Chwalik and Brad Goehle. "What the Top Innovators Get Right." Tech & Innovation. *Strategy + Business*, October 30, 2018. https://www.strategy-business.com/feature/What-the-Top-Innovators-Get-Right?gko=e7cf9.

Mumford, Lewis. *Technics and Civilization*. New York: Harcourt Brace & Company, 1934.

New York Plan for the Resolution of Jurisdictional Disputes: In the Matter of Arbitration between IBEW Local #3 and Plumbers Local #1. § 100-O. 1-4. (2009).

New York Plan for the Resolution of Jurisdictional Disputes, In the Matter of the Arbitration between Local Union No. 3, IBEW and New York City District Council of Carpenters. § 100-S. 1-4. (2011).

Plan for the Settlement of Jurisdictional Disputes in the Construction Industry: In the Matter of Arbitration between IBEW Local #3 and United Association of Journeymen and Apprentices and Pipe Fitting Industry of the United States and Canada, and Tishman Construction Corp. § 100-P (Appeal to 100-O). 1-7. (2010).

Plan for the Settlement of Jurisdictional Disputes in the Construction Industry: In Arbitration between IBEW Local Union No. 3, and New York City District Council of Carpenters. Case No. H10-047. 1-6. (2011). (Robert M. Hirsch, Arbitrator).

Putzier, Konrad. "Momentum Builds for Automation in Construction." Real Estate. *Wall Street Journal*, July 2, 2019.

Pye, David. *The Nature and Art of Workmanship*. New York: Bloomsbury Academic. (Also Chapter 11.)

Rittel, Horst W. and Melvin M. Webber. *Dilemmas in a General Theory of Planning*. Berkley, CA: Institute of Urban and Regional Development, University of California, 1973.

Romer, Paul M. "Economic Growth." Econlib. *Concise Encyclopedia of Economic Growth*, 2nd ed. Carmel, IN: The Liberty Fund, 2007. https://www.econlib.org/library/Enc/EconomicGrowth.html.

Semuels, Alana. "The Role of Highways in American Poverty." Business. *Atlantic*, March 18, 2016. https://www.theatlantic.com/business/archive/2016/03/role-of-highways-in-american-poverty/474282/.

Stiglitz, Joseph. "Inequality is Holding Back the Recovery." *New York Times*, January 20, 2013.

Teicholz, Paul. "Trends in Labor Productivity in the Construction Industry." Paper presented at the Project Production Institute Symposium, San Francisco, CA, December 9, 2015.

Vitullo-Martin, Julia and Hope Cohen. *Construction Labor Costs in New York City: A Moment of Opportunity*, report. New York: Regional Plan Association, June 2011. https://rpa.org/uploads/pdfs/RPA-CUI-Construction-Costs.pdf.

Woodbury, Robert S. "The Legend of Eli Whitney and Interchangeable Parts." *Technology and Culture* 1, no. 3 (Summer, 1960): 235–253.

Chapter 9

Asquith, Lindsey and Marcel Vellinga. *Vernacular Architecture in the Twenty First Century: Theory, Education and Practice*. New York and Ontario: Taylor & Francis, 2006.

Blaser, Werner. *The Rock is My Home*. New York: Van Nostrand Reinhold Co., 1977.

De Lucca, Denis De. *A Living Tradition? Maltese Vernacular Architecture*. New York and London: Routledge, 1993.

Frampton, Kenneth. "Adolf Loos and the Crisis of Culture." Quoted in *Modern Architecture: A Critical History*. New York and Toronto: Oxford University Press, 1980.

Frampton, Kenneth. *Studies in Tectonic Culture*. Cambridge, MA: The MIT Press, 1995. (Also Chapter 10)

Habraken, N.J. and Jonathan Teicher. *Supports: An Alternative to Mass Housing*. London: Urban International Press, 2011. (Also Chapter 10)

Heynen, Hilde. *Architecture and Modernity: A Critique*. Cambridge, MA and London: MIT Press, 2000.

Kahn, Louis. "1973: Brooklyn, New York." *Perspecta 19* (1982): 92. Accessed September 23, 2020. doi:10.2307/1567053.

Kleinman, Kent and Leslie Van Duzer. *Mies van der Rohe: The Krefeld Villas*. New York: Princeton Architectural Press, 2006.

Loos, Adolf. *Spoken into the Void: Collected Essays*. Cambridge, MA and London: MIT Press, Cambridge, 1982.

Loos, Adolf. *Ornament and Crime: Selected Essays*. Riverside, CA: Ariadne Press, 1998.

Richards, J.M Richards. "Is There a Modern Vernacular?" Quoted in *A Companion to Contemporary Architectural Thought*. Edited by Michael Manser. New York and London: Routledge, 1993.

Rudofsky, Bernard. *Architecture without Architects*. Garden City, NJ: Doubleday and Company, 1965.

van der Rohe, Ludwig Mies, Brick Country House, project, Potsdam-Neubabelsberg, Plan, 1964, ink on illustration board, 30 in x 40 in (76.2 cm x 101.6 cm), Museum of Modern Art, New York, New York, https://www.moma.org/collection/works/780.

Winters, Jennifer. "Director's Column: 100 Years of Blocks: Why Blocks Continue to Be a Cornerstone in the Curriculum." Stanford, Bing Nursery School. Last modified August 6, 2013. https://bingschool.stanford.edu/news/director-s-column-100-years-blocks-why-blocks-continue-be-cornerstone-curriculum.

Chapter 10

"Dieter Rams: 10 Principles for Good Design." *Shuffle Magazine*. Accessed June 20, 2020. https://readymag.com/shuffle/dieter-rams/.

"Instagram by the Numbers: Stats, Demographics & Fun Facts." OmnicoreAgency.com. Last modified February 10, 2020. https://www.omnicoreagency.com/instagram-statistics/.

"Internet Usage Statistics: The Internet Big Picture." *Internet World Stats*. Last modified July 20, 2020. https://www.internetworldstats.com/stats.htm.

"TikTok Statisics," 99 Firms (blog). Accessed June 20, 2020. https://99firms.com/blog/tiktok-statistics/#gref.

"White City of Tel-Aviv – The Modern Movement." UNESCO. Accessed June 20, 2020. https://whc.unesco.org/en/list/1096/.

Buras, Nir H. Buras. "Joseph Neufeld in Eretz Israel: Romanticism in Modernism." Doctoral thesis, Israel Institute of Technology, 2000.

Chayka, Kyle. "What's the Deal with George W.S. Trow." Culture. *Nation*, April 17, 2019. https://www.thenation.com/article/archive/george-trow-context-no-context-book-harpers-reviewing-social-media/.

Foxwell, Bella, "A Guide to Social Media Influencers: Mega, Macro, Micro, and Nano," Iconosquare (blog), last modified February 17, 2020, https://blog.iconosquare.com/guide-to-social-media-influencers/.

Funk, Matthias "How Many YouTube Channels Are There?" Tubics (blog), last modified January 31, 2020, https://www.tubics.com/blog/number-of-youtube-channels/

Martineau, Paris. "The Wired Guide to Influencers." Business. *Wired*, December 6, 2019. https://www.wired.com/story/what-is-an-influencer/.

Maulden, Robert. *Tectonics in Architecture: From the Physical to the Meta-Physical*. Massachusetts Institute of Technology, 1986.

Moneo, Rafael. "A Talk with Rafael Moneo: The Beck's Architect Finds in Houston a Plane Truth." Interview by Carlos Jiménez. *Cite*, no. 24 (Spring 2000): 23–23.

Roose, Kevin. "Don't Scoff at Influencers. They're Taking Over the World." Technology. *New York Times*, July 16, 2019. https://www.nytimes.com/2019/07/16/technology/vidcon-social-media-influencers.html.

Seabrook, John. *Nobrow: The Culture of Marketing, The Marketing of Culture*. New York: Random House, 2001.

Seabrook, John. *Frontline*. By PBS affiliate WGBH. Channel 13, November 18, 2015.

Trow, George W.S. *Within the Context of No Context*. Boston, MA: Little, Brown and Company, 1997.

Weill-Rochant, Catherine. "Myths and Buildings of Tel Aviv." Bulletin du Centre de recherche français à Jérusalem (English translations). Published December 2003. https://journals.openedition.org/bcrfj/672?amp%3Bid=672.

Chapter 11

"Environmental Health in Emergencies." World Health Organization. Accessed June 22, 2020. https://www.who.int/environmental_health_emergencies/natural_events/en/.

"New Approaches to Help Businesses Tackle Climate Change." Research News. *University of Cambridge*, February 22, 2020. https://www.cam.ac.uk/research/news/new-approaches-to-help-businesses-tackle-climate-change.

"Who We Are." MHI Manufactured Housing Institute. Accessed June 22, 2020. https://www.manufacturedhousing.org/who-we-are/.

"Work." Summit ID Industrial Design. Accessed June 22, 2020. http://www.summitid.com/.

Arendt, Hannah. *The Human Condition*. Chicago, IL: University of Chicago Press, 1956.

Berlin, Isaiah. *The Hedgehog and the Fox*. London: Weidenfeld & Nicolson, 1963.

Flavelle, Christopher, "U.S. Flood Strategy Shifts to 'Unavoidable' Relocation of Entire Neighborhoods." *New York Times*, August 26, 2020. Accessed August 28, 2020. https://www.nytimes.com/2020/08/26/climate/flooding-relocation-managed-retreat.html?action=click&module=Top%20Stories&pgtype=Homepage

Kunzelman, Michael and Michael Biesecker. "Lessons Learned from Katrina, FEMA Says It Won't Rely on Trailers for Irma, Harvey Victims." News. *Advocate*, September 19, 2017. https://www.theadvocate.com/baton_rouge/news/article_19ecca5c-9d4c-11e7-845b-7f0edcb8d0a7.html#:~:text=FEMA%20purchased%20more%20than%20140%2C000,or%20in%20makeshift%20trailer%20parks.

Masters, Jeff. "Earth's 40 Billion-Dollar Weather Disasters of 2019: 4th Most Billion-Dollar Events on Record." Opinion. *Scientific American*, January 22, 2020. https://blogs.scientificamerican.com/eye-of-the-storm/earths-40-billion-dollar-weather-disasters-of-2019-4th-most-billion-dollar-events-on-record/#:~:text=In%20the%20U.S.%2C%20there%20were,to%20both%20Aon%20and%20NOAA.&text=The%201980%E2%80%932019%20annual%20inflation,than%20doubled%2C%20to%2013.8%20events.

Weiner, Jonah. "Jerry Seinfeld Intends to Die Standing Up." *New York Times Magazine*, December 23, 2012.

Project Team Credits

GBM System R&D

David Wallance
Jason Buchheit
Karl Hirschmann
Vincent Huang
Gary Zaid

Consultants
Structural Engineers: LERA Consulting Engineering
Acoustical: Shen Milsom & Wilke
Overseas Procurement: Axis Sourcing USA
Façades: Axis Facades
Energy and Environmental: Jamy Bacchus

372 Lafayette Street

David Wallance
Jason Buchheit
Karl Hirschmann
David Fung
Stuart Allen

Consultants
Structural Engineers: LERA Consulting Engineering
Mechanical Engineers: Plus Group
Fire Protection: Schirmer Engineering
Acoustical: Shen Milsom Wilke
Historic Preservation: Higgins Quasebarth

Hi-Rise Student Housing Feasibility Study

David Wallance
Dan Kaplan
Brian Fanning

Consultants
Structural Engineers: LERA Consulting Engineering
Mechanical Engineers: Dagher Engineering

Philadelphia Mixed-Use Project

David Wallance
Dan Kaplan
Juan DeMarco
Sidhant Seth

Consultants
Structural Engineers: LERA Consulting Engineering

UrbanMODe

David Wallance
Jack Robbins
Amy Shell
Ben Abelman
Emau Vega

The Prefabricator's Toolbox Façade System

David Wallance
Sidhant Seth
Emma Le Lesle
Serena Stedeford

Façade Consultant
Gabrielle Brainard

Image Credits

Figure 2.1 Denys Nevozhai, aerial photography of concrete roads, June 9, 2016 via Unsplash, accessed April 14, 2020.

Figure 2.2 Jean-Philippe Delberghe, Untitled, January 18, 2020 via Unsplash, accessed April 14, 2020.

Figure 3.1 Snark/Art Resources, NY.

Figure 3.2 Left: Josue Isai Ramos Figueroa, Untitled, July 17, 2018 via Unsplash, accessed August 24, 2020. Right: Lenny Kuhne, Untitled, September 6, 2019 via Unsplash, accessed August 24, 2020.

Figures 3.3, 3.4, 3.8 © 2020 David Wallance.

Figure 3.5 Courtesy of Resolution: 4 Architecture.

Figure 3.6 © 2020 CMH Services, Inc.

Figure 3.7 Courtesy of Stephen B. Jacobs Group.

Figure 4.1 Lewis Hine, July 1937, Federal Works Agency. Work Projects Administration. National Research Project, accessed August 24, 2020 via Wikimedia Commons.

Figure 4.2 U.S. Marine Commission Photograph (1946), Library of Congress, accessed 24 August 2020 via Wikimedia Commons.

Figures 4.3–4.6 Public Domain; United States Patent Office.

Figure 4.7 Courtesy of Maersk.

Figure 4.8 Source: OECD International Transport Forum.

Figures 5.1, 5.2 Public Domain.

Figure 5.3 Alden Jewell, March 24, 2017, accessed August 8, 2020 via Flickr.

Figure 5.4 Courtesy of KDN Films.

Figures 5.5–5.7 © Ezra Stoller/Esto.

Figure 5.8 Courtesy of David Meerman Scott.

Figure 5.9 © McGraw Hill, *Architectural Systems: A Needs, Resource and Design Approach*, by Ezra Ehrenkrantz.

Figures 6.1–6.24, 6.45, 6.50–6.60, 6.62–6.64 Courtesy of David Wallance Architect.

Figures 6.25–6.28, 6.46, 6.65–6.70 Courtesy of FXCollaborative and David Wallance Architect.

Figures 6.29–6.44, 6.47–6.49 © 2020 David Wallance.

Figure 6.61 Source: Dagher Engineering.

Figure 7.1 Source: Natural Resources Defense Council.

Figure 7.2 Source: Athena Sustainable Materials Institute.

Figure 7.3 Source: EcoTransIT.

Figure 7.4 Sources: EcoTransIT, Athena Sustainable Materials Institute, Buro Happold.

Figure 7.6 Courtesy of FXCollaborative.

Figure 7.7 Source: LERA Consulting Engineers.

Figures 7.8–7.10, 7.12, 7.15 © 2020 David Wallance.

Figure 7.11 Source: Jonathan Rose Companies.

Figure 7.13, 7.14 Source: Jamy Bacchus PE, LEED AP BD+C, BEMP.

Figure 7.16 Left to right, top to bottom: Josuelsai Ramos Figueroa, July 17, 2018, Lenny Kuhne, September 6, 2019, Vivint Solar, August 26, 2019, Peter Osmenda, December 14, 2018, Matthew T. Rader, November 11, 2018, Diego Fernandez, October 16, 2019. All images via Unsplash, accessed August 24, 2020.

Figure 8.1 © 2020 David Wallance.

Figure 8.2 Source: Project Production Institute.

Figure 8.3 Source: Idea to Value.

Figure 9.1 La-Real Easter, Untitled, November 8, 2018 via Unsplash, accessed August 24, 2020.

Figure 9.2 Samuel Penn, Poulnabrone Dolmen, September 3, 2019 via Unsplash, accessed August 24, 2020.

Figure 9.3 D. Challita, Habitat 67 Montreal, April 20, 2011 via Wikimedia Commons, accessed August 24, 2020.

Figure 9.4, 9.5 © The Museum of Modern Art/Licensed by SCALA/Art Resource, NY. © 2020 Artists Rights Society (ARS), New York / VG Bild-Kunst, Bonn.

Figure 9.6 Courtesy of FXCollaborative and David Wallance Architect.

Figure 10.1 © CNAC/MNAM/Dist. RMN-Grand Palais / Art Resource, NY, permission from the Superstudio Archive.

Figure 10.2 Dennis Schrader, Untitled, January 20, 2019 via Unsplash, accessed August 24, 2020.

Index